Controversial Issues
in Aging

Controversial Issues in Aging

Edited by
Andrew E. Scharlach
University of California, Berkeley

Lenard W. Kaye
Bryn Mawr College

Series Editors
Eileen Gambrill
Robert Pruger
University of California, Berkeley

ALLYN AND BACON
Boston • London • Toronto • Sydney • Tokyo • Singapore

Series Editor, Social Work: Judy Fifer
Editor in Chief, Social Sciences: Karen Hanson
Editorial Assistant: Mary Visco
Marketing Manager: Quinn Perkson
Sr. Editorial Production Administrator: Susan McIntyre
Editorial Production Service: Ruttle, Shaw & Wetherill, Inc.
Composition Buyer: Linda Cox
Manufacturing Buyer: Suzanne Lareau
Cover Administrator: Suzanne Harbison

Copyright © 1997 by Allyn & Bacon
A Viacom Company
160 Gould Street
Needham Heights, MA 02194
Internet: www.abacon.com
America Online: keyword: College Online

Library of Congress Cataloging-in-Publication Data
Controversial issues in aging / edited by Andrew E. Scharlach, Lenard
  W. Kaye.
     p. cm.
  Includes bibliographical references.
  ISBN 0-205-19381-1
  1. Aged—United States. 2. Aged—Government policy—United
States. 3. Aged—Services for—United States. I. Scharlach,
Andrew E. II. Kaye, Lenard W.
HQ1064.U5C61138 1997
305.26'0973—dc20   96-16322
                                                             CIP

Printed in the United States of America

10 9 8 7 6 5 4 3   01 00 99

Contents

1 Policy and Program Issues

II Age-Based Politics

III Health and Quality-of-Life Issues

IV Family Issues

V The Field of Gerontology

VI Aging in the Future

About the Editors

Andrew E. Scharlach, Ph.D., is Professor of Social Welfare at the University of California at Berkeley, where he holds the Eugene and Rose Kleiner Chair in Aging, coordinates the Gerontology specialization in the School of Social Welfare, and directs the Center for the Advanced Study of Aging Services. He received his B.A. in mathematics from the University of California at Berkeley, his M.S. in social service from Boston University, and his Ph.D. in psychology from Stanford University.

Dr. Scharlach has published extensively on the needs of older adults and their families, particularly with regard to employee elder care responsibilities and adults' reactions to parental death. He is a leading national expert on work and family issues and the author of *Elder Care and the Work Force: Blueprint for Action* (Lexington Books, 1991). His current research examines innovative solutions for meeting the long-term care needs of older adults and their families, including a public-private partnership for organizing and financing long-term care services and an HMO-sponsored Caregiver Resource Center.

Dr. Scharlach is Vice President of the California Council on Gerontology and Geriatrics and a member of the editorial board of *Generations,* the journal of the American Society on Aging. He also serves on the advisory committees of numerous local, state, and national aging organizations. He is a Diplomate in Clinical Social Work, a Fellow of the Gerontological Society of America, and is included in *Who's Who in California, Who's Who in the World, Who's Who of Emerging Leaders in America,* and *Who's Who in Gerontology.*

Lenard W. Kaye, D.S.W., is Professor of Social Work and Social Research at Bryn Mawr College Graduate School of Social Work and Social Research in

Bryn Mawr, Pennsylvania. He received his bachelor's degree from the State University of New York at Binghamton, his master's degree from New York University School of Social Work, and his doctorate from the Columbia University School of Social Work. He is the editor of *New Developments in Home Care Services for the Elderly: Innovations in Policy, Program, and Practice* (The Haworth Press, 1995), the author of *Home Health Care* (Sage Publications, 1992), the co-author of *Men as Caregivers to the Elderly* (Lexington Books, 1990), the co-editor of *Congregate Housing for the Elderly* (The Haworth Press, 1991), and the co-author of *Resolving Grievances in the Nursing Home* (Columbia University Press, 1984). His forthcoming books include: *Part-Time Employment for the Lower Income Elderly: Experiences from the Field* (Garland Publishing), *Self-Help Support Groups for Older Women* (Taylor and Francis), and *Elderly Men: Problems and Potential* (Springer Publishing). He has published approximately 100 journal articles and book chapters on issues in elder caregiving, long-term care advocacy, home health and adult day care, marketing techniques in the human services, retirement lifestyles, and social work curriculum development.

Dr. Kaye sits on the editorial boards of the *Journal of Gerontological Social Work* and *Geriatric Care Management Journal.* He is a board member of numerous community organizations, the Past President of the New York State Society on Aging and of Understanding Aging, Inc., and a Fellow of the Gerontological Society of America. He has recently conducted an economic analysis of telemedicine in home health care and, with the support of the AARP Andrus Foundation, research on self-help support groups for older women and on the delivery of high-technology home health care services to older adults. His current research includes an assessment of a continuum of independent living program providing traditional and high-technology home care services in combination with an alternative model of case management.

Preface

Controversies regarding aging are emerging throughout our society. Aging-related issues are being debated in the halls of Congress, in the media, and in the privacy of our own homes. These issues are as public as whether the Social Security Trust Fund is solvent, as private as whether we have saved enough for our retirement; as abstract as whether the elderly are benefiting at the expense of younger generations, as immediate as whether we can afford to care for our parents and also send our kids to college; as political as whether the government or private business should be responsible for long-term care, and as personal as who will care for us in our old age. Moreover, these are issues that affect those who are old now and their families, as well as those who will be old someday—in short, these issues affect all of us.

The emergence of aging issues is in large part caused by major changes in the age composition of our society. Representing just 4 percent of the American population in 1900, persons aged sixty-five years and older numbered approximately thirty-one million in the 1990 census, or almost 12.6 percent of the population (AARP, 1991). By the year 2030, those sixty-five years of age and older will more than double to sixty-six million, comprising more than one of every five Americans. By that time, it is estimated that there will be more Americans aged sixty-five years and older than children younger than age eighteen years (AARP, 1991).

Interest in the elderly also is a result of fundamental structural and economic changes affecting the United States and the entire world. With the emergence of a global economy and increased international competition have come threats to the seemingly unlimited economic growth that marked the post–World War II era in the United States. Retraction rather than expansion is the focus. Given this perception of scarcity, "entitlements" are giving way to an emphasis on "individual responsibility." Although this is true for all members of society, the elderly, on whose behalf more than 30 percent of government dollars are spent, are receiving particular scrutiny. In this context, the basic rationale for the elderly receiving special rights and privileges is being examined. Questions are being raised as to what, if anything, older persons are entitled to simply because of their age.

Contributing to questions regarding the status of the elderly is the realization that age seems of decreasing importance in structuring societal opportunities and social interactions. With a shift from predominantly a manufacturing economy to a service economy, physical labor has become less important in determining productivity or even the ability to work. At the same time, technological advances have made it possible for even persons with substantial disabilities to remain productive contributors to society. Meanwhile, improvements in health and living conditions enable persons in their seventies and eighties to retain the capabilities of persons ten or twenty years younger in their parents' generation.

Yet, today's elderly persons are far from a unitary lot. Seventy-five percent of elderly persons own their own homes, so that the average older person heads a household whose net worth is more than double that of households headed by the average adult younger than age sixty-five years. More older adults have annual household incomes over $50,000 than do individuals in any other age-group. Yet 28 percent of older persons have incomes below or just above the federal poverty level, and almost 60 percent of older persons live on less than $10,000 a year (Davis & Rowland, 1991). Poverty is especially prevalent among nonwhite elderly persons, with more than one-third of African Americans and Native Americans having incomes below the poverty line. Moreover, as a result of immigration patterns and decreasing mortality rates, the number of nonwhite elderly is expected to grow significantly in the coming years, from approximately 10 percent of the elderly population today to more than 20 percent by the middle of the next century (U.S. Senate Special Committee on Aging, 1991).

These emerging social, economic, and demographic realities have shaken the very foundation of existing paradigms regarding the elderly. Questions are arising from all corners regarding the responsibility of society with regard to its elderly members, as well as the rights and obligations of the elderly themselves. Given this changing context, Fernando Torres-Gil, U.S. Assistant Secretary of Health and Human Services, has suggested a new conception of aging, based on the politics of diversity rather than on the politics of entitlement (Torres-Gil, 1992). This "New Aging" argues that common political interest should replace age as a primary determinant of societal policies and programs. Moreover, it asks how the elderly and other generations can contribute to the larger society, rather than only what services older persons require.

Contents of This Book

In this volume, we have assembled debates that address twenty controversial issues that arise from the changing context of aging in the United States. Each debate includes position statements arguing for and against the given proposition, rebuttals to those position statements. This format allows for an exciting and stimulating exchange that offers readers an opportunity to consider divergent views on central issues affecting an aging society. It is hoped that these debates will be interesting and informative, while also encouraging you to consider in a new light your own basic assumptions regarding life in an aging society.

The book is divided into six sections: Policy and Program Issues, Age-Based Politics, Health and Quality-of-Life Issues, Family Issues, The Field of Gerontology, and Aging in the Future. Part I, Policy and Program Issues, addresses fundamental questions regarding this country's social and legislative policies with regard to its elderly members. Central to this discussion is the issue of what, if anything, older persons are entitled to, just because of their age. Among the issues addressed are whether Social Security benefits should be reduced for high-income individuals (Debate 1), whether Medicare should be means-tested (Debate 2), whether the network of programs and services for the elderly should be dismantled entirely (Debate 3), whether there should be affirmative action for hiring older persons (Debate 4), whether long-term care should be financed primarily with public or private dollars (Debate 5), and the fundamental question of whether age should be abandoned entirely as a basis of eligibility for public programs and services (Debate 6).

Two underlying themes provide the context for the issues discussed in Part I: (1) whether age or need should be the primary criterion for allocating scarce societal resources, and (2) whether public-sector or private-sector solutions are preferable. Arguments on both sides of these issues are rooted in practical realities such as an apparent lack of adequate resources to pay for age-based entitlements, as well as moral and philosophical positions regarding what older persons deserve relative to other age-groups.

Part II, Age-Based Politics, examines the relative political strength of the elderly in the United States. Given dramatic improvements in the overall economic well-being of America's elderly in the last thirty years, these debates examine to what degree these advances are a result of age-based interest group politics. Issues addressed include whether older adults are benefiting at the expense of younger persons (Debate 7), and whether the elderly really have as much political clout as is often assumed (Debate 8).

Part III examines a variety of issues regarding health and quality of life in the later years. Questions addressed include whether older persons should have the right to commit suicide (Debate 9), whether health care for older adults should be rationed (Debate 10), whether managed care is beneficial for older persons (Debate 11), and whether aging is more problematic for women than for men (Debate 12). These debates elucidate the tension between individual autonomy and the needs of society in general, while highlighting those groups whose needs and well-being are most apt to be compromised in the name of societal goals.

Part IV examines various family issues that arise in the context of an aging society. Issues include whether use of formal services leads to families relinquishing care of their elderly relatives (Debate 13), whether family members themselves should be paid to provide care (Debate 14), whether older adults should be able to give assets to family members to qualify for Medicaid (Debate 15), and whether grandparents should assume full parental responsibility for their grandchildren (Debate 16). Underlying these issues are basic questions regarding the proper role of families in an aging society, including what families should be expected to do, what they are capable of doing, what rights older adults and their families have to control their own fates, and what supports they need from the larger society.

Part V addresses two issues that arise in the field of gerontology: whether gerontology itself is inherently ageist (Debate 17), and whether gerontology should be considered a separate profession (Debate 18). These debates illustrate the lack of consensus even among gerontologists with regard to the very nature of the practice of gerontology. In so doing, they reflect the larger society's ambivalence regarding its older members and those who study and serve them.

The final section, Part VI, considers aging in the future. Issues examined include whether future elderly persons will experience more years of disability (Debate 19), and whether in general tomorrow's elderly will be better off than are today's elderly (Debate 20). In examining current trends to discern what they portend for the physical and economic well-being of future cohorts, these debates provide us with a glimpse at our own future. At the same time, they show the difficulty of predicting a future that is in many ways still of our own making.

The twenty debates included in this book address issues that ultimately will affect all of us. Whatever our race, ethnicity, gender, sexual orientation, socioeconomic status, or place of birth, one thing is certain: we all are aging. And so is the society in which we live. The aging of society brings with it new controversies. Many are difficult issues, often involving complex moral, philosophical, cultural, economic, political, and ultimately personal dilemmas. How we resolve these issues now will have implications not only for today's elderly, but for how we and our children age in the future.

It is our belief that only through increased public, family, and personal awareness and discussion of these difficult and sometimes painful issues can we assure the best possible future for ourselves and our children. We offer this book in the hope that it, in some small way, contributes to that discussion.

We would like to thank our contributors for the quality and thoughtfulness of their debates. This book is more theirs than ours, and whatever constructive impact this book may have is a direct result of their fine work. We also want to thank our contributors for their willingness to work within the debate format of this book, which sometimes required them to argue positions that went far beyond their own beliefs, as well as their cooperation with the restrictions imposed by space limitations. Finally, we would like to express our appreciation to Kris Duermeier and Lorretta Morales, without whose editorial, organizational, and word-processing skills this book could never have been produced.

References

American Association of Retired Persons (AARP). (1991). *A profile of older Americans, 1990.* Washington, DC: AARP.

Davis, K., & Rowland, D. (1991). Old and poor: Policy challenges in the 1990s. *Journal of Aging and Social Policy, 2,* 37–59.

Torres-Gil, F. (1992). *The new aging: Politics and change in America.* New York: Auburn House.

United States Senate. Special Committee on Aging. (1991). *Aging America: Trends and projections.* Washington, DC: U.S. Department of Health and Human Services.

Controversial Issues
in Aging

Should Social Security Benefits Be Reduced for High-Income Individuals?

EDITORS' NOTE: Social Security has been a topic of escalating political interest in recent years. This public program, which provides for the economic security and welfare of individuals and their dependents, was first established as part of the Social Security Act of 1935, a hallmark of President Franklin Roosevelt's New Deal Program. It has since been repeatedly amended and now represents a national program of compulsory taxation on wages and salaries for the purposes of paying old age retirement, survivors, disability insurance, and health insurance benefits. Depending on the side of the debate you take in the argument, the Social Security system may be seen as being either a major cause of this country's growing economic deficit, or its savior, given its current status as a major source of substantial surplus funds. In similar fashion, some argue that the Social Security system is destined to collapse outright in the not-too-distant future, and others maintain that relatively minor adjustments in the formulas dictating payroll tax deductions and beneficiary payouts will assure its integrity well into the twenty-first century. Whatever the position you assume in the debate, no one can deny that Social Security, traditionally considered an extremely successful government entitlements program, has now become exceedingly controversial, misunderstood by much of the public, and subject to increasing critical scrutiny. Should eligibility criteria for Social Security be modified substantially? Should the benefits available through the program be differentially assessed based on the relative economic status of its prospective beneficiaries?

Martha H. Phillips, M.A., says *YES*. She is the Executive Director of the Concord Coalition, a nonpartisan nationwide grassroots organization dedicated to eliminating the federal budget deficit. Its co-chairs are former Senators Warren Rudman and Paul Tsongas. Before her current position. Ms. Phillips was the Republican Staff Director for the Committee on the Budget in the U.S. House of Representatives.

Teresa Ghilarducci, Ph.D., says *NO*. She is an Associate Professor of Economics at the University of Notre Dame. Ghilarducci is the author of *Labor's Capital: The Economics and Politics of Employer Pensions*. In September 1995 she was appointed by President Clinton to the Pension Benefit Guaranty Corporation's advisory board.

YES

MARTHA H. PHILLIPS

The Social Security program must be overhauled, and reducing benefits for high-income people should be a substantial part of that reform effort. There is no point in debating whether Social Security should be changed. The current program is unsustainable. Doing nothing is not an option. Here's why:

Social Security is a pay-as-you-go program. That is, the payroll taxes paid by today's workers are used for the monthly benefits that are sent to today's retirees. Just like a chain letter scheme, the Social Security system depends on having enough new people at the bottom of the pyramid to support those at the top. At first, this worked fine. When the system began, a little before World War II, there were plenty of workers to support each retiree, and workers had to pay in only 1 percent of their first $3,000 in earnings. In the 1950s, there were more than seven workers for each retired person, and taxes climbed to 2 percent of the first $4,200 of earnings. By the 1970s, there were only 5.2 workers per retiree.

It will get worse. Before long, about 2010 or so, the baby boomers will begin retiring. When the full force of this demographic tidal wave hits Social Security, there will be fewer than three workers for each retiree. These are not wild or exaggerated predictions. They are calculations based on figuring out when people who have already been born will be retiring.

Unless we want to ask every three workers to adopt a retiree, our options are limited: trim benefits, increase taxes, or both. Forget about raising taxes. Payroll taxes are already high—too high, according to many. More than three-fourths of working people pay more in payroll taxes, including both the employer's and employee's share, than they pay in federal income taxes. For Social Security, 5.6 percent is taken out of each paycheck up to the first $60,600 in wages. The *employer* pays in an equal amount for each employee. Thus, the tax on wages is really 11.2 percent.

Adding even another 1 percent to payroll tax may sound like a small incremental change, but for many families, especially those dependent on two workers, it would be the straw that breaks the camel's back. Restoring full solvency to the Social Security Trust Fund would require a whopping *4 percent* payroll tax increase by 2030. Clearly, this is out of the question. Such an added burden would erode workers' take-home pay, slow the pace of job creation, and lead to layoffs, and drag down economic growth. Moreover, generational equity demands that *all* generations share the burden of shoring up Social Security. Payroll taxes fall entirely on those still young enough to be in the workforce, whereas today's retirees, who paid much lower tax rates during their working years, would not be affected by payroll tax increases and thus would be exempted from helping to solve the Social Security problem.

Well then, if raising payroll taxes is out, what about trimming benefits? If benefits are reduced for everyone, the well-off will hardly notice the difference, but the reduction could spell disaster for retirees who are just barely scraping by as it is. Seventeen percent of people aged sixty-five to sixty-nine in 1992 had annual family incomes of under $15,000, as did a third of beneficiaries in their eighties and older. Across-the-board benefit reductions, even modest reductions in cost-of-living adjustments, would hit these retirees hard.

This leaves the alternative of reducing benefits for those who have comfortable retirement incomes. Workers with higher incomes must pay income taxes at a higher rate. Paying lower benefits to retirees who are comfortably well off is in keeping with this progressive way of arranging our affairs.

Many of today's retirees are doing better economically than their younger neighbors who are paying their Social Security benefits. Thirty percent of married couples aged sixty-five to sixty-nine receiving Social Security had family incomes of $40,000 or more in 1992. These 900,000 retirees were clearly among the economically fortunate in our society—of any age.

A Roper Starch national poll in 1994 found that retirees can and do live comfortably on the same income that younger working families need just to get by. Retirees, in most cases, no longer have to pay for mortgages, child care, college educations, commuting, and other expenses associated with going to work every day. In addition, they can take advantage of seniors' discounts, and use their disposable time to save money by doing projects themselves, traveling and dining at nonpeak times, and shopping longer for bargains. Even though medical expenses may be higher for seniors, their reduced living costs are why people aged sixty years and older report that, on average, they can live comfortably on a little more than $30,000 per year and can fulfill all their dreams on $79,000, whereas people age thirty to fifty-nine years need about $30,000 a year just to get by.

Families with children are, on the whole, the poorest economic group in the nation, with per capita total household income after taxes in 1992 of $10,300 for all households with children and $6,600 for single-mother households. In comparison, households with elderly members averaged $16,600 per capita, a figure

61 percent higher than that for all households with children (Howe and Jackson, 1994). Solving the Social Security problem or balancing the budget by asking families with children to shell out more money is simply out of the question. In fact, if they fully appreciated how the system works, they probably would be irate at the thought of sending money they can scarcely afford to part with to add to an already comfortable or even luxurious retirement for someone who no longer has to go to work at all.

At one Concord Coalition debate on this matter, a woman volunteered the fact that she and her husband would willingly give up their Social Security benefits to help solve some of the critical problems facing our nation today. This fortunate couple simply did not need their benefits. In fact, each month when their Social Security check of more than a thousand dollars arrived, they went to Las Vegas and gambled until it was gone. For them, Social Security was "play money." Literally.

Some of this wealthy couple's play money probably came from people whose incomes meet the official definitions of poverty or near-poverty: single mothers doing their best to raise children on barely more than minimum wage; college students working their way through; or couples who are both working, paying child care and double commuting costs, and still not earning enough to afford a home of their own. Requiring them to turn over 11.2 percent of their wages to retirees who live far more comfortably and securely than they do flies in the face of common sense and our idea of justice.

Reducing or eliminating Social Security benefits for upper-bracket retirees can be accomplished in a number of ways. The Concord Coalition has proposed a sliding scale starting at $40,000 or $50,000 of annual income, using 1990 dollars indexed for inflation (Concord, 1995). For every $10,000 of income above the starting point, beneficiaries' entitlements would be trimmed by an additional 10 percent. Therefore, if a retired couple had $40,000 of "other" income from investments and private pensions and $15,000 of Social Security, the Social Security would be reduced by $2,000 a year (10% × $10,000 plus 20% × $5,000). Their total income would be $63,000 instead of $65,000. Under Concord's proposal, families with incomes of $120,000 or more would be permitted to receive payments equal to 15 percent of their entitlement. This recognizes the fact that retirees who have high incomes now may suffer reverses in the future; the underlying entitlement to benefits would remain intact in case their future economic circumstances declined.

Means-testing of Social Security involves administrative complications, but they are not insurmountable, as Australia, New Zealand, and other nations have discovered. For example, it will be necessary to define income or wealth in a comprehensive way so that income counted for purposes of benefit determination is not artificially shifted into forms of income that do not count, and so that couples and families do not rearrange their financial affairs or even their marital status to qualify for more benefits than warranted by their economic circumstances; but, administrative complexities should not be an excuse for not asking wealthier retirees to contribute more than lower-income retirees and working citizens toward shoring up the Social Security program and solving the federal budget deficit situation.

Providing lower benefits for wealthy retirees would require a reconceptualization of the Social Security program. Currently, people who have paid FICA taxes and survived to age sixty-two or sixty-five can claim their benefits, no questions asked. The system is something akin to an *annuity* that is purchased in one's younger years and guarantees periodic payment of specific amounts in one's older years. The annuity payout has nothing to do with the owner's other sources of income. However, if Social Security is perceived as an *insurance* policy, then people would expect to be paid only if the "insured event" occurred—in this case, retirement income of less than $40,000 or $50,000 per year. When we purchase automobile insurance or health insurance, we hope we never have to use it. Similarly, if Social Security were viewed as insurance against insufficient retirement income, people with high retirement incomes would not expect to receive it.

This change in expectations would have a further desirable effect: it would tend to increase savings. When people plan for their retirement, they generally have in mind a target retirement income that they hope to attain through a combination of investment income from their assets and savings, private pensions, continued earnings, and Social Security. If they understand from the outset that their target retirement income is so high that they will receive little or no Social Security, then they will have to save more to reach that retirement income. Not only will retirees benefit from these increased savings, the entire American economy in coming generations will be better off as a result of increased capital available for needed investments in transportation, communications, plants and equipment, and a well-educated and highly trained workforce.

Also, the Social Security system itself would be strengthened financially and politically by trimming benefits for the wealthy. On its current course, the Social Security Trust Fund will begin taking in less in FICA taxes each year than it pays out in benefits beginning in about 2012. Reducing the amount of benefits paid to better-off retirees by $23 billion to $24 billion annually would cure nearly two-thirds of the Social Security solvency problem (Bipartisan Commission on Entitlement and Tax Reform, 1994).

Standing by while politicians debate endlessly about who is to blame for Social Security going bankrupt is unacceptable. Anyone who has looked at even the most conservative projections for the Trust Fund can see that Social Security is heading over an actuarial cliff. The sooner we make a decision, the more gradual, fair, and equitable the change of course can be. The time is soon approaching when the course correction must be decided. Asking financially well-off retirees to shoulder a significant portion of this burden should be part of any solution. By ignoring the looming insolvency of Social Security and the unjust distribution of the current system, we are also ignoring the future economic well-being of this country.

References

Bipartisan Commission on Entitlement and Tax Reform. (1994). *Final Report to the President.* Washington, DC: U.S. Congress.

Concord Coalition. (1995). *The zero deficit plan: A plan for eliminating the federal budget deficit by the year 2002.* Washington, DC: The Concord Coalition.

Congressional Budget Office. (1994). *Reducing entitlement spending.* Washington, DC: U.S. Congress.

Howe, N., & Jackson, R. (1994). *Entitlements and the aging of America.* Washington, DC: National Taxpayers Union Foundation.

Rejoinder to Ms. Phillips

TERESA GHILARDUCCI

Martha Phillips proposes to reduce Social Security benefits for high-income people. I agree that the federal tax structures and programs need to be more progressive. I also agree that doing nothing is not an option. This is where our agreements end.

My disagreement with Phillips is not about her modest proposition; she ridicules the very nature of the Social Security system. It is important to view her piece in two sections. The first is a direct attack on the entire system. The second is a proposal for mild reform. Her arguments are inherently contradictory. Means-testing Social Security would transform the program into welfare, subjecting retirees to having to ask for transfers every budget year. Means-testing would divide the population along class lines and exacerbate growing income and wealth inequality.

Her attack on Social Security is filled with sound bites. Social Security is "just like a chain letter scheme," and "restoring full solvency to the Social Security system would require a whopping 4 percent of payroll tax increase to the Social Security Trust Fund. Clearly, this is out of the question." Why is it "out of the question"?

In 1960, Social Security payroll taxes doubled. In 1973, they increased by 55.6 percent, and in 1984, Old Age Survivors and Disability Insurance (OASDI) taxes went up by 42 percent. A 2 percent increase would be a relatively modest 16 percent increase. Is a 14.6 percent rate too high? Far more successful and productive economies than the United States have sustained far greater levels of payroll tax much longer. The average old age pension tax rate is 16.11 percent. Germany's old age pension tax rate is 16.3 percent, Japan's over 14 percent, and Switzerland's over 20 percent. The percentage of the population older than sixty-five years in Japan will go up dramatically in the near future; there is no political pressure in Japan to turn its social insurance system into a welfare system.

Despite common (non) wisdom, the Social Security system is financially sound—it has enough revenue and savings to pay benefits for thirty-six years! No corporation or government is put to a thirty-six year solvency test. No entity would define insolvency as being in surplus for the next thirty-six years. In fact, minor reforms and a 1 percent increase in the payroll tax would restore the Social Security system to solvency for seventy-five years!!

Phillips says that a 1 percent tax increase would hurt the lowest-income workers—"the straw that breaks the camel's back." Again, nice sound bite, but what does it mean? Perhaps if low-income workers did not have access to the earned income tax credit (EITC), it would break the backs of the working poor. But the EITC makes the Social Security tax less regressive—in fact, it makes it progressive. The EITC gives back what the lower end of the workforce pays in FICA, so a tax increase would not "break their back."

In addition to the argument that the system is somehow flawed structurally, Phillips argues that the retirees are better off than current workers. Indeed the standard of living for 90 percent of American families fell every year from 1989 to 1993—even in an economic recovery! The fact that our institutions protected at least one group, the elderly, is testimony to the success of the system. Her rhetoric for more equal income is strong, but she hides deep and worsening divisions of each social economic group by manufacturing generational warfare.

Generational warfare is a contrived battle. The young and old are not divided—all young will be old. Not even a meaningful fraction of the poor will be rich. If Phillips and the Concord Coalition are sincerely concerned about income equality, the Concord Coalition would advocate taxing the wealthy, old or young, more than the poor. A progressive federal income and corporation tax would reverse the deleterious impact Republican tax reform had on income distribution in the 1980s.

NO

TERESA GHILARDUCCI

Means-Testing Proposals

The Concord Coalition has proposed cutting Social Security benefits to the higher-income elderly by gradually decreasing Social Security benefits to elderly with incomes over $40,000. One result would be loss of income to the system because of the loss of taxes. The total savings would be an overkill of savings—a huge 3.4 percent of payroll—which is more than the projected 2.17 percent of payroll that the system needs to be in balance for the next seventy-five years. This assumes, of course, that the higher-income elderly will stay in the system (Goss, 1994). Another way to "means-test" the system is to change "bend points" (the calculation of Primary Insurance Amount). Persons with steady and maximum earnings (now approximately $61,200) would have a 20 percent decline in benefits in 2055, and those with average and steady earnings would get a 8 percent decline. This would save the system 0.61 percent of taxable payroll.

Why Not Means-Test?

Most Social Security analysts oppose means testing because it violates the basic principles of insurance, social or not. Insurance programs pay if the insured contingency is met. In the case of Social Security, the insured contingency is reaching retirement, becoming disabled, or dying and leaving dependent survivors. Programs—tax, transfer, and social insurance—are fair if they treat people in similar situations in similar ways. If not, "moral hazard" or "gaming" takes place. If people with similar earnings histories are means-tested at retirement, the saver with assets would lose benefits, and the spender would receive them. People would spend down right before retirement or not save. This already happens because we have no long-term nursing home care except means-tested Medicaid (International Labour Office, 1984; Myers, 1993; Steurle & Bakija, 1994).

Younger workers who earn the highest wages will receive historically low ratios of predicted benefits over predicted contributions. This is a feature of a mature social insurance system that pays progressive benefits—lower-income workers receive a higher replacement rate on preretirement earnings than do higher-income workers. If Social Security benefits for high-income seniors are reduced, the ratio could turn negative, and so could support from this most influential group.

For this reason, universal income maintenance programs are more politically stable than welfare programs. If one group pays taxes and another distinct group receives, the taxpayers end up judging and resenting the beneficiaries. Judging and screening for the deserving poor is the main reason welfare programs are difficult to administer. Aid to Families with Dependent Children (AFDC) costs 10 percent of revenue to administer, whereas Social Security administration costs are less than 1 percent.

The bottom line is that means-testing the truly wealthy elderly does not yield a lot of savings. To get meaningful savings, benefits for those in the $30,000 range have to be cut. There are better ways to promote progressive taxation, without risking the system's fundamental universal nature. No industrial nation—except Australia—has a means-tested old-age income security program as its primary system.

Can Social Security Be Made More Progressive without Means-Testing?

There are many ways Social Security can be more progressive and bring revenues into the system. (The Social Security system is already mildly progressive because low-income earners' preretirement income replacement rate is 60 percent compared with high-income earners' 25 percent rate.)

Earnings Test and Delayed Retirement Credit

Some have argued that we turn the system back to a true retirement program by cutting back on benefits to those who still work. Now, Social Security recipients aged sixty-two to sixty-four years lose $1 for every $2 earned over $8,040, and those between ages sixty-five and sixty-nine years lose $1 for every $3 earned over $11,160, whereas people who work past age seventy lose nothing. We could save a substantial amount by tightening the earnings test—people lose $1 for every $1 they earned. Studies show that this would not decrease work effort very much, because most people think the reduction is more severe than it is. This would be politically very unpopular because it would be seen as a work disincentive (though it really is not—it is just a boon to those that can keep on working). A possible alternative would be to eliminate the second and third tiers and extend the first tier to all ages.

In 1983, efforts were made to further encourage people to work past age sixty-five by giving "Delayed Retirement Credits" (DRC) to post–age-sixty-five workers. The DRC is scheduled to increase every two years until it reaches 8 percent for each year worked by 2008 (when the normal retirement age becomes sixty-six). The DRC was 1 percent (for every year worked), and it was increased to 3 percent between 1982 and 1992. Freezing the DRC at 4.5 percent saves 0.06 percent of payroll. Ironically, unlike any other pension system, where delayed retirement helps the in which people working more does not save the system money! Twenty-seven percent of those older than sixty-five work, and they are the higher-income elderly. If the earnings test were tightened, the primary impact would be to reduce benefits to higher-income elderly—those who have family incomes above $63,500 (back door means testing).

Raise the Taxable Wage Ceilings

A second way is to remove the taxable ceiling for the employer contribution. Now employers and employees pay no more tax on earnings above $61,200. This would save the system 1 percent of payroll (out of a 2.13 percent deficit). Or, we could increase the taxation of Social Security benefits as ordinary income. Now, singles and couples with incomes over $34,000 and $44,000, respectively, include

85 percent of their Social Security benefits as ordinary income. Lowering the thresholds to $25,000/$32,000 would save 0.02 percent of payroll. Other proposals include taxing all Social Security benefits like private pension annuities (that is approximately 85 percent of the benefits regardless of income) and raising the maximum wage ceiling on employee and employer contributions.

Conclusion

Means-testing Social Security has laudable goals and fatal consequences. Progressivity is a means and not the most important end. "Taxing the rich" out of context is a knee-jerk populist position that, in this case, is used cynically to erode, divide, and conquer Social Security participants.

The Social Security system is a dynamic program that evolves to meet the needs of a changing economy. It has major support of workers in all age-groups mainly because it is a long-standing "contract" each generation has with each other, which, in sixty years, has always paid benefits by the third of the month.

REFERENCES

Goss, S. (1994). [Memo to Harry Ballantyne, Chief Actuary, Social Security Administration, April 19, 1994.]

International Labour Office (ILO). (1984). *Into the 21st century: The development of Social Security.* Geneva: ILO.

Myers, R. (1993). *Social Security* (4th ed.). Philadelphia, PA: Pension Research Council.

Steurle, C. E., & Bakija, J. (1994). *Retooling Social Security for the 21st century: Right and wrong approaches to reform.* Washington, DC: Urban Institute Press.

Rejoinder to Professor Ghilarducci   MARTHA H. PHILLIPS

The major argument advanced against entitlements means-testing is that it would erode political support for Social Security and that curtailing payment of benefits to upper-income retirees will cause them to leave the system. Experience with the federal income tax indicates that this is not the case. In the 1930s through the 1950s, extremely steep progressivity, including a 90 percent marginal top rate, engendered anger and resentment among many in the monied classes, but they could no more "leave the system" than can taxpayers today.

Even with today's flattened rate structure, income taxes are still quite progressive. In 1991, individuals with adjusted gross incomes of $40,000 or more accounted for 24 percent of all tax returns but paid 76 percent of all individual income taxes. Taxpayers in the top 1 percent of adjusted gross income paid more than 42 percent of all individual income taxes. This level of progressivity has been roughly maintained throughout the last 20 years despite repeated arguments in favor of flat taxes and national sales taxes. The disproportionately affected upper-income taxpayers do not leave the system. Indeed, they cannot without risking serious financial penalties or imprisonment. Neither can they just leave Social Security. The penalties for not paying FICA tax are just as strong as those for not paying income tax. Of course, they can, and do, lobby for lower taxes on themselves, but for decades, the interests of the broader middle class and the common good have prevailed.

It is argued that once Social Security is means-tested by phasing it down between $40,000 and $120,000 (indexed) of annual family income, it will receive the same puny support as the AFDC "welfare" program. However, the sheer size of Social Security virtually guarantees that this will not be the case. Ninety-four percent of all elderly families receive Social Security benefits and 29 percent of all families. Although means-testing would reduce these percentages, most retirees would still receive their full Social Security benefits. During their working years, many people no doubt hope and plan for comfortable retirement incomes in excess of $40,000 annually or even into the six-figure range, but most are worried that their hopes may not be realized because of misfortune, financial reverses, illness, or plain bad luck. Therefore, it is likely that people in their working years will continue to support even a means-tested retirement insurance program that pays full benefits to any retiree with less than $40,000 of retirement income and half benefits for retirees of incomes above $80,000 (both figures indexed). This is because, under a means-tested system, the contingency against which Social Security is insuring is not retirement, but rather not having enough income to be comfortably well off during retirement, defined as $40,000 or better.

The discussion against means-testing argues both that means-testing produces federal budget savings overkill and that it does not save enough. This is called trying to have it both ways. Ghilarducci states that Concord's means test starting at $40,000 would yield savings equal to 3.4 percent of payroll, far more than what is needed to cover the payroll deficit. Later, she argues that means testing Social Security yields little savings, and to get meaningful savings, benefits must be cut for those below the $30,000 range. The Congressional Budget Office analysis, which is probably on the conservative side, concludes that immediately implementing Concord's means test would yield savings of nearly $25 billion annually in the 1996 to 1999 period, and increasing amounts as the baby boom generation hits the retirement rolls (Congressional Budget Office, 1994). The Bipartisan Commission on Entitlement and Tax Reform calculated that Concord's means test, implemented with a five-year phase-in starting in 2000, would cure 64 percent of the long-term Social Security imbalance. Raising the age for receiving full retirement benefits (while retaining the early retirement age of sixty-two) would cure the remainder of the solvency imbalance (Bipartisan Commission,

1994). How one judges the fact that Concord's means-testing proposal solves only 64 percent of the problem depends on whether one sees the glass as 64 percent full or 36 percent empty. Either way, however, means-testing solves a large part of the problem fairly and equitably.

References

Bipartisan Commission on Entitlement and Tax Reform. (1994). *Final Report to the President.* Washington, DC: U.S. Congress.

Congressional Budget Office. (1994). *Reducing entitlement spending.* Washington, DC: U.S. Congress.

Should Eligibility for Medicare Be Means-Tested?

Editors' Note: The soaring costs of health care in the United States combined with the improved economic status of growing numbers of the elderly has created a climate that encourages a rethinking of the major premises behind some of our well-established older adult benefit programs. Included among those programs whose eligibility philosophy is being questioned is Medicare. The Medicare program, authorized in 1965 through Title XVIII of the Social Security Act, consists of a compulsory hospital insurance and a voluntary supplementary medical insurance program. These programs are financed through the Social Security payroll tax, general revenues, and participant-paid monthly premiums. During the life of the Medicare program, a series of amendments to the Social Security Act have been enacted to address the escalating costs of health care delivery and the expanding numbers of Medicare beneficiaries. More recently, the Medicare debate appears to have grown more intense, including serious consideration concerning modifying the very structure of the program and its eligibility criteria. Strong voices can now be heard advocating that benefits be reduced for selected subgroups of the older adult population. Should the benefits of Medicare be restricted to economically vulnerable older Americans?

William A. Niskanen, Ph.D., says *YES.* A former defense analyst, business economist, and professor, Dr. Niskanen has been Chairman of the Cato Institute since stepping down as Acting Chairman of President Reagan's Council of Economic Advisors in 1985. He has written and lectured on a wide range of issues, including budget policy, defense, education, government organization, health care, international trade, productivity, regulation, and taxes. He is the author of *Bureaucracy and Representative Government* and *Reaganomics: An Insider's Account of the Policies and the People.*

Marilyn Moon, Ph.D., says *NO*. She is a Senior Fellow with the Health Policy Center of the Urban Institute. Before this she served as Director of the Public Policy Institute of the American Association of Retired Persons and as a Senior analyst at the Congressional Budget Office. Dr. Moon has written extensively on health policy, policy for the elderly, and income distribution. She has recently published *Medicare Now and in the Future.* Her current work focuses on health system reform and financing.

YES

WILLIAM A. NISKANEN

Don Regan, then Secretary of the Treasury and a former chairman of Merrill Lynch, once asked me in exasperation, "Why the hell should I be eligible for Medicare?" Indeed. Instead of insuring people for medical expenses that are high relative to their income, the government created an entitlement to health insurance for all those aged sixty-five and older regardless of income. This basic feature of Medicare should now be reconsidered.

The status quo is not an option. Medicare must be substantially restructured because it is in serious financial trouble. Spending from the Part A trust fund is expected to be higher than revenues in 1996. More importantly, federal expenditures for Medicare are now $157 billion and are expected to increase at a 10 percent annual rate, doubling as a share of national output in 15 years, despite a temporarily slow growth of the eligible population. Moreover, the rapid increase in Medicare expenditures will continue to fuel the relative increase in the price of medical care to all groups. And these problems will become substantially worse when the baby boomers begin to retire in about 2010.

Something must give. The economist Herb Stein reminds us that any trend that is unsustainable will not be sustained; that is correct but not very reassuring. For the government has already implemented several exotic policies to restrain Medicare spending—hospital reimbursement by diagnosis-related group, physician reimbursement on a relative value scale, a restricted drug formulary, volume performance standards, and restrictions on balance billing—without demonstrable success. And there is no apparent consensus on the policies that would be necessary to make Medicare sustainable.

It is clear that a major reduction in Medicare *benefits* will be necessary to restrain Medicare spending. Almost all of the cost control measures implemented have been some form of squeeze on the suppliers of medical care. Such measures have not been very effective, have shifted some costs to other health insurance carriers, and are likely to be less effective in the long run as suppliers withdraw from serving the Medicare population.

The least disruptive way to reduce Medicare benefits would be to income-test the deductible. The federal tax code now allows a tax deduction for only those medical expenses over 7.5 percent of adjusted gross income. Using that same rate, for example, a retired couple with an annual income of $10,000 would pay the first $750 of medical expenses out of pocket, and a couple with an annual income of $100,000 would have a deductible of $7,500. For comparison, the current deductible for Medicare Part B is now $100 regardless of income. Medicare thus would be transformed from a comprehensive health insurance plan to a catastrophic plan for which the deductible is proportional to income.

Several other features of an income-tested Medicare policy should also be considered:

1. The policy should probably include an annual physical examination, not subject to the deductible, to encourage some contact with a physician by all of the Medicare-eligible population.

2. The increase in the deductible should probably be phased in, maybe by 1.5 percent of income per year over five years, to ease the adjustment to the higher deductible.

3. Expenses beyond the deductible should be reimbursed based on the lowest price for a specific test or therapy in the region. Most of Medicare's costs are incurred by a small share of the eligible population, so it is important to maintain some copayments on expenditures above the deductible. All restrictions on balance billing should be eliminated, restoring the right of providers to charge fees that are higher than the Medicare reimbursement rates. This change will prove necessary to maintain the opportunity of the Medicare population to use fee-for-service medical care. Otherwise, the most likely future is that the Medicare-eligible population will be assigned to health maintenance organizations (HMOs) that will make the decisions about what medical services to provide. All charges above the Medicare reimbursement rates thus would be the responsibility of those patients choosing the higher-priced services.

The combination of these provisions thus would lead to a three-part payment structure. The Medicare-eligible population would pay nothing for the standard cost of an annual physical, the full price of the incremental services up to the income-tested deductible, and a copayment for services above the deductible equal to the difference between the provider fee and the Medicare reimbursement rate. The primary effects of this payment structure would be to encourage an annual physical, reduce the amount of routine medical services demanded (especially by those with higher incomes), and to reduce the use of higher-priced medical services for expenditures above the deductible. The amount by which Medicare benefits would be reduced would be a function of both income and the relative use of higher-priced medical services. Eliminating the restrictions on balance billing would ensure a continued supply of medical services to the Medicare population. The reduction of medical services demanded by the Medicare-eligible population would also reduce the relative inflation in medical services to all groups.

Any health insurance policy creates a "moral hazard" problem to the extent that people use more medical services when they pay less than the full price. The changes proposed in this note would substantially reduce the overuse of medical services by those insured by Medicare, also reducing the tax rate on earnings necessary to finance Medicare.

At the same time, it is important to acknowledge that any income-tested transfer program creates another problem by increasing the effective marginal tax rate on higher income. In this case, an income-tested deductible for Medicare would somewhat reduce the rate of return on preretirement savings and the net income from any postretirement earnings, depending in part on one's expected use of medical services after retirement.

The balance of these two problems, in part, is an empirical issue. The magnitude of the first problem is a function of the price elasticity of demand for medical care after retirement and the net interest elasticity of preretirement earnings. The magnitude of the second problem is a function of the net interest elasticity of preretirement saving, and the net wage elasticity of postretirement earnings. My own judgment is that the first problem is substantially larger than the second, but I acknowledge that the balance of these problems may differ among people with different behavior patterns.

All of us, if we are lucky, will become old someday. So it is misleading to characterize the policy debate on Medicare (and Social Security) as a generational conflict between those who are now young and those who are now old. (Those who are now covered by Medicare have no inherent right to current benefits, because most of these benefits are financed by those now working.) The choice of policies should be based on the expected effects over a whole lifetime. Do you favor the *combination* of high Medicare taxes, high relative medical care inflation, and high Medicare benefits on retirement—regardless of your expected income on retirement? In that case, you have reason to prefer the current structure of Medicare. However, do you favor lower Medicare taxes, lower relative medical care inflation, and Medicare benefits on retirement that decline with your postretirement income? In that case, you have reason to favor the changes in Medicare policies summarized in this note.

Rejoinder to Dr. Niskanen Marilyn Moon

Although changes in Medicare are indeed needed over time, the proposal by William Niskanen is not a reasonable or even feasible approach. Although not strictly means-testing Medicare in the usual way, the income-tested deductible proposed by Niskanen would be cumbersome to administer, raise burdens on low- and moderate-income elderly substantially, and undermine two basic strengths of Medicare: (1) the proposed deductible would mean that even very-low-income families would receive no protection from Medicare until their expenses exceeded 7.5 percent of income; (2) by allowing providers who now accept Medicare as payment in full to go after beneficiaries for higher payments, beneficiaries would face higher burdens.

This proposal raises a broad range of practical questions. Who would certify income? If it is the IRS, millions of elderly who now are not required to file income tax returns would suddenly have to do so. What about families with modest incomes but substantial assets? Should they not pay more if we are anxious to means-test benefits? Are there any protections for low-income beneficiaries, because 7.5 percent is a very high burden for people on very tight budgets? What does the beneficiary pay when he or she goes to a hospital?

Niskanen cites the federal tax code, which allows deductibility for expenses that individuals incur over 7.5 percent of adjusted gross income as a rationale for setting a deductible at that percentage. But a typical elderly person already spends approximately 21 percent of family income on health expenses today—nearly three times the federal tax limit. And Niskanen's proposal would raise that amount substantially beyond the current level. His justification for this high a deductible thus seems flimsy at best.

Moreover, the outlook is even worse for those with low and moderate incomes, who now typically devote nearly one-third of their incomes to medical expenses. Although the deductible would be lower for these families because it would be tied to their incomes, their high expenses would mean that many of them would be likely to have burdens exceeding the $500 to $1,000 deductible, and hence most would have to pay that amount before getting any help from Medicare. Adding another 7.5 percent to their existing burdens would be simply unaffordable for many.

Ultimately, this proposal would cause Medicare to be viewed as very different from private insurance. One of Medicare's strengths has always been that it offers insurance similar to that offered under employer-based insurance. This proposal violates that pairing. Moreover, the universal nature of Medicare is an advantage that we should not lightly eliminate. An income-related deductible would discourage high-income beneficiaries from participating in the Medicare program because they would benefit little. It would rather quickly establish an upper bound on who would enroll in a program of substantially reduced benefits.

Medicare will need to face some serious adjustments in the future, but this proposal is not a desirable option. There is no credible evidence that such a deductible would lead to more efficient provision of care. And the program would be substantially undermined by putting low-income persons at risk and alienating higher-income families. Taxing people who are sick and old or sick and disabled is not the best way to finance this program; rather the Niskanen prescription would implicitly lead to a gradual dismantling of a successful public program.

NO

MARILYN MOON

Medicare ranks as one of the most successful federal programs. Today Medicare stands as the largest public health program in the United States, providing the major source of insurance for acute care for the elderly and disabled populations. In its nearly 30-year history, Medicare has contributed substantially to the well-being of America's oldest and most disabled citizens. Its administrative costs are low, and it is popular with both its beneficiaries and the population as a whole. But perhaps most important is the principle that nearly everyone contributes and thus eventually becomes eligible to participate in the program.

It is not surprising, given its popularity and effectiveness, that Medicare is one of the fastest growing programs in the federal budget, gobbling up new resources at a double-digit rate. Medicare has grown at an average rate of just over 12 percent each year since 1975. Nonetheless, with the growing demand to cut back the federal budget and bring down the deficit, Medicare has become an obvious target. This is also reinforced by the financial crisis facing the major trust fund that supports the program.

Among the many proposals about how best to cut the rate of growth of Medicare, one of the more dramatic is to means-test the program. The argument is simple: in a time of tight resources, we should make Medicare's subsidies available only to persons whose resources are below some prescribed limit. Let the rich carry their own burden and help only the poor.

Should eligibility for Medicare be means-tested? I argue "NO" for five important reasons:

First, Medicare is already a very progressive program. Persons pay into the system an amount related to their earnings. So a person who earns $60,000 per year pays twice as much as someone who earns $30,000 per year for the *same* ultimate benefit. And, in 1993, the upper bound on earnings to which the payroll tax was applied was eliminated so that now someone with $250,000 in wages, for instance, will pay ten times what someone earning $25,000 will pay. We need not go as far as means-testing the benefits. If more progressivity is desired, other approaches are possible.

Second, if means-testing were adopted, a major strategic dilemma would arise between saving enough dollars to make a means-test worthwhile and maintaining support for Medicare by allowing many to continue benefiting from the program. If the cutoff is set very high—some proposals suggest $100,000, for example—the number of older and disabled persons who would be excluded from eligibility would be very small. This is likely to be more politically acceptable but would save little for the federal government. A major philosophical shift in the program seems unwise if it is not going to do much to reduce the fiscal pressures facing Medicare. Conversely, if the income cutoff is set at a level low enough to produce substantial savings to the government, the program would eliminate from eligibility many middle class persons who are currently supporters of the program. Medicare would simply become another welfare program—a genre so much in disfavor in the 1990s.

To determine where to set a cutoff for eligibility, we might ask at what income an elderly person is capable of footing the bill for the full costs of Medicare. Consider 1994 levels of spending. The average Medicare subsidy was over $4,000. This new burden would be added to the over $2,500 the noninstitutionalized elderly already contribute to the costs of their care. In 1993, median per capita income—that is, the income level for the average elderly person—was about $12,500. Certainly, at least half of the elderly would not be good candidates for paying for all of their own care because health care costs would effectively command more than half of their incomes.

If the means-tested policy were set so that the average expenditures on health care should not total more than 15 percent of an individual's income, the cutoff for eligibility for Medicare would be set at about $43,500. If the figure used instead were 12 percent, the income cutoff would rise to about $54,200. These levels would mean that very few elderly persons would be excluded from Medicare. In 1992, for example, fewer than 5 percent of the elderly had per capita incomes in excess of $45,000, and fewer than 3 percent had incomes in excess of $55,000.

In addition, further changes would be needed to reduce the disruption from means-testing the program. To avoid the problem of an enormous "notch," where people just above an income cutoff receive nothing and people just below receive the full subsidy, a phase-out would be needed. For example, the subsidy could be reduced beginning with those whose incomes were $40,000 or more and then eliminated at, say, $50,000. Nonetheless, all of these types of adjustments add to the complexity of the program and the need for administrative oversight.

The administrative costs and hassle associated with means-testing Medicare would also erode support in the system—a third reason for opposing such an approach. Welfare systems that require complex eligibility determinations are demeaning and serve as a barrier to participation even by those whom welfare programs are intended to help. For example, just as individuals must apply at the Social Security office for coverage under the Supplemental Security Income program, participation in Medicare might require individuals to fill out forms essentially declaring their inability to provide for themselves.

Alternatively, the current income tax system could be used to require Medicare beneficiaries to pay the full costs of the program if their incomes are above a given taxable income. A similar effort was envisioned for the short-lived Medicare Catastrophic Act in 1989 and led, in part, to the unprecedented repeal of that law. The administration of the income-related premium was viewed as an unfair tax on seniors. To again seek to couple Medicare with the IRS would likely undermine the popularity of Medicare.

A fourth reason to oppose means-testing is the breakdown of the pooling of risk for the 36 million elderly and disabled participants in Medicare. The average costs of providing health care are lowest when the burdens of any one high-cost patient can be spread across the entire population. Much of the rest of our health care system is fragmented and hence more expensive than it would be if risks were better pooled. In this way, Medicare provides an advantage over the rest of our health care system. Eliminating a substantial share of older persons from eligibility and hence participation in Medicare would begin to fragment a risk pool where such sharing is particularly important. Efficiencies from this pooling of risk should not be lost in a rush to means-test the program.

Finally, by totally eliminating high-income persons from eligibility you penalize people who have saved all their lives. Persons aged sixty-five and older with high levels of income generally are either still in the labor force (and hence probably relying more on a private employer-subsidized plan rather than Medicare) or they have substantial amounts of asset income. In the latter case, eliminating them from eligibility for Medicare would occur explicitly because they had saved during their working years. A major challenge facing the United States in the coming years is to find ways to enhance the incentives for individuals to save for their retirement. Penalizing them through the Medicare program when they do so consequently seems counterintuitive to all of the efforts we are making to encourage such activity elsewhere.

Since Medicare started as a tax in 1966, most Americans have for most of their working lives paid into the system and factored Medicare into their long-term retirement behavior. This system—in both the short and the long run—has worked well and ought to be retained. Means-testing would prove a dramatic and unnecessary change in what has been a popular and smooth-running program. There is a great deal of political risk. Means-testing would constitute a major shift in philosophy from a universal program in which we all have a stake to a program with all the stigmas associated with "welfare."

The goal should be to find the right balance between progressivity and universality for Medicare. For example, directing revenue from the taxation of Social Security benefits into the Medicare Hospital Insurance trust fund implicitly serves as a progressive premium for Medicare. There are plenty of other ways to save Medicare money over time, and to keep this effective program in balance, *without* eliminating some from eligibility to save very little money.

Rejoinder to Dr. Moon   WILLIAM A. NISKANEN

Wow! Marilyn Moon regards the rapid increase in expenditures for Medicare as a measure of its success rather than as the major problem to be addressed. Yes,

Medicare, like Social Security, is quite popular among the current recipients and for the same reason: both of these programs are intergenerational chain letters. Those at the head of the chain receive benefits that are far higher than their own contributions, a system that can be sustained for a while only by forcing each new generation to make progressively higher contributions. A private company offering such a chain letter scheme would be subject to criminal prosecution. Such schemes must be stopped in the interests of the next generation; the political challenge is to do this without harming the most vulnerable of the current recipients.

Moon's objections to means-testing Medicare range from perplexing to bizarre. She complains that means-testing would make Medicare more "progressive"; the major alternative to increasing the effective price of medical services to the higher-income elderly, however, is to increase the tax on all labor earnings. She worries that means-testing would reduce the political support for Medicare, but so would a substantial increase in the Medicare tax rate or the Part B premium. She claims that means-testing would increase costs and reduce the efficiency of risk pooling; income-testing the deductible would be only a minor change to the current administrative process, and the pooling of people with different *ex ante* risks involves an inefficient cross-subsidy among risk groups. Finally, she asserts that "there are plenty of other ways to save Medicare money over time" without a hint about these other ways or any analysis to suggest that they would be superior to means-testing. My opponent does not favor means-testing, but compared with what? and why?

Should the Aging Network Be Dismantled?

EDITORS' NOTE: The Older Americans Act (OAA), passed by Congress in 1965 and amended in 1973, created a national network of federal, state, and local entities to plan, monitor, organize, and deliver services to older persons. These public entities, along with the broad array of nongovernmental agencies and organizations that are funded in part by OAA monies, have come to be known as "the aging network." The aging network has received increasing criticism in recent years. Some have questioned its ability to impact significantly the underlying problems faced by America's elderly, suggesting that the aging network is at times more concerned with professional self-interest than with truly improving the lives of senior citizens. Others have argued that senior citizens no longer need a separate network of aging programs and services. Given these criticisms, has the aging network outlived its usefulness? Is there a better way to meet the needs of senior citizens? Or, as some have argued, does the unusual character of the aging network make it particularly well suited to meeting the needs of elderly persons in a society that is at best ambivalent and at worst hostile to the notion of public support for aging programs and services?

Elias S. Cohen, J.D., M.P.A., says *YES,* the aging network should be dismantled. He is associated with Community Services Systems, Inc., a nonprofit consulting service engaged in the development of educational materials, events, and video documentaries. He was Pennsylvania's first Commissioner on Aging and has been a faculty member at the University of Pennsylvania Medical School and Temple University's Long Term Care Gerontology Center. He has received the Arthur Fleming Award for National Achievement in Law, Aging and Social Policy, and the National Association of State Units on Aging's (NASUA) Award as Administrator of the Decade (1960s).

Donna L. Wagner, Ph.D., says *NO*. She is Vice President for Research and Development at The National Council on the Aging (NCOA) and is Director of the National Institute on Consumer-Directed Home and Community-Based Care Systems. Dr. Wagner was a university professor of gerontology before coming to NCOA. Her research has been in the area of community-based services for the elderly, with special attention to corporate responses to employee caregiving.

YES

Elias S. Cohen

Apart from the difficulty of dismantling something that does not exist, my response to the question of whether the aging network should be dismantled is a resounding "Yes!"

The Fundamental Failure of Purpose

The fundamental flaw in the organization of services and programs for the elderly under the leadership of the Administration on Aging has been and continues to be a failure to carry out the objectives set by Congress in the Older Americans Act. The Older Americans Act (42 USC §3001 et seq) declares that "...it is the joint and several *duty and responsibility* of the government(s)...to assist our older people to secure equal opportunity" to objectives such as the following: (1) an adequate income; (2) the best possible physical and mental health without regard to economic status; (3) affordable housing; (4) a comprehensive array of community-based, long-term care services; (5) participation in the widest range of civic, cultural, educational, and training, and recreational opportunities; and (6) "freedom, independence, and the free exercise of individual initiative in planning and managing their own lives, full participation in the planning and operation of community-based services and programs, provided for their benefit, and protection against abuse, neglect, and exploitation."

The Older Americans Act goes on to impose the following affirmative duties on the Administration on Aging: coordinating Federal programs and activities (Sec. 202[11]), convening conferences of public officials and nonprofit private organizations (Sec. 202[13]), conducting evaluations of programs and activities related to the purposes of the Act (Sec. 202[15]), and developing a national strategy for meeting the needs for trained personnel related to the purposes of the Act (Sec. 202[17]). Beyond those explicit references to the purposes of the Act, it is clear from the comprehensive set of duties and functions imposed on the Administration on Aging (AoA) that the Congress intended AoA and the instruments in the states to be vigorous intervenors in behalf of America's elderly.

The Aging Network Has Failed to Focus on Important Major and Minor Issues

The "aging network," with AoA at the head of the parade, has never fulfilled its duties as a major leader or advocate for the elderly, either with the states or with its sister agencies. It has neither undertaken nor provided resources for evaluation of federal programs affecting the elderly, for example, the programs of the National Institutes of Health, the Social Security Administration (e.g., disability determinations of persons aged fifty-five to sixty-two years), and the Civil Rights Commission (e.g., employment discrimination).

State agencies on aging have been no more courageous than AoA, accepting virtually without comment the routine determinations by federal and state agencies that people with Alzheimer's disease are not "mentally ill" or entitled to state mental health services. And Area Agencies on Aging (AAA) have been relatively silent for their part, scattering small grants to fund small programs and ignoring major issues and agencies to avoid controversy. Although they have not funded "bad" programs or squandered funds, none has taken Title I of the Older Americans Act as its mission statement.

Title I of the Older Americans Act laid out an admirable agenda that AoA and its progeny could have seized on as their mandate. To do so would have meant the deliberate insinuation of AoA and State Units into the policy and fiscal debates going on at the state and federal levels on such matters as mental health, income maintenance, housing, long-term care, programs for the disabled, and so on. At best what occurred was the participation of the public aging agencies in some interdepartmental councils and in the White House Conference activities, beating a retreat to the comfort of administering Title III grants, taking on a relatively narrow approach to the real problem of nutrition, and promoting some efforts for subsidizing senior centers and transportation. Doing so produced a pattern and practice that clearly conveyed the impression that AoA, the State Units, and the Area Agencies were minor players in the human services system. The major and minor organizations of older people never looked to the AoA or to the state units on aging as centers of the national or state systems.

The fundamental flaw in the aging network is its lack of relationship to the population of older adults. Early on it abdicated any commitment it may have had to community organizing and group service, which could have developed some kind of network. The aging organizations early on elected to operate without relationship to public welfare agencies and, *mirabile dictu,* without relationship to the Social Security Administration. Neither federal, state, nor local aging agency executives have used the "bully pulpit" of their offices to change the major service or economic systems dealing with the elderly.

The Aging Network Is Not a "Network"

The term *aging network* suggests that there is a *network* of organizations and agencies that share a common view of the world of older Americans, that these groups somehow are bound up together into a relationship that is good for old people, that this *network* toils on their behalf, and that it delivers social and economic goods to them. One might suggest evidence of the network in the federal/state/AAA funding stream (a trickle when it comes to doing something for 35 million senior citizens), viz. the organizations that have been created to reify the "network" (e.g., the National Association of Area Agencies on Aging and the National Association of State Units on Aging). However, a funding stream does not a network make. Neither the National Council of Senior Citizens, nor the American Association of Retired Persons, nor the Gerontological Society of America, nor the American Society on Aging, nor the Association for Gerontology in Higher Education, nor the National Council on Aging, nor the organizations making up the so-called Leadership Council in the nation's capitol are in any kind of "network" relationship.

At federal, state, and local levels there are gaping holes where there is little or no relationship between and among welfare and Medicaid agencies and state or local AAA's, or between emergency medical services, the Medicaid agency, the police, and the AAA—and certainly the state agency is not promoting better coordination. As for Federal regional personnel, there no longer are staff to work with regional federal programs or even to meet with state personnel.

The Aging Network Obstructs Basic Empowerment Strategies for the Elderly

The Aging agencies at all levels continue to organize programs on agency models rather than on the basis of consumer-oriented models. No lessons have been learned from the independent living movement. Case management, dominated by agency direction, is the program of choice in direct service. The aging network is the boulder in the road toward the independence so clearly dictated in Title I.

The Aging Network Is Unresponsive to Major Changes in the Aging Population

What has the aging network spawned? Its largest program, the nutrition program, is a modern-day soup kitchen without the "nosedive" of the skid row mission. Senior centers reach a small proportion of elderly and have neither group service programs nor the richness of the Settlement House Programs that served early immigrants so well. An array of limited in-home services funded less through Older Americans Act programs than through Medicaid waivers obtained from the formerly reviled public welfare programs—important, but woefully insufficient.

If the current programs and administrative structure were ever useful, Torres-Gil's analysis (1992) of changed demographics, reexamination of intent and principles underlying the current system of some services for the aging, and the issues of generational claims, longevity, and diversity suggest they are no longer so.

Time for a Major Paradigm Shift?

What ought to be done? Can it be fixed? Can it be scrapped? Is there a substitute for what we have, and what will it take to get there?

Concern about life in old age requires broad-based solutions to achieve full employment in our economy throughout one's working life, rejection of an unemployment standard of 6 percent as acceptable, elimination of hunger and poor health for children and adults, reduction of violence, crime, and neglect, and correction of the horrendous disparities in the life situations of older women and older people of color when compared with men and majority populations, respectively. Neither the Administration on Aging nor the State Units and their AAAs are equipped or inclined to take on those issues. They are constrained by their history and the expectations of the small constituencies they have garnered. It is time to recognize that we need something different in purpose, function, behavior, and structure.

Dismantling the AoA/State Units on Aging (SUA)/AAA Structure

One thing is certain: neither amendments tinkering with the Older Americans Act nor a new block grant to the states is the answer. We seek nothing less than massive system reform on behalf of the elderly, based on a new view of old age in America. Addressing the issues of the hospitable society for the elderly requires explicit acknowledgment (1) that organizational arrangements are *not* the critical factor and can in no way assure substantive outcomes for older Americans; (2) that a generation of AoA/SUA/AAA structure has been ineffective in terms of intervening programmatically in the major areas affecting what life will be like in old age; and (3) that past improvements in the status of today's elderly are attributable to post–World War II commitments to educational benefits and other GI Bill provisions, improvements in investment technologies, as well as improvements in Social Security and Medicare.

That the reform will take a long time, I have no doubt. But I was at the White House when Lyndon Johnson signed the Older Americans Act, and I have toiled in the vineyard as an administrator of programs under the Act, a researcher and educator under the terms of the Act, and as an advisor to and evaluator of programs delivered under the Act. Now I am a potential beneficiary under the Act. Let's save Title I and to the extent possible scrap the structure, and let's try again.

REFERENCES

Torres-Gil, F. M. (1992). *The new aging: Politics and change in America.* Westport, CT: Auburn House.

Rejoinder to Dr. Cohen
DONNA L. WAGNER

Cohen's argument for the dismantling of the aging network rests on assumptions that this network has been responsible for a fundamental failure of purpose, a failure to focus on major issues facing older persons, that the network is not a true network, and that the network obstructs empowerment strategies and is unresponsive to changes in the aging population. With the exception of the fundamental failure of purpose argument—a function I believe of structural legislative restrictions outside of the control of the aging network—I take issue with all of the assumptions proposed. The network is addressing empowerment strategies and responding to the new aging cohorts—perhaps not as quickly as Mr. Cohen may like, but nonetheless it is making progress.

The aging network is, in my experience, a network and one that works well in response to various external forces affecting older persons and changes within the aging population. It is not, as is becoming increasingly apparent, necessary for a network to be centralized to be a functioning network. And, in the current political climate, federal solutions to social issues will continue to be limited and at odds, sadly, with the "Great Society" days of old.

The architects of the aging network had, as their goal, a coordinated system of services for older persons that would be free of duplication, efficient, and accessible. In an ideal world with unlimited resources and the will to make Older Americans Act (OAA) services a true entitlement for all older Americans, this network may have been successful in reaching this goal. Today the aging network is often described as fragmented and inaccessible and therefore a failure. However, this description is more a function of the limitations of public policy and finance than of the structure of the network. And, certainly, this "failure" is not a function of the thousands of dedicated and hard-working aging network professionals. It is, however, a function of the goal itself.

Americans have placed a good deal of confidence in the private market and tend to view the government's role as limited. This is hardly an ideal context for centralized, coordinated problem solving. The aging network is, in effect, a reflection of this persistent belief system. One can argue that the fragmentation of services that is present is a necessary "evil" of this system. Perversely, this fragmented and loose-knit network may prove to be the ideal structure for a society that places its trust in the private marketplace and resists government solutions to social problems.

The aging of America will require both private sector and public sector solutions, and the current structure of the aging network to some extent supports this partnership. Lacking this partnership, it is likely that the OAA programs will increasingly serve those unable to purchase services in the private marketplace, thus creating a two-tier system of services. The aging network is working to address this problem and, if history is any indication, will be successful in doing so.

NO

DONNA L. WAGNER

No! The Administration on Aging, state Units on Aging, Area Agencies on Aging, and the thousands of programs nationwide that receive Older Americans Act (OAA) funding and make up the aging network have provided an infrastructure for service and advocacy for older Americans. The OAA legislation established a separate and distinct network for older persons at a time in our history when options for the aged were limited and needed. This network has developed and expanded over time in spite of structural, regulatory, and funding limitations and remains vital and necessary today. And, as the aging population continues to grow, this infrastructure will be an even more important resource for older persons, their families, and other human service networks seeking workable options to enhance the quality of life of older Americans. The aging network has demonstrated resiliency and strength during its thirty-year existence and, although by no means a perfect system, has the capacity to sustain a tradition of service and advocacy on behalf of the growing and changing elderly population.

During the past thirty years, the aging network has made significant contributions to older Americans, both directly and indirectly. In a relatively short period, the aging network has designed, tested, and implemented a range of community services and options that address the Older Americans Act mandates of continued independence, employment opportunities, and meaningful participation in the community for and by older Americans. This network has also addressed program standards and practice and continues to actively balance what has become a dual role of the network—advocacy and service.

The past accomplishments of the network are many and demonstrate the potential for the future. In arguing against the dismantling of the aging network, selected accomplishments will be reviewed, including examples of resiliency and innovative responses to rapidly changing service trends and challenges. The first, and perhaps the most important, accomplishment of the aging network is the development of an array of community services and resources for older persons with chronic illness. When the Older Americans Act was first enacted in 1965, the options available to older persons were primarily medical model options: hospitals and nursing homes. Since then a range of nonmedical model options have been developed by the network. And, the aging network has been unrelenting in its advocacy for community-based long-term care models with funding sources, so that today almost every state in America has some form of Medicaid waiver program that provides access to these services for income-eligible elderly.

A second success story of the aging network involves the expansion of employment and volunteer opportunities for older persons. Through Title V of the Older Americans Act, each year more than 100,000 older persons have the benefit of supported employment. Not only do these employment opportunities provide added, and much needed, income to the older workers, the workers are receiving training, experience, and a chance to upgrade skills and expand their future employment opportunities. The aging network has also advocated for and structured volunteer opportunities for older persons through a variety of programs. Programs such as Family Friends, an OAA program that matches older volunteers with families with special needs children, directly address the OAA goal of meaningful community participation.

A third accomplishment of the aging network is support for organized advocacy efforts of and on behalf of older persons in a number of ways. First, the network provides resources and, in many cases, a home for grassroots aging organizations. Second, aging network members are a source of information about public policy issues affecting the older population. And, third, the aging network adds its voice to the voice of older Americans about important public policy issues. Anyone who doubts the strength of this voice need only remember the Catastrophic Health Care fiasco of the 1980s or the wariness of today's Capitol Hill denizens when it comes to framing the debate about Medicare or Social Security.

A fourth and final accomplishment is one that is predictive of the tenacity of the network and its future ability to withstand the massive changes now taking place in Washington. That is the ability of the aging network to leverage the diminishing federal dollars to support services needed by an expanding older population. In spite of a maze of federal regulations that restrict local initiatives, fluctuations on the national level in service emphasis and focus, and a steadily decreasing stream of federal dollars for OAA programs—or perhaps because of it—local aging network organizations have demonstrated resiliency and flexibility in their approach to financing needed services.

Today, on average, only approximately 20 percent of the support needed by senior center programs comes from OAA. The remainder of the funds needed are received from local community sources and special programs as well as fund-raising efforts. And yet the senior center movement has remained strong and displayed creativity in its programming. Health promotion and intergenerational and educational programs have replaced the bingo and ceramics classes of yesterday. Adult day care receives extremely limited OAA support and is now the fastest-growing service in the aging network. Both senior centers and adult day care have developed their own set of standards for practice and professional development in the absence of federal or state mandates. And both are actively planning for new cohorts of elderly in the future.

The demographic imperative faced by our nation as the baby boom generation lurches toward old age is unprecedented in history. The role of the aging network and services in the future will largely be an exercise in improvisation over time, an exercise in which the aging network is currently engaged. Managed care and consumer choice are just two trends that are producing bold and innovative approaches to service within the aging network today, even under the current restrictive regulatory environment. For example, in Indiana and Oregon, the area agencies are serving both the aging and the disability populations and, through special financing packages, are able to offer more choice to consumers. In Oregon, a consumer-directed option is also available to older persons. And many community programs are experimenting with approaches to integration of their services within the managed care environment as well as providing vital educational material to older persons who are being recruited into managed care systems.

The aging network provides a communication system through national organizations that allows the exchange of ideas and best practice models necessary to keep consumers informed and to make modifications in service approaches—as a result of both new trends and changes in the elderly population. Every place the aging network meets, professionals are discussing the implications of managed care, consumer choice, and quality improvement on the existing practice standards. Local and state aging network participants are exploring ways in which there can be closer ties between the disability and aging communities and discussing what lessons are transferable to each other to strengthen the life chances of those served by these two service networks.

There is no doubt that change is taking place—on all levels of the network. The Administration on Aging is an active participant in the newly formed National Coalition on Disability and Aging and, in partnership with the Assistant Secretary for Planning and Evaluation, recently announced its intention to fund a National Institute on Consumer-Directed Community-Based Long-Term Care. This Institute represents an investment in the future of the aging network and the recognition that changes are needed to better address the needs of today's elderly and those of future cohorts.

Although the aging network should be kept intact, change in the aging network is still needed. The changes, however, should be made based on some new assumptions. Rather than clinging to the belief that federal solutions are the answer for the future, and that the barrier to achieving an effective federal intervention is the elimination of fragmentation in the aging network, we need to think about ways in which the aging network can be supportive of families and community solutions. Focusing on the consumers of home- and community-based care is one way the aging network can better address the needs of older persons. Educating consumers and developing more consumer-friendly and consumer-directed services may hold more promise for the future than obsessing about coordination, fragmentation, and centralization of the network. Opening up the network to be inclusive of private and proprietary services will minimize the likelihood of a two-tier system of services, one for poor elderly and one for the elderly who can compete in the open marketplace. And, finally, adaptation of approaches developed in other service networks like that of the disability network, with its emphasis on personal choice and lifestyle preferences, may be particularly useful in addressing the needs of a changing cohort of elderly.

Solutions to the problems facing older persons cannot rest entirely with the aging network, however. The cause of many of the problems facing older persons lies in the structure of our society—our economic system, health care system, and prevailing negative stereotypes about old age—as well as in the choices made by individuals around lifestyle practices. The aging network can provide some help with the accommodations necessary to enhance independence, but it can hardly be expected to provide a solution to all of the diverse and difficult problems encountered by older persons and their family members.

Rejoinder to Dr. Wagner

ELIAS S. COHEN

My opponent in this debate assumes that calling the agglomeration of State Units on Aging and the Area Agencies on Aging a "network" or an "infrastructure" makes it so. It is neither. The agglomeration has virtually nothing to do with the structure or administration of the most fundamental programs reaching most of the elderly—Social Security, Supplemental Security Income, Medicare, Medicaid, housing assistance, or the array of antidiscrimination programs concerned with fair housing, employment, and pension management. It has tinkered, tested, and tried a wide variety of programs—many of them useful, helpful, compassionate, and creative. It has not brought forth a single program that is statewide and uniformly available to all who might be eligible. The programs remain small in terms of both the numbers reached and the resources commanded. To speak of 100,000 engaged in employment programs generated by the "network" is to speak of a program reaching *twenty-eight hundredths of 1 percent* (0.28 percent) of the elderly population of the country.

My worthy opponent has her history wrong. The wide array of options for long-term care were not the product of the "aging agglomeration." Rather, it was programs passed and financed under the Social Security Act that gave impetus to community-based services, notably the Service Amendments of 1963 and Title XIX (Medicaid). For the agglomeration to take credit for what the Medicaid program or health maintenance organizations (HMOs) have done borders on presumption of a high order.

That the elderly of America may on occasion flex their political muscle (to wit the Catastrophic Health Care fiasco) is hardly a testament to the efforts of the agglomeration. In fact, what major legislative programmatic achievement can the agglomeration point to over the last thirty years? Has it made any impact on housing? Has it been able to preserve the highly successful 202 direct loan program? Has it been effective in stemming erosion in the Supplemental Security Income program? Has it been effective in breaking the horrendous backlog of age discrimination programs before the Civil Rights Commission? Did it even raise its voice over the administration policy to deny findings of disability under the Social Security program, a policy that was reversed in 80 percent of the cases that went to court—a policy which had an enormous impact on the young old? Indeed, did the components of the agglomeration routinely provide advocates for elderly individuals who wanted to appeal their denials of home-based services, or was that advocacy task left to others? If the agglomeration points to its record of advocacy, it has precious little to show for its efforts either for individuals or for programs.

The role of the agglomeration has been, currently is, and will continue to be "an exercise in improvisation," a survival dance, often doing good, but more often participating in the maintenance of the status quo, or like a will-o'-the-wisp, flowing with whatever current is moving along. Perhaps the best evidence that the agglomeration is played out may be garnered from the recommendations of the 1990s White House Conference on Aging, best characterized as pablum and pap. Truman, Kennedy, Johnson, and Nixon all delivered messages on aging to the Congress. In 1981, President Reagan sent a televised message to the State Conferences on Aging in which he barely mentioned programs for the elderly. No president has bothered with a message on aging since. The agglomeration has been unable to force its attention on any administration.

Having said all that in rebuttal, I do agree with my opponent about the resiliency of the agglomeration: it has survived! It is a cheap sop provided by the Congress and Republican and Democrat administrations alike. It has never cost very much, it has never produced an entitlement, it is satisfied to experiment, and fortunately, so far (from Congress' point of view), it has never produced any scandals, significant demonstrations, or stirred up trouble. Moreover, I would not quarrel with the assertion that there are some remarkable programs that have been developed under the leadership of some state units and some area agencies, including the Options program in Wisconsin, Case Management in Philadelphia, protective services in Puma County, Arizona, and the On Lok program in San Francisco. But even a hundred such do not a network make.

The time has come for advocates for the elderly to address the hard questions about how problems ought to be addressed without reference to organizational preservation and maintenance. The issues are issues of how we can meet the needs of the legions and cohorts of elderly who through the blessings of less poverty, better medical care, better education, and a richer life experience are marching into our present and our future. One generation of the network is a fair trial period. One generation of the "network" is enough!

Should There Be an Affirmative Action Policy for Hiring Older Persons?

EDITORS' NOTE: It is an undeniable fact that discrimination in the workplace based on age exists. Age-related job discrimination is evidenced at various points, including during the job search itself and after employment has been secured. It has been documented to be a significant variable in explaining layoffs, extended job hunting, and passed-over promotions. It can impact the lives of older male and female workers and blue- and white-collar employees in a wide variety of job categories. The Age Discrimination in Employment Act of 1967, amended in 1974 and 1978, prohibits the discrimination against older persons between the ages of forty and seventy years at the point of referral, hiring, and discharge and in relation to decisions regarding classification, pay, and benefits. Since the Act went into effect, the number of age discrimination charges filed with the Equal Employment Opportunity Commission has increased annually and at a faster rate than complaints about sex and race discrimination. In the face of this disturbing trend, one is left to ponder whether enacting preferential policies on behalf of the older job seeker are warranted. More precisely, should there be an affirmative action policy for the hiring of older persons?

Anthony A. Sterns, M.A., and Harvey L. Sterns, Ph.D., say *YES*. Anthony A. Sterns is the Director of Data Management for Lifespan Associates, Inc., a market research firm in Akron, Ohio. He is a doctoral candidate in industrial and organizational psychology at the University of Akron. Harvey L. Sterns is Professor of Psychology and the Director of the Institute for Life-Span Development and Gerontology at the University of Akron. He is also a Research Professor of Gerontology at the Northwestern Universities College of Medicine. He received the 1994 Clark Tibbits Award for outstanding contributions to the advancement of gerontology in higher education, which includes authoring more than seventy-five articles and chapters and giving more than two hundred presentations.

Phillip Longman says *NO*. He is currently Senior Editor of *Florida Trend Magazine* in St. Petersburg. Mr. Longman has written extensively on aging, entitlements, and public finance issues. He is the recipient of numerous journalism awards, including U.C.L.A.'s 1995 Gerald Loeb Award for Distinguished Financial Journalism. Longman is the author of *Born to Pay: The New Politics of Aging in America* and *The Return to Thrift: Surviving the Coming Collapse of the Middle-Class Welfare State.*

YES

Anthony A. Sterns
Harvey L. Sterns

The impact of an aging workforce raises the biggest issues facing employers today. Like other minorities, middle-aged and older workers will become increasingly prevalent in the workplace. Research supports the notion that older workers have the capacity to continue making contributions to work. Despite the performance of older adults, there are still approximately 5.4 million, about 10 percent of older adults, who would prefer to work and are unable to find suitable jobs. This large number of individuals includes two million people fifty-five to sixty-four years of age, 2.3 million people sixty-five to seventy-four years of age, and 1.1 million adults age seventy-five and older (The Untapped Resource, 1993). Most of these individuals have long employment histories and decades of experience.

Where these individuals are underrepresented in the workforce or past discrimination has been demonstrated, preference should be given over someone equally qualified. The preference is given to overcome institutionalized discrimination that keeps older adults from working when they want to work.

People may not only wish to work longer, they may have to. A recent survey of 12,600 Americans, undertaken by F. Thomas Justice on behalf of the National Institute of Aging, the University of Michigan, and the Alliance for Aging Research, showed that a significant proportion of the next generation of potential retirees have few resources on which to retire. The survey results indicated that, in the 1990s, 40 percent of Americans fifty-one to sixty years of age who were still working would have no pension income other than Social Security were they to retire. Twenty percent of all households had no assets (house, investments, or savings). The survey also indicated that 14 percent of the respondents had no health insurance, and 20 percent were disabled. All of these individuals, regardless of their health and disability status, will feel the financial pressure to continue working.

People will have to fight harder to remain in the workforce longer. Current fifty- and sixty-year-olds were hired at a time when they could choose among jobs. They were a part of the workforce when there was accelerated growth and numerous promotions. They had to deal with the slower promotions and salary increases of the 1980s but still expected that they would have control over how long they worked and when they exited the workforce. At the peak of their careers, they now have much less control or no control at all. Older adults have many different reasons for staying longer in the workforce. They want to earn money and have the opportunity to be productive.

Older workers certainly will have to compete, but they should enter the door with equal opportunity for a position. Older people who enjoy work will want to continue to maintain the social interactions and relationships they enjoyed with co-workers, and they will want to continue to participate in meaningful activities. They should not be discriminated for doing so.

Affirmative action has continued to evolve since its inception after the passage of Title VII of the 1965 Civil Rights Act. Affirmative action is a goal-oriented program to achieve diversity in the workforce. When candidates are of equal merit, preference is given to the members of the underrepresented group to achieve the goals of diversity. Affirmative action currently applies to all women and defined racial groups (African Americans, Asians, Hispanics, and Native Americans). The basis of affirmative action for these groups is employment discrimination, which has been and continues to be demonstrated in thousands of cases annually in the local, district, and federal courts.

Similar in intent and language to Title VII and the CRA of 1965 is the Age Discrimination and Employment Act (ADEA). It is illegal to use age-related stereotypes or assumptions concerning abilities, physical status, or performance. According to the most recently revised Age Discrimination in Employment Act (ADEA) of 1986, it is illegal to discriminate against a worker older than age forty on the basis of age, for any employment decision. There are exceptions for key leadership positions for individuals who would receive a pension greater than $44,000. In originally recommending this law, President Johnson stated that in 1965 the Secretary of Labor reported to Congress that approximately half of all private job openings were barred to applicants older than age fifty-five, and a quarter were closed to applicants older than forty-five (Edelman & Siegler, 1978).

In addition to a parallel system of legislative protections from discrimination, older adults are also a clear minority in the workforce. Over the past thirty or so years, there have been significant changes in the workforce participation of older adults. In 1990, 65 percent of men and 42 percent of women between the ages of fifty-five and sixty-four were in the workforce. For individuals aged sixty-five and over, 14 percent of men and 7 percent of women were still working. The percentage of these individuals in the workforce has decreased, although the absolute number has increased (Kutscher & Fullerton, 1990). The expanding population of older workers may experience diminished opportunities (Sterns & Sterns, 1995), and discrimination is widespread and pervasive (Rix, 1990). Employee charges filed with federal and state agencies have continued to increase. Between 1990 and 1993, there was an increase of 26 percent—to 30,600 age discrimination cases nationwide (Epstein, 1993).

Today, many human resource (HR) managers consider older workers to be excellent workers (Dennis, 1988). However, HR managers tend to expect older workers to cost more than younger workers. In the current economic climate, HR managers are understandably concerned with cost containment and may look less favorably on current and new older workers. And negative stereotypes do remain. Older workers are often considered less flexible people who are unwilling to learn or change their ways. Some HR managers subscribe to the notion that older workers have a different work style, which clashes with the work style of younger workers (Hochstein, 1992). The literature over a fifty-year period documents a pattern of well-established discrimination regarding older workers. Like women and racial minorities, older workers are equally deserving of affirmative action programs that formalize an equal playing field for all prospective job candidates.

There have been more than a dozen Supreme Court cases dealing with affirmative action issues both in the public and private sector. From these decisions, Barrett and A. Sterns (1994) have developed a set of general principles. These principles guide current affirmative action programs and seem reasonable to apply to any group who is experiencing discrimination, such as older workers. The first principle requires that evidence of underrepresentation or past discrimination exist. In this case, the underrepresentation is determined with respect to the number of qualified older adults in comparison with the qualified workforce. Discrimination must be specific to a company. Once a problem has been identified, then it is possible to formulate an affirmative action plan.

The second principle is that an affirmative action plan must be implemented to remedy a specific problem. It should not be an across-the-board program but should be narrowly focused on the problems that have been identified. Just as sex and race are now taken into account, the age of an applicant can be taken into account without violating Title VII. Some variation of the "Harvard plan" endorsed in the Regents of the University of California v. Bakke (1978) is probably the preferred approach. If a work group was composed of only young employees, then an older qualified job candidate would be given preference to increase the diversity of the group. Following this reasoning, age is just one factor taken into consideration in the personnel decision.

A third principle of affirmative action is that there should be goals and timetables, but there should be no quotas. Goals should be established to achieve proportional representation of qualified older adults in the workforce. A reasonable time should be allowed to achieve these goals. The goals and timetables should be reviewed annually. The Supreme Court has repeatedly warned that goals and timetables are not quotas. The goal must be to obtain but not to maintain a balanced workforce. Affirmative action programs should be of limited duration and are not intended to maintain proportional representation by race, sex, or in this case age.

Fourth, like quotas, affirmative action programs also should not unnecessarily trample the rights of nonminorities. Remedial plans that set aside a specific number of slots for minorities, females, or the elderly would be suspect, particularly if competitive testing had been the model in the past for obtaining these positions. Courts have recently cited the need to attempt race-neutral policies before implementing race-based policies (Podberesky v. Kirwan, 1994), and we would support the attempt of age-neutral policies before implementing age-based affirmative action plans.

In addition, minorities cannot be considered in a separate process from nonminorities. We would encourage the evaluation of older candidates alongside their younger competition. The comparative evaluation of all individuals together must be accomplished for the protection of individual rights under the Fourteenth Amendment. However, when age-neutral policies fail to achieve equal representation, an affirmative action program should be the next alternative, rather than court-imposed quotas.

REFERENCES

Age Discrimination in Employment Act of 1967, 29 U.S.C. Sec. 621 et seq. (1976 & Supp V. 1981 & 1986).

Barrett, G. V., & Sterns, A. A. (1994, April 10). *Legal and personnel perspectives on affirmative action and quotas.* Accepted to the Ninth Annual Conference of the Society of Industrial and Organizational Psychologists, Nashville, Tennessee.

Dennis, H. (1988). *Fourteen steps in maintaining an aging work force.* Lexington, MA: Lexington Books.

Edelman, C. D., & Siegler, I. C. (1978). *Federal age discrimination in employment law: Slowing down the gold watch.* Charlottesville, VA: Michie.

Epstein, A. (1993, May 16). Age discrimination increasing in workplace. *The Akron Beacon Journal,* p. A5.

Hochstein, M. (1992). *Overview.* Textbook Authors Conference Presentations. Washington, DC: American Association of Retired Persons.

Kutscher, R. E., & Fullerton, H. N., Jr. (1990). The aging labor force. In I. Bluestone, R. J. Montgomery, and J. D. Owen (Eds.), *The aging of the American work force* (pp. 37–54). Detroit: Wayne State University Press.

Podberesky v. Kirwan, 38 f.3d 147 (4th Cir. 1994).

Regents of the University of California v. Bakke, 438 U.S. 265 (1978).

Rix, S. E. (1990). *Older workers: Choices and challenges.* Santa Barbara, CA: ABC-CLIO.

Sterns, H. L., & Sterns, A. A. (1995). Health and employment capability of older Americans. In S. A. Bass (Ed.), *Older and active: How Americans over 55 are contributing to society.* New Haven, CT: Yale University Press.

The untapped resource: The final report of the Americans over 55 at work program. New York: Commonwealth Fund.

Rejoinder to Professor Sterns and Mr. Sterns

PHILLIP LONGMAN

Sterns and Sterns have failed to show that older Americans as a whole are a victim class, much less that affirmative action is the proper remedy. Many, if not most, members of the age-group currently approaching retirement age practiced or at least indirectly profited from age discrimination during their younger years. Similarly, many if not most members of this age-group benefitted, directly or indirectly, from systematic discrimination against racial minorities in decades gone by. Thus, a typical 65-year-old white man who believes he is entitled to age-based affirmative action has a much weaker claim than do members of historically victimized groups. Indeed, if African Americans and women have any claim to affirmative action themselves, it is largely because of the history of discrimination practiced against them by today's older white men and their forebears.

Why, then, create affirmative action preferences that benefit white men just because they happen to reach a certain birthday? This approach is especially absurd because any such preference will come at the expense of all other groups, including those that have actually been victims of discrimination in the past. Every job awarded to a sixty-five-year-old white man on affirmative action grounds is a job that cannot be offered to a young black man, for example.

It does no good to assert distinctions about goals being different than quotas. Discrimination against blacks, women, and the elderly existed in the past without any need for formal quotas. Whether an affirmative action program uses quotas or simply extends preferences to certain favored groups, the result is still discrimination, or "reverse discrimination," as the case may be. Age-based affirmative action would be no different, except that it would lead to a result perhaps better characterized as "reverse reverse discrimination." This is because white men would be prime beneficiaries of such a scheme, whereas groups historically victimized by discrimination would see the value of their own affirmative action preferences diluted.

Age discrimination exists in our society. Individuals who are actual victims of it are entitled, under current law, to sue for redress. This policy allows for justice in individual cases, without conferring still more windfall benefits on the undeserving.

NO

PHILLIP LONGMAN

Two contradictory ideas drive the ideology of the modern senior power movement. The first, deriving from Francis Townsend and the movement he led during the 1930s, holds that older Americans ought to be universally provided with special benefits on the basis of their seniority alone. "Age for Leisure, Youth for Work," Townsend declared, in pushing his plan to entitle every American older than age sixty to the then-princely sum of $200 a month. Today, this idea continues to manifest itself in the opposition of virtually all senior power groups to any reduction of windfall Social Security and Medicare benefits even for the well-to-do.

The other defining idea of the senior power movement, influenced by the New Left and the civil rights movement, as well as by changing biological reality, stresses the diversity of the elderly. Chronological age is meaningless, goes the common assertion; many seniors are frail and needy, many more are active, alert, and well able to contribute to society. This idea manifests itself in opposition to mandatory retirement and other forms of age discrimination in employment. A pervasive "ageism"—or "gerontophobia," as the Gray Panther's Maggie Kuhn called it—excludes the elderly from full participation in American life on the basis of their age alone.

The senior power movement makes little attempt to resolve this contradiction at its core. Indeed, in recent years, some activists have actually found a way to combine both warring strains of thought in a single policy proposal. The penultimate expression of the inherent contradiction in senior power ideology is the recent call for establishing affirmative action policies for older persons.

The proposal begs certain unavoidable questions. If indeed there are significant numbers of older Americans who are able and eager to contribute to the workforce (and I suspect there are), why do we as a society spend hundreds of billions of dollars every year essentially subsidizing early retirement across the board through Social Security, Medicare, and a myriad of other age-based entitlements? Today, more than 60 percent of all federal entitlement spending goes to the 14 percent of the population aged sixty-five years and older, with most of this money flowing to middle-class families.

If, however (and I do not believe this for a minute), the older population is so consistently needy and frail that it makes sense to distribute social benefits on the basis of age alone, is it not to be expected that employers would make little use of older workers? If one grants this dubious premise, then the rarity of older workers in our society can hardly be attributed to systematic discrimination, and as such, policies to combat age discrimination are hardly worth the effort.

In reality, of course, today's older population tends to be more diverse—in its distribution of income, education, and health status—than the population as a whole. If there is any single generalization that characterizes the old, it is that no generalization holds true for all of them. As the economist Joseph Quinn has warned:

> Never begin a sentence with 'The elderly are...' or 'The elderly do....' No matter what dimension of the aged you are discussing, some are, and some are not; some do, and some do not. The central characteristic to be remembered is the diversity of the aged. The least interesting summary statistic about the elderly is their average, because it ignores the tremendous dispersion around it. Beware the mean (Quinn, 1983, p. 2).

This reality, which is likely to become even more pronounced in the next century given the greater racial diversity and widening disparity of income among today's young, argues strongly against using seniority as a basis for distributing benefits. Age-based transfer programs such as Social Security do play a critical role in reducing poverty among the elderly but do so inefficiently, because most of the resources these programs extract from the economy wind up being transferred to the nonneedy in the form of windfall benefits.

Similarly, the fact that the elderly are such a diverse group argues against the creation of new group rights for senior citizens, such as affirmative action preferences in hiring. True, as the graying of the population inevitably causes programs such as Social Security and Medicare to be cut back in the next century, Americans will be compelled to remain in the workforce for a longer proportion of their lives. But these Americans will include professionals as well as menial workers, whites, blacks, Hispanics, Asians, men and women, debtors and savers, homeowners and renters, saints and sinners, etc. Perhaps the least important detail about any of these future workers will be the date of their birth.

Why then should generational membership in itself become an occasion for special treatment? It is absurd enough that the Social Security Administration mails Ross Perot and thousands of other multimillionaires Social Security checks each month. It would be even more absurd for the Electoral College to double-count Ross Perot's votes merely because he is two decades older than Bill Clinton.

But do not older Americans face discrimination in the workforce? Sure, many do. But that hardly makes affirmative action the appropriate remedy. One reason derives from the fact that age discrimination is not a new problem. This means that the group who would receive preferences from the advent of age-based affirmative action (today's older Americans) includes many individuals who previously committed (and profited from) the very injustice the policy is supposed to remedy. Far from a requirement of social justice, seniority-based affirmative action would in many instances reward those who discriminated against the elderly in the past.

Would seniority-based affirmative action at least bring appropriate benefits to future senior citizens? Unlikely. Instead, such a policy would worsen what is likely to be an already highly strained relationship between the generations in the next century, with the elderly being the ultimate losers.

Affirmative action for blacks and women has had only a marginal effect in raising the economic or social status of these groups but has inspired broad resentment among nonfavored groups, adding fuel to the already raging fire of the conservative backlash. The most common complaints against existing affirmative action programs are that they punish individuals for wrongs they did not commit, that they often reward underqualified individuals, and that they often exclude or discriminate against groups that have also suffered during long periods of history, such as, most notably, Jews and Chinese Americans. Seniority-based affirmative action would provoke similar charges of unfairness and would present an equal, if not greater, threat to social harmony.

Consider, for example, that in criticizing preferential hiring of blacks, not even the most ardent Michigan militia member would complain that African Americans, as a group, are already better off than Caucasians as a group. But those who suffered reverse discrimination under seniority-based affirmative action plans would be losing out to a group that commands significantly higher per capita wealth than the population as a whole. As Daniel Patrick Moynihan has pointed out, the United States has now become "the first society in history in which a person is more likely to be poor if young rather than old."

The comparative affluence of older Americans as a group is not a circumstance that is likely to change soon. The poverty rate among children is now one-in-five. Worse, the slow growth and mounting indebtedness of the American economy threaten to make downward mobility a more or less permanent feature of American society. Indeed, many observers have looked at these trends and at the long-term cost projections for Social Security, Medicare, and other age-based entitlements and concluded that some sort of generational war is inevitable in the next century.

In 1995, President Clinton's Entitlements Commission found, for example, that unless appropriate policy changes are made in the interim, outlays for entitlements and interest on the national debt will consume all tax revenues collected by the federal government within 17 years. By 2030, the Commission projects, spending for Medicare, Medicaid, Social Security, and federal employee retirement programs alone will consume all federal tax revenues. This would leave the federal government with no role except subsidizing old people, providing health care for the poor, and paying interest to bond holders.

These projections are echoed by the warnings the White House has published annually during the first half of the 1990s as part of its analysis of the U.S. federal budget. At the last count, this analysis concluded that if current trends in entitlement spending and federal borrowing continue, today's toddlers will pay fully half of what they earn during their entire lives in taxes, and children not yet born may pay as much as 82 percent. (This 82 percent is in *excess* of all future benefits they are currently promised to receive.)

Long before America ever gets to this point, of course, entitlements will be severely cut. Nonetheless, the burden of supporting an aging population will weigh heavily on the shoulders of the next century's workers, and the potential for serious backlash against the elderly is real. Especially for those of us who are members of the baby boom generation, the last thing we need is a policy that will give today's children even more reason to resent us in old age. The debt bomb we are passing to the next generation is bad enough. We should not add insult to injury by institutionalizing reverse discrimination against the young as well.

REFERENCES

Bipartisan Commission on Entitlement and Tax Reform. (1995). *Final Report to the President.* Washington, DC: U.S.G.P.O.

Longman, P. (1987). *Born to pay: The new politics of aging in America.* Boston: Houghton Mifflin.

Longman, P. (1996). *The return of thrift: Surviving the coming collapse of the middle-class welfare state.* New York: Free Press.

Quinn, J. F. (June 24-25, 1983). "The economic status of the elderly: Beware of the mean." Keynote address for the 1983 Family Economics–Home Management Workshop, Madison, Wis.

World Bank. (1994). *Averting the old age crisis: Policies to protect the old and promote growth.* Oxford, UK: Oxford University Press.

Rejoinder to Mr. Longman

ANTHONY A. STERNS
HARVEY L. STERNS

Mr. Longman makes the mistake of assuming that affirmative action is an issue related to entitlements when in fact it is a mechanism to stop institutional discrimination. Relying on his own version of "generational solidarity," he invokes resentment toward older adults for collecting Social Security and Medicare benefits, two programs that are in fact entitlements. On the contrary, if older adults were able to find employment or remain employed into late life, they would collect a salary and be covered by a company health plan rather then receive these entitlements.

Mr. Longman asserts without evidence that "affirmative action (programs) have had only a marginal effect in raising the economic or social status of (women and black) groups." This implies that raising economic status is a goal of affirmative action programs, which is not the case. Affirmative action programs are intended to help companies who have an underrepresentation of protected groups achieve a correct representation. Furthermore, affirmative action programs have had a dramatic impact on bringing minorities and women into management positions.

Mr. Longman lists common complaints about affirmative action programs, including trampling the rights of third parties and rewarding underqualified individuals. These common complaints are really common misunderstandings about what affirmative action programs do. Implemented properly, voluntary affirmative action programs give consideration to an underrepresented class only when these individuals are qualified for the job. The usual practice is to consider the three most qualified candidates. If a person is in a protected class, this is then given due consideration along with other important hiring considerations. An affirmative action program is not a court-imposed quota requiring a company to hire a certain number of minority individuals, women, or older adults. When courts do impose quotas, it is a result of a judge finding past discrimination.

Affirmative action seeks to equal the playing field where minorities are underrepresented. Affirmative action is not an entitlement. Affirmative action does not cost the taxpayer anything. Pervasive discrimination, as demonstrated by the thousands of cases won by older adults against companies every year, does exist and prevents older adults who want to work (anywhere between two and five million) from doing so.

Affirmative action for minorities, women, and older adults is a win-win proposition. It breaks down discrimination, allows individuals to work and be promoted, and keeps those individuals off the welfare, unemployment, and Social Security roles. Once one understands what affirmative action is, how it is properly and legally implemented, and what its benefits are, this conclusion is clearly evident.

Are Private Sector Solutions to Long-Term Care Financing Preferable to Expansion of Public Long-Term Care Programs?

EDITORS' NOTE: Current and projected future growth in the number of older persons with disabilities has prompted concern about how society will be able to afford the cost of long-term care. Currently, more than half of all long-term care expenditures are from public dollars, primarily Medicaid. However, many question the adequacy of a social policy that requires older persons to impoverish themselves before any public assistance becomes available. Some see private sector solutions as the best answer. They point to the potential of long-term insurance to meet the needs of middle-class and affluent elderly persons, just as private health insurance covers medical care for most working Americans. Others see an expansion of public programs such as Medicare as the best solution. But, is long-term care a public responsibility, or is it best left to marketplace forces as are other insurable events such as illness, automobile accidents, and death? Conversely, can private sector solutions ever serve more than a small proportion of elderly persons in need of long-term care? And, can they do so in an equitable manner, without benefiting primarily affluent persons and ignoring the needs of the poor?

Stanley S. Wallack, Ph.D., says *YES*. He is the Director of the Institute for Health Policy at Brandeis University. He also is Chairman of the Board and Chief Executive Officer of LifePlans, Inc., a Boston-based long-term care risk management company, and Chairman of the Coalition for Long Term Care Reform. Dr. Wallack developed the concept of the Social Health Maintenance Organization, which integrates the financing and delivery of acute and long-term care services, and he currently is developing Medicare voluntary volume performance standards for physician groups and a capitated program for end stage renal dialysis (ESRD) patients.

Joshua M. Wiener, Ph.D., says *NO*. He is a Senior Fellow in the Economic Studies Program at the Brookings Institution, where he specializes in research on health care for the elderly. He has done policy analysis and research for the White House Task Force on National Health Care Reform, the Health Care Financing Administration, the Massachusetts Department of Public Health, and the Congressional Budget Office. He is the author or editor of seven books and forty-five articles on long-term care, health reform, health care rationing, and maternal and child health.

YES

STANLEY S. WALLACK

One Perspective

The question at hand is whether the government should introduce a new social insurance program or perhaps broaden Medicare to include long-term care services, or whether private sector solutions such as private long-term care health insurance are preferable. It is my belief that solving the social problems of the elderly cannot be accomplished using public dollars only. Most social welfare programs for this population, such as retirement income, are provided through a combination of public and private funds. There is general agreement that this should occur for long-term care as well, rather than through an expansion of public programs. Believing we should have the private sector go as far as possible in solving social problems before we use scarce public dollars moves me to embrace a solution in which the government leads in policy and the private sector leads in financing.

In our society, "goods" are presumed to be private unless there is a reason to make them a public responsibility. However, the limited size of the private long-term care insurance market indicates that a major obstacle exists to having a meaningful private market. This obstacle is Medicare and Medicaid, which are viewed as the preferred financing alternative for long-term care by most elderly. The past growth and expansion of these programs has created among the elderly a feeling that public dollars are now paying or should in the future pay for such care. This expectation can be changed only by government actions that result from a new policy, based on shifting the government role from one of financier to leader.

The Rationale for Public Financing: Does Long-Term Care Fit It?

Many advocates for the elderly want to establish a new government program or a social insurance system for financing long-term care service needs of chronically ill individuals. The argument appears to be that because the elderly have Social Security to provide income and Medicare to finance their acute care costs, it follows that the government should finance their long-term costs. Long-term care, however, is far from a public good. It corresponds to one's lifestyle and quality of life, because it incorporates social and housing environments as well as the provision of personal care services, such as bathing and dressing. Not surprisingly, most long-term care services are provided by family members. Our national preference has been to let individuals make their own choices with regard to private goods and personal services. Other life cycle events, cost of rearing children, purchasing a home, and insuring against early death or disability, are the responsibility of individuals. What is so different about long-term care to assume it is the public's responsibility?

Some argue that the cost of long-term care is a compelling reason. However, although becoming disabled is a likely consequence if one is fortunate enough to live to eighty or ninety years of age, only a small percentage of individuals experience very large out-of-pocket long-term care expenses. A year in a long-term care institution is very expensive; if paid directly by individuals, very few could afford it. Nevertheless, approximately half of the revenue of nursing homes is paid directly by individuals. When a few individuals suffer huge expenses, this is an appropriate opportunity for insurance, private or social. Private insurance is preferred except when: (1) there is market failure as represented by an inadequate number of qualified private alternatives; (2) the cost of private insurance is so high as to offer a very limited solution; or (3) the government would be unwilling to care for those having inadequate resources.

With regard to the third reason for social insurance, the general population's reluctance to adequately support the needy, some argue that by having a social insurance program we can assure services for the poor because of its broad-based popularity. No one can question the public support for Social Security or Medicare. With no overall budget constraint, this argument for social programs has carried the day in the past. However, if we believe that we will have to live within a constrained or fixed public budget in the future, the argument is less convincing. Finally, there is the political argument that we will not support long-term care only for the indigent population. The fact that nursing home care is the largest single service expenditure in the Medicaid program and that approximately half of nursing home revenue comes from Medicaid suggests that, at least for the elderly, income status is not associated with the public's willingness to help.

Market Failure with Significant Private Alternatives?

In the 1970s, a social insurance program made a good deal of sense. In fact, both Josh Wiener and I contributed to a Congressional Budget Office Analysis of the long-term care problem and the need for a Part C of Medicare; a social program was the only option because no private policies existed, and we did not have adequate data to determine whether long-term care was an insurable risk. These factors changed in the 1980s. As data became available on the incidence and duration of nursing home use and disability, the number of private insurance companies offering policies rose from seventy-five in 1987 to more than 140 in 1990. There was significant interest among private insurers, particularly those selling the related products of health and disability insurance.

Although the long-term care products of the mid-1980s were very restrictive, policies now have become more comprehensive, and benefits have grown in duration. The value of the policies has risen. Today, the typical policy costs approximately $125 a month (which is not that different from a Medigap policy) and covers more than five years of long-term care in a broad array of settings—nursing homes, assisted living facilities, and in one's home. This duration of benefits covers the expected long-term care stays for more than 90 percent of the population. Moreover, a significant percentage of the elderly have the financial wherewithal to purchase such policies (Cohen, Kumar, & Wallack, 1993). These product improvements reflect the pressure of the marketplace, because individuals want insurance to assure choice and independence.

Rethinking Government Responsibility from Social Insurance to Social Leadership

But even with the private sector responding to consumer preferences, the number of individual policies sold is still very small; only approximately 3 percent of the elderly have purchased a policy. If the elderly are the target market for long-term care insurance, then it is interesting to learn why those with sufficient incomes choose not to purchase a product that provides choice and catastrophic protection. When asked, the answer is not surprising. Some individuals state that they believe the government will pay under Medicare, and those who know Medicare will not pay believe the government should. It is certainly very difficult to sell a private policy to someone who thinks they already have "purchased" the necessary protection (Cohen, Kumar, & Wallack, 1992). These beliefs and preferences are not surprising in light of the past largesse and expansions in Medicare and Medicaid.

A preferable strategy for the Federal government to adopt is to assume social leadership on the financing problem without making it another large public expenditure. Leadership could take the form of federal long-term care standards to assure consumers of protection and tax incentives for the purchase of private insurance. The government also would have to consider how the Medicare and Medicaid programs compete against the private sector. A good example is the recent rapid growth in Medicare's home health expenditures, which have largely resulted from providing less skilled services to individuals for a longer period, indicating a shift toward serving more chronically ill long-term care patients. Imposing a visit limit of 100 or 150 visits per episode of illness would be a straightforward way of reducing the rate of growth in home health expenditures and limiting the program to those with acute illnesses. These actions would send a signal to individuals that the federal government wants to support a private long-term care market and that all individuals, including the elderly, need to assume more financial responsibility. Because these actions are likely to change the expectations of individuals, the impact of such steps would go way beyond that expected from premium reductions resulting from tax law changes. Without these and other federal actions, a private long-term care market cannot develop anywhere close to its potential. In fact, failure of a private long-term care market is the necessary result of the failure of the government to lead.

Balancing Private and Public Financing

Financing for long-term care must take the form of a private/public partnership; those with inadequate incomes must be supported in part by the public sector. A private/public sharing of responsibility could include having the government pay for some portion of long-term care, either the first or the last dollars spent for services (Cohen, Kumar, McGuire, & Wallack, 1992). If a philosophy of encouraging private choices undergirds policy, then it follows that a last-dollar program would be preferable because a first-dollar program could discourage private insurance and could be difficult to integrate with private polices. The public sector could assume financial responsibility after private payments, perhaps covering three, four, or five years of services or some dollar amount, $100,000 or $150,000. Such a program could be viewed as a government reinsurance or catastrophic insurance program. The Robert Wood Johnson Foundation long-term care partnership program in New York fits this description, although in this case individuals become eligible for Medicaid if they have a policy that covers three years of nursing home care (Meiners, 1993).

Implementing New Forms of Social Responsibility

It is becoming clear to most policy makers that we cannot maintain our current approach to social programs for the elderly. Although social insurance approaches have the advantage of assuring us that the program will continue because of its popularity, there is no assurance of adequate benefits, particularly to poorer individuals. Social insurance programs will have to be trimmed back or slashed in the future because we cannot continue to tax a shrinking number of middle income workers to provide benefits to a growing number of middle class retirees.

Policy makers and analysts need to ask themselves a simple question with regard to solving the financing problem in long-term care: will having 50 percent of the population privately insured leave them dissatisfied because it falls far short of a 100 percent solution, or will such a large private market be welcomed because it provides the opportunity to focus financial support on the 50 percent without private insurance?

REFERENCES

Cohen, M., Kumar, N., & Wallack, S. (1992). Who buys long-term care insurance? *Health Affairs, 11*(1), 208–223.

Cohen, M., Kumar, N., & Wallack S. (1993). New perspectives on the affordability of long-term care insurance and potential market size. *The Gerontologist, 33*(1), 105–113.

Cohen, M. A., Kumar, N., McGuire, T., & Wallack, S. (1992). Financing long-term care: A practical public-private mix. *Journal of Health Politics, Policy and Law, 17*(3), 403–423.

Meiners, M. R. (1993). Paying for long-term care without breaking the bank. *Journal of American Health Policy, 3*(2), 44–48.

Rejoinder to Dr. Wallack

JOSHUA M. WIENER

In his contribution, Stanley Wallack challenges the arguments favoring expansion of public long-term care programs and instead supports reliance on private sector solutions. But private sector solutions are unlikely to work for more than a small minority of the population; serious long-term care reform must depend on public sector programs.

Private long-term care insurance is too expensive for most elderly persons. A good quality insurance policy costs more than $2,000 a year if bought at age sixty-five. Lower-cost products lack critical inflation protection and assume that large percentages of policyholders will drop their insurance before they use services. Policies bought by the working-age population are substantially cheaper, but few younger people are interested in buying them. Thus, a major dilemma is that older people are interested in long-term care insurance, but they cannot afford it; younger people can afford long-term care insurance, but they are not interested.

Rejecting the argument that public financing of long-term is a logical extension of Social Security and Medicare, Wallack contends that long-term care is somehow fundamentally different from income security and medical care. But it is not clear how. Although long-term care obviously relates to lifestyles, so does the income that Social Security provides. Moreover, virtually no one argues that the sick or even terminally ill should use all of their income and assets to pay for hospital or physician care, yet doing so is routine in long-term care. If one is "lucky" enough to have heart disease, then the sky is the limit in terms of Medicare expenditures. However, a person with Alzheimer's disease can obtain government help only after becoming impoverished. Such distinctions could be reduced or eliminated by expanding the role of government long-term care programs.

In addition, Wallack argues that more universal programs do not have greater public support than do means-tested programs such as Medicaid. Yet, in efforts to balance the federal budget in 1995, the social insurance programs did far better than the welfare programs. Cuts in Social Security were never considered, and proposed Medicare cuts were much smaller proportionately than the reductions in Medicaid and Aid to Families with Dependent Children (AFDC). Reliance on private long-term care insurance will further divide the financially comfortable from those who are not.

Finally, Wallack proposes that the Federal government should "assume social leadership on the financing problem without making it another large public expenditure." True consumer protection, however, will require standards that make policies more expensive, thus reducing the market. Tax incentives are likely to be an inefficient way of encouraging the market because they provide benefits mostly to people who would have bought the insurance policy anyway. Making private long-term care insurance more desirable by reducing government benefits, such as Medicare-covered home health care, will adversely affect the population with disabilities that depend on them.

In sum, private long-term care insurance will grow, but will probably never play a major role in the financing and delivery of long-term care. In contrast, expanded public programs offer the possibility of universal coverage, a more balanced delivery system, strong public support, and improved access to services and quality of care.

NO

JOSHUA M. WIENER

The current system of long-term care financing is broken and needs to be fixed. The United States does not have, either in the private or public sector, satisfactory mechanisms for helping people anticipate and pay for long-term care. With the average cost of a year in a nursing home exceeding $40,000 a year, it is not surprising that long-term care is a major cause of catastrophic out-of-pocket health care costs for the elderly. The disabled elderly and nonelderly find, often to their surprise, that neither Medicare nor their private insurance covers the costs of nursing home and home care. Instead, the disabled must rely on their own resources or, when these have been exhausted, turn to welfare in the form of Medicaid, the federal–state health care program for the poor. Finally, despite the strong preference of the disabled for home- and community-based services, the available financing is highly skewed toward institutional care.

Although the debate over long-term care has many facets, it is primarily an argument over the relative merits of private versus public sector approaches. Private sector solutions, especially private long-term care insurance, are unlikely to ever play a major role in financing long-term care. Although the current unpopularity of government programs makes their expansion more politically difficult, public sector strategies are much more likely to reduce catastrophic out-of-pocket costs, lessen dependence on Medicaid, provide benefits for lower- and middle-income elderly rather than the well-to-do, and reorient the delivery system toward home care.

The Limits of Private Long-Term Care Insurance

Private insurance against the potentially devastating costs of long-term care is very recent and still quite rare. As of 1993, only about 2.4 million policies, mostly sold on an individual basis to the elderly, were in force (author's estimate based on Coronel & Fulton, 1995). Thus, only 5 to 6 percent of the elderly have policies, which account for only 2 percent of total nursing home financing (Levit et al., 1994). Thus, the hard reality of 1995 is that private long-term care insurance plays an extraordinarily small role in paying for nursing home and home care. The burden of proof is on private long-term care insurance advocates as to why this will change radically in the future.

Numerous barriers stand in the way of widespread use of private insurance to finance long-term care. First, good-quality long-term care insurance is expensive; in 1993, the average annual premium for good-quality policies offered by the thirteen companies with the largest sales was $2,137 if purchased at age sixty-five and $6,811 if purchased at age seventy-nine (Coronel & Fulton, 1995). Most studies find that only a relatively small minority of the population—generally 10 to 20 percent—can afford private long-term care insurance (Crown, Capitman, & Leutz, 1992; Families USA Foundation, 1993; Friedland, 1990; Rivlin, Wiener, Hanley, & Spence, 1988; Wiener, Illston, & Hanley, 1994; Zedlewski & McBride, 1992). Moreover, simulations done using the Brookings-ICF Long-Term Care Financing Model suggest that private long-term care insurance sold to the elderly will play only a small role in financing nursing home and home care for the elderly well into the future. Using fairly generous assumptions about the willingness of the elderly to pay for insurance, Wiener, Illston, and Hanley estimated that, in 2018, long-term care insurance targeted on the elderly will be affordable by only 20 percent of the elderly and will account for only 9 percent of total long-term care spending for the elderly (Wiener, Illston, & Hanley, 1994). Moreover, it will reduce Medicaid nursing home spending by only 2 percent, and the proportion of nursing home patients who incur catastrophic out-of-pocket costs by only 6 percent. In addition, 70 percent of private insurance benefits would go to elderly with incomes greater than $40,000.

Another possible solution is for younger people to purchase policies and employers to help pay for long-term care insurance as an employee benefit. Long-term care insurance policies are cheaper when purchased at younger ages and in a group setting. In 1993, fewer than 400,000 policies sold through the employer market were in force, and virtually all were offered on an employee-pay-all basis (author's estimate based on Coronel & Fulton, 1995). Simulations of this approach suggest that purchase by younger persons through employer groups can substantially solve the affordability problem, but other barriers arise (Wiener, Illston, & Hanley, 1994). Working-age adults are unlikely to want to buy the insurance. They have numerous competing demands on their disposable income, such as child care, mortgage payments, and college education for their children. And often they deny the risk of needing long-term care or believe that Medicare or Medicare supplemental insurance will cover its costs. On the employer side, many companies already face huge unfunded liabilities for retiree acute care health benefits and are unlikely to want to take on another costly and unpredictable expense.

Why Public Strategies Should Take the Lead

The limits of the private sector mean that greater attention should be given to reforming our public programs. There are two broad approaches to publicly financing long-term care. Medicaid can continue as the principal government program to finance care, but be liberalized so that it does not require total impoverishment, or more long-term care can be provided on a non–means-tested basis through programs that cover everyone in need, regardless of their financial status.

Proposals for Medicaid reform generally include using more lenient financial eligibility standards—raising the level of protected assets and increasing the amount of income nursing home patients can retain for personal needs—and expanding home care coverage. In general, Medicaid requires single individuals in nursing homes to use up all but $2,000 in liquid assets and to contribute all of their income toward the cost of care except for roughly $30 to $50 a month. By liberalizing Medicaid, the safety net can be cast more widely so that fewer people face complete impoverishment before receiving benefits and the range of services can be expanded.

A social insurance approach explicitly recognizes long-term care as a normal risk of growing old. There is no cogent reason why long-term care should be financed primarily through a welfare program, whereas acute care and income support for the elderly are financed through the non–means-tested programs of Medicare and Social Security. Moreover, social insurance is the only approach that guarantees universal or near-universal coverage, covering the able-bodied and the currently disabled, the young and the old, and people of all levels of income and wealth. In this way, social insurance does not exclude less-well-off people who cannot afford private insurance or persons with disabilities to whom private insurers will not sell policies. As a result of more extensive coverage of the population than private insurance, public programs would do better in protecting the elderly against catastrophic out-of-pocket costs (Wiener, Illston, & Hanley, 1994). In addition, because social insurance programs provide benefits without regard to income, they have the political advantage of including middle- and upper-income beneficiaries as part of their constituency. These beneficiaries generally wield more political power than the poor, and programs benefiting them, such as Social Security and Medicare, tend to be more politically stable than programs for the poor. Social insurance can also deliberately create a more balanced delivery system by providing broad coverage of home care.

The primary disadvantage of a social insurance approach is its cost. The combination of an intractable federal budget deficit and resistance to new taxes makes this a formidable barrier. Nonetheless, most of the costs of additional public programs will be incurred by society, with or without such a program. Much of what a public program would do is to shift individual nursing home and home care expenditures from the private sector to the public sector, rather than create new spending. To the extent that the presence of public insurance would increase overall costs to society by increasing use of nursing home and home care, the same is also true for the wide-scale purchase of private insurance.

Because social insurance provides benefits regardless of the recipient's income, critics argue that it will be a windfall to upper-income elderly who could otherwise afford to pay for long-term care themselves. But most nursing home patients have low levels of income and assets, suggesting that this argument is much overstated (Wiener, Harris, & Hanley, 1994). Moreover, evaluation of prototype public insurance policies suggest that the overwhelming majority of new expenditures would go to people with quite modest financial means (Cohen, Kumar, & Wallack, 1992; Wiener, Illston, & Hanley, 1994).

Detractors also contend that it would be unfair to create yet another program—in addition to Social Security and Medicare—that benefits the elderly but is financed mostly by younger people. As such, it is argued that a major new program for long-term care would be "generationally inequitable." There are at least three responses to such concerns. First, many disabled persons are not elderly; and virtually all proposals would benefit the nonelderly disabled as well as the elderly. By some estimates, as much as 40 percent of the community-based population with disabilities is younger than age sixty-five (Adler, 1995). Second, be-cause family care is the backbone of community-based long-term care, middle-aged caregivers will benefit from an expanded home care program. Third, gener-ational equity concerns are based on a narrow, cross-sectional perspective of ben-efits and tax payments at one moment in time rather than over a lifetime. Like public education for children, social insurance for long-term care responds to a need that exists across the course of life and thus benefits all groups. Indeed, the current nonelderly population is likely to live much longer—and need more long-term care.

Conclusions

Because it is so expensive, private insurance is unlikely to cover very many peo-ple or to pay for a very high proportion of nursing home care. Nor is it likely to reduce Medicaid expenditures or to diminish the number of nursing home pa-tients who incur catastrophic out-of-pocket costs. Moreover, most benefits will go to upper-income elderly. During the early 1960s, it was considered intolerable that only half of the elderly had some form of acute care insurance; yet, private long-term care insurance is unlikely to ever reach even that level of market pene-tration. Private sector initiatives cannot be the engine of reform.

REFERENCES

Adler, M. (1995). Population estimates of disability and long-term care. *ASPE Research Notes.* Washington, DC: U.S. Department of Health and Human Services.

Cohen, M. A., Kumar, N., & Wallack, S. S. (1992). Financing long-term care: A practical mix of public and private. *Journal of Health Politics, Policy and Law, 17,* 403–423.

Coronel, S., & Fulton, D. (1995). *Long-Term Care Insurance in 1993.* Washing-ton, DC: Health Insurance Association of America.

Crown, W. H., Capitman, J., & Leutz, W. N. (1992). Economic rationality, the af-fordability of private long-term care insurance, and the role for public poli-cy. *The Gerontologist, 32,* 478–485.

Families USA Foundation. (1993). *Nursing home insurance: Who can afford it?* Washington, DC: Foundation.

Friedland, R. B. (1990). *Facing the costs of long-term care.* Washington, DC: Employee Benefit Research Institute.

Levit, K. R., Sensenig, A. L., Cowan, C. A., Lazenby, H. C., McDonnell, P. A., Won, D. K., Sivarajan, Stiller, J. M., Donham, C. S., & Stewart, M. S. (1994). National Health Expenditures, 1993. *Health Care Financing Review, 16*(1), 247–294.

Rivlin, A. M., & Wiener, J. M., with Hanley, R. J., & Spence, D. A. (1988). *Caring for the disabled elderly: Who will pay?*. Washington, DC: The Brookings Institution.

Wiener, J. M., Harris, K. M., & Hanley, R. J. (1994). *The economic status of elderly nursing home users.* Washington, DC: The Brookings Institution.

Wiener, J. M., Illston, L. I., & Hanley, R. J. (1994). *Sharing the burden: Strategies for public and private long-term care insurance.* Washington, DC: The Brookings Institution.

Zedlewski, S. R., & McBride, T. D. (1992). The changing profile of the elderly: Effects on future long-term care needs and financing. *Milbank Quarterly, 70,* 247–275.

Rejoinder to Dr. Wiener Stanley S. Wallack

In this debate, we cannot forget principles: do we prefer a primarily public or private solution, and how should limited public dollars be targeted? I believe that a private approach is preferable when we are concerned with the provision of private, personal services. Private sector suppliers have to respond to consumer interests. The evolution of private long-term care insurance from a limited posthospital benefit to a very comprehensive benefit is in sharp contrast to Medicaid's failure to evolve, as pointed out by Josh Wiener. Moreover, rather than needing a social insurance program to cover home care, just the opposite may be true. Because the inclusion of home care as a benefit can lead to substantial inappropriate use, a managed care system seems more appropriate.

Josh Wiener bases his argument, first and foremost, on the notion that most elderly cannot afford a "good" policy, which is said to cost more than $2,100 for a sixty-five-year-old and more than $6,800 for a person at age seventy-nine. However, the *actual* average premium for a sixty-five-year-old is approximately $1,400. A major reason for this difference between actual premiums and what Josh Wiener stated would be a good policy, is that many purchasers do not want to buy inflation insurance, which requires them to pay premiums up front for higher benefits in future years. Interestingly, when Josh Wiener discusses social insurance, he does not talk in terms of actuarially sound premiums, but a pay-as-you-go financing scheme. I am troubled by the implication of Josh Wiener's idea that middle- and upper-class elderly are unable to afford private long-term care insurance when society can afford social insurance through an increasing level of intergenerational transfers.

Wiener argues that only a few elderly can afford to buy private long-term care insurance and that, therefore, there will be little impact on the number insured and Medicaid costs. Empirical evidence—not simulations—shows that the purchasers of long-term care insurance are often middle-class elderly who are most worried about covering a catastrophic expenditure. Using data on the income and asset level of actual purchases and the level of benefits they select, my colleagues and I found that between 29 and 38 percent of policy holders that use nursing homes would have gone on Medicaid if they did not own a policy.

Josh Wiener and I do not disagree that the current level of private policies sold is very low and that if this level is maintained, a private solution holds little hope for solving a major part of this social problem. However, I sometimes think that the existence of any private policies is rather remarkable in light of the existence of Medicaid and Medicare and nonexistence of public support for a private solution. There is no doubt that a private solution requires public leadership and policies encouraging individuals to purchase private plans. A strong signal needs to be sent to the general public about the need to protect against this risk. Private solutions with public leadership are the best way to achieve this.

Should Age Be Abandoned as a Basis for Program and Service Eligibility?

EDITORS' NOTE: Virtually every society has provided a special status for its older members, typically including honorific roles, relief from physically onerous tasks, and the receipt of assistance based on age or disability. In the United States, older adults are entitled to income support through Social Security, health care through Medicare, even discount bus passes and movie tickets. Yet, the dramatic improvement in the economic and physical well-being of America's elderly in the past thirty years has led many to question whether it is appropriate for older adults to receive such special treatment based solely on age. Moreover, some gerontologists such as Bernice Neugarten have suggested that the United States is becoming an "age-irrelevant society," in which chronological age makes little difference in terms of what one can do or what benefits one should receive. They argue that age should be replaced by more appropriate measures of need as the criteria for allocating societal resources. Yet, is there nothing that a person is entitled to based simply on reaching an advanced age? Are there no rights and privileges that should be available to all elderly persons, regardless of need? Should age-based programs be abandoned altogether?

John H. Skinner, Ed.D., says *YES.* He is Associate Professor of Gerontology and Director of the Ph.D. in Aging Studies program at the University of South Florida in Tampa, Florida. He has served as Associate Commissioner on Aging for Research, Demonstrations, and Evaluations in the Administration on Aging, has been Vice President of the Gerontological Society of America, and has held leadership roles in a variety of other policy, program development, and research organizations.

Elizabeth A. Kutza, Ph.D., says *NO*. She is Director of the Institute on Aging at Portland State University. Dr. Kutza's special interest is in the field of federal aging policy. Author of *The Benefits of Old Age: Social Welfare Policy for the Elderly* (University of Chicago Press, 1981) and editor of *Diversity in Aging: Challenges Facing Planners and Policymakers in the 1990s,* Dr. Kutza also has written widely in the area of long-term care and community-based aging services.

YES

John H. Skinner

In an increasingly diverse society facing scarce resources and constrained public spending, age-based programs have a number of shortcomings: (1) exacerbation of intergenerational tensions; (2) reduction of resources available to persons in greatest need; and (3) inattention to the heterogeneity of the elderly. This article explores these issues and argues in favor of abandoning age-based programs in favor of more clearly defined need-driven programs.

Age Stigmatization

Although age-based programs offer the advantage of garnering broad political support from older people, these programs also have the negative side effect of aggravating intergenerational tensions (Minkler, 1991). At a time when the population of persons older than sixty-five years of age is rapidly growing and younger members of the labor force are declining, the emphasis on age-based programs only further exacerbates concerns about intergenerational conflict. It is difficult to promote programs for one age-group, independent of need, without creating the appearance of selectivity and bias.

Proponents of universality have argued that special targeting of programs by need creates a welfare stigma for those program participants, especially when those programs are means-tested. However, age-based programs stigmatize an entire group of people as ill, frail, poor, lonely, depressed, or demented. Age-based programs also stigmatize older persons as "greedy geezers" wanting programs they do not really need. Need-based programs, however, reflect a humane, ethical, and caring society responding to its most disadvantaged citizens.

Universality versus Targeting Resources

Age-based programs confer special privileges on a population group based on dubious claims of entitlement. Specifically, using age as the sole criterion of entitlement produces problems when resources are limited. For all older persons to receive benefits, even if not needed, those persons in greatest need will inevitably receive less than they should.

Is it more fair to have universal eligibility that will include a large percentage of false positives (people who are eligible for services but who do need them), or is it more fair to target eligibility that focuses public resources toward those who truly need them (a large percentage of true positives)? Universal eligibility faces the risk of alienating large numbers of older persons by raising false expectations for services that cannot be met with scarce resources. Need-targeted eligibility focuses scarce resources on the most needy, providing a rational allocation of benefits.

Age Is a Poor Proxy for Need

Age is a poor proxy for need, because of the heterogeneous nature of the elderly population in the United States. Although old age is often associated with the loss of vitality and health, many elders are vital and healthy even at advanced ages (partly because of the availability of Medicare). Although older people as a group have median incomes that are lower than those of most middle-aged adults, many older persons have substantial incomes and assets (predominantly as a result of Social Security and private pensions). Before the establishment of Social Security and the growth of private pensions after World War II, age was a better predictor of low income and poverty among the elderly than it is now (Achenbaum, 1994). Even when the public is asked to rank Social Security, Medicare (both age-based programs), and Supplemental Income (age-based), they consider the poverty status of the recipient in their ranking (Cook & Barrett; 1992). This implies that the public is employing a need-based reference in their ranking.

The use of age as a categorical proxy indicator is based on the assumption that most older persons are needy; however, the evidence indicates that they are not. The use of age as a proxy indicator of need may be relatively efficient and even convenient, but it is not effective, equitable, or fair. Categorical proxy indicators are notorious in not only capturing the needy but also including large segments of the less needy or even those with no need at all.

A Broader Definition of Need

In arguing that age be replaced by need as a basis for program and service eligibility, it is important to consider what criteria should be used for determining need. Classically, need-based programs have relied on means-testing as the basis of determining eligibility; however, there are other needs that should be considered in any debate of need-based programs. However, it may be more useful to categorize needs as immediate or anticipated. Immediate needs require responses to address a current status or condition, whereas anticipated needs offer the advantage of taking actions now to prepare for needs that are expected to occur in the future.

Taking into consideration our conceptualization of immediate and anticipated needs, it is possible to reframe needs into three types:

1. Prevention of poverty
2. Improving functional and social conditions
3. Maintenance of lifestyle through deferred income

Prevention of Poverty

Income needs associated with the prevention of poverty most closely relate to those identified with existing means-tested "welfare" programs such as Medicaid, Food Stamps, Supplemental Security Income, etc. These programs are explicitly designed to reduce the effects of poverty by providing income assistance designed to enable persons to live at subsistence levels. These programs may provide benefits through direct payments to beneficiaries, subsidies, or payments to providers on behalf of beneficiaries.

Improving Functional and Social Conditions

Functional and social needs relate to the ability of individuals to live as independently as possible in the society, thereby reducing further public involvement at a greater cost later. Examples include the Older Americans Act and community-based long-term care programs (Torres-Gil and Puccinelli, 1994). Programs addressing functional and social needs give priority to individuals with these needs, although income and the ability to pay also may be taken into consideration.

Maintenance of Lifestyle through Deferred Income

Maintenance of lifestyle needs are long-term projections of income needs in old age for which individuals at younger ages forego current income for benefits in the future. Examples include Social Security (Old Age Survivors Insurance) and Medicare (Hospital Insurance), both of which require workers to make lifetime contributions in the expectation that they will receive benefits when they need them in retirement. Binstock (1994) has indicated that these programs can be categorized as beginning to combine age and economic status as policy criteria for eligibility. Even though Social Security is more properly described as an (intergenerational) income transfer program, it has been sold to the American public by name and is still popularly thought of as a retirement insurance program. The fact that it uses the terminology of insurance programs (coverage, benefits, beneficiaries, etc.) contributes to this confusion (Skinner, 1991).

Conclusion

Age-based programs are less equitable and efficient than programs based on need. Need-based programs, especially those designed to maintain people's lifestyles through deferred income programs, exemplify the American values of self-sufficiency, autonomy, and independence by having citizens contribute to their future well-being.

Existing programs considered to reflect universal age-based entitlement (e.g., Social Security, Medicare, and Medicaid) are not truly universal. They, in fact, are targeted programs that segment the population into subsets (the elderly, the disabled, the poor), based on proxies of needs for services and benefits in the underlying populations. Because these programs do not explicitly identify the underlying needs or population segment that they ultimately target, they are less efficient and effective in achieving their objectives than are programs that are explicitly need based.

Programs in health and social welfare that are truly universal are required to end the age-versus-need debate. Truly universal programs would provide services to all citizens and legal residents in the United States, regardless of age or other demographic characteristics. These programs must be need driven, providing services to all those who require their benefits and services.

REFERENCES

Achenbaum, W. A. (1994). U.S. retirement in historical context. In A. Monk (Ed.), *The Columbia retirement handbook* (pp. 12–28). New York: Columbia University Press.

Binstock, R. H. (1994). Changing criteria in old-age programs: The introduction of economic status and need for services. *The Gerontologist, 34*(6), 726–727.

Cook, F. L., & Barrett, E. J. (1992). *Support for the American welfare state: The view of Congress and the public.* New York: Columbia University Press.

Minkler, M. (1991). "Generational Equity" and the new victim blaming. In M. Minkler. & C. Estes (Eds.), *Critical perspectives on aging: The political and moral economy of growing old* (pp. 67–79). Amityville, NY: Baywood Publishing Co.

Skinner, J. H. (1991, Fall/Winter). Entitlements: What do they mean? *Generations,* pp. 16, 19.

Torres-Gil, F. M., & Puccinelli, M. A. (1994). Mainstreaming gerontology in the policy area. *The Gerontologist, 34*(6), 749–752.

Rejoinder to Professor Skinner   ELIZABETH A. KUTZA

My colleague John Skinner seems to put forward some compelling arguments for abandoning age as a basis for program and service eligibility. However, on closer examination, these arguments are built on some questionable assertions and shaky generalizations.

The assertion that age-based programming exacerbates intergenerational tensions, for example, assumes that what the media trumpets as sentiment of the young toward the old is in fact true. Terms such as *greedy geezers,* however, come from the mouths of journalists, not from younger citizens. When younger people are directly asked questions about their support for age-based programming, it is generally positive. Recently, for example, the American Association of Retired Persons (AARP) did a telephone survey with one thousand people older than eighteen years of age, asking them whether Social Security and Medicare should be cut to reduce the federal deficit. In the age-group eighteen to thirty-four, 86 percent opposed such cuts; in the thirty-five to forty-nine age-group, 89 percent were in opposition (AARP, 1994). In addition to viewing these programs as very important, the younger generations did not believe that recipients were getting more than their fair share. Ninety-five percent of respondents held this view, hardly evidence of impending intergenerational warfare around resource sharing.

Dr. Skinner also asserts that age-based programs stigmatize the elderly as needy and frail. I would counter that these societal attitudes are formed quite independently of whether one knows about age-based programs. Another AARP study looked at the differences in attitudes toward aging of 423 students, aged six to eleven years. Children were asked to draw a picture of an older person and a younger person. Those who drew an older person they knew, like a grandparent, were more likely to portray the older person in positive ways. Children with generalized drawings of older persons they did not know often drew negative stereotypes. The older the child, the more negative the portrayal (AARP, 1995). It is not the existence of age-based programming that leads to these views, but rather the deeply ingrained attitudes embedded in our society. It is only when the status of older persons, now so devalued, is again given legitimacy that these negative stereotypes will abate.

There is one area on which my colleague Dr. Skinner and I agree—the debate about substituting "need" for "age" needs better specification. What is need? How can it be measured? Neither of these is a simple question with a simple answer. The answers also have implications for the scarce resources to which Dr. Skinner alludes.

Part of the appeal of age-based programming is its administrative efficiency. Any form of needs-testing increases a program's administrative costs because it requires labor-intensive eligibility determination—whether a financial review or a functional assessment screening. One need seriously question whether it is better to expend scarce resources on administrative and personnel costs directed at making sure only the "truly needy" are served, or provide benefits to a few "false positives." Until these questions are answered, I would support the latter.

REFERENCES

American Association of Retired Persons. (1994, December). *Horizons: Research Newsletter,* 4(6).
American Association of Retired Persons. (1995, April). *Horizons: Research Newsletter,* 5(2).

NO

ELIZABETH A. KUTZA

Arguments in favor of retaining age as a basis for program and service eligibility stand on a broad foundation, one found in the social, moral, and political structures of American society. Our economic institutions, for example, largely exclude older persons from meaningful work and substantial gainful employment. Covert and overt age discrimination in the private sector may even restrict the opportunities for employment available to persons in their forties and fifties. Thus, income security in late life needs to come from other, predominantly public, sources. In addition, an organized and civilized society brings with it a moral obligation to respect its older members. Mutual obligations between generations have always been assumed. From the standpoint of contributions made by persons across a lifetime, as reflected in the social capital they leave behind, older persons deserve special consideration and respect. And finally, American political structures encourage the development of age-based programs. Older persons have a right to organize in their own behalf, and if the outcome of this organizing is age-based programming, such programming should remain as a reflection of this political preference.

Influence of Social Structures

A substantial part of the social structure of modern society is reflected in our work roles. Increasingly, these work roles are performed outside the home. Through the middle years, most men and two-thirds of all women work in the labor force full-time (Schulz, 1992). Thus, the primary source of support for individuals in today's society is through trading one's labors on the open market for wages and salaries that provide for income needs. This contrasts to earlier agricultural and pre-industrial periods, when individuals received economic security through the production of their own goods, which they could sell or barter.

Accompanying this change in the nature of work has been a change in the nature of how one ends his or her work life. Instead of continuing to contribute to the economic viability of the family in late life, albeit through reduced effort, individuals in late life today are abruptly terminated from their work through retirement. As Zena Blau has noted: "The social expectation that older people must give up their jobs at some fixed age, therefore, often represents a marked and sudden discontinuity for the individual, particularly for men, whether they themselves accept this norm or not" (Blau, 1981, p. 34).

Although retirement is no longer mandatory, policies in the public and private sectors do provide incentives to individuals that encourage withdrawal from the workplace. And, individuals have been responding to these incentives. For men aged fifty-five to fifty-nine years, labor force participation rates have dropped from over 90 percent to less then 80 percent during the period 1964 to 1989. For men 60 to 64 years of age, partly in response to eligibility for Social Security benefits and the growing availability of early retirement options in private pensions, labor force participation rates have plummeted from 80 to 55 percent over this twenty-five–year period (Quinn, Burkhauser, & Myers, 1990).

Thus, the social structure of modern society has defined older persons as out of the economic mainstream. And, as compensation for the results of such exclusion, public income maintenance programs such as social security must continue to be, and logically must remain, age based.

The Moral Imperative

A second argument for the retention of age as a basis for program and service eligibility is based on the ethical principle of "just reward." The elderly deserve special programs because of their past contributions to society, both personal and economic. The society is maintained through the children they have raised and the things they have contributed. It is thus argued that programs for support of older persons are right and just (Kutza, 1981).

Albert Jonsen, a Jesuit philosopher, has written:

> The elderly themselves, as members of society, even though not necessarily as individuals, have participated in the creation of these social goods. The state of science, technology, medicine, and culture are effects of the elderly having lived communally through their histories. Effective recognition of their autonomy requires the application of that science, technology, medicine, and culture on their plight. This is due to them in justice (Jonsen, 1976, p. 101–102).

Another way this principle is sometimes presented is as "veteranship." The elderly, *by virtue of their age,* have a veteranship status in society that should be honored and attended to. In most traditional or "preindustrial" societies, the appearance of respect for the elderly prevails, and they receive public marks of deference (Perlmutter & Hall, 1992). Achenbaum (1979) notes a long-standing historical belief among Americans that years of experience make older persons sagacious and exemplary. The adjective *venerable,* for example, was often used in the writings of pre–Civil War America to "identify relatively obscure aged men and women who were considered upright and respected members of their community" (p. 18). As Maggie Kuhn has said, "Old age is not a disease—it is strength and survivorship, triumph over all kinds of vicissitudes and disappointments, trials and illnesses" (Hessel, 1977, p. 54). Thus, a second rationale for the retention of age-based programming is found in ethical imperatives.

Influence of Political Structure

A final argument is found in our political structure. Ours is a representative form of government. Under such a structure, the political process usually responds to the power of a particular constituency. The elderly are a constituency of some influence because of their increasing numbers and because of their voting behavior (a higher percentage of older persons vote than any other age-group). Some observers think that the growth of programs for the elderly can be understood as a response to the visibility of older people as a political constituency.

If the political structure encourages groups to organize in their own behalf, it is to be expected and accepted that older persons will pursue age-based programming. As farmers support programs targeted toward themselves, and the oil industry supports programs targeted toward themselves, so too the elderly should be able to politically agitate in their own behalf and pursue age-based policies and programs. Although unlimited support for the elderly may not be possible, the public readily acknowledges a willingness to support services considered "life-supporting"—such as income and health care—through taxation.

Cook and Barrett (1992) report on the results of a random nationwide sample of 1,209 residents of the United States who were asked in-depth questions aimed at measuring their support of specific social welfare policies and programs. When asked whether benefits for Social Security, Medicare, and Supplemental Security Income (SSI) programs should be increased, decreased, or maintained at current levels, between 96 and 97 percent of respondents indicated that they wanted benefits to be either maintained or increased. In addition, the researchers found that social security was what they termed "doubly blessed"—it has both supporters who are more actively committed and opponents who are less active—compared with other social welfare programs examined. Moreover, when respondents were asked to rank-order six recipient groups as to their preference to provide them with financial support, disabled elderly who were poor ranked first and poor elderly who were not disabled ranked second. Poor children and poor or disabled adults were ranked lower than these elderly recipient groups. Thus, the public itself seems to support age-based programming and may provide continued political support for such programs.

Conclusion

The circumstances of the elderly are determined by and embedded in societal context. When societal institutions and institutional arrangements disadvantage a person of advanced age, public policies and programs must step in. The capacity of the elderly to remain integrated into our dominant economic system has been compromised over time through decisions made by the larger society. Older persons are not welcomed in the labor force, resulting in the need for an alternate income maintenance system such as social security or SSI. And as it is age by which people are excluded, it is appropriate that age be an eligibility criterion for receipt of benefits from this alternate, compensatory system.

Society's ethical responsibilities to those who have contributed to the physical, human, and social capital of the nation also supports the appropriateness of policies that are age based. And finally, full participation in the benefits of the political process leads to policies that are targeted to special interest groups, including older Americans.

References

Achenbaum, W. A. (1979). *Old age in the new land: The American experience since 1790.* Baltimore: Johns Hopkins University Press.

Blau, Z. S. (1981). *Aging in a changing society* (2nd ed.). New York: Franklin Watts.

Cook, F. L., & Barrett, E. J. (1992). *Support for the American welfare state: The views of Congress and the public.* New York: Columbia University Press.

Hessel, D. (ed.). (1977). *Maggie Kuhn on aging: A dialogue.* Philadelphia: Westminister Press.

Jonsen, A. R. (1976). Principles for an ethics of health services. In B. Neugarten & R. J. Havighurst (Eds.), *Social policy, social ethics, and the aging society.* Washington, DC: U.S. Government Printing Office.

Kutza, E. A. (1981). *The benefits of old age: Social welfare policy for the elderly.* Chicago: The University of Chicago Press.

Perlmutter, M., & Hall, E. (1992). *Adult development and aging.* (2nd ed.). New York: John Wiley.

Quinn, J. F., Burkhauser, R. V., & Myers, D. A. (1990). *Passing the torch: The influence of economic incentives on work and retirement.* Kalamazoo, MI: W. E. Upjohn Institute for Employment Research.

Schulz, J. H. (1992). *The economics of aging* (5th ed.). New York: Auburn House.

Rejoinder to Dr. Kutza
John H. Skinner

Since the early 1980s, the forces intent on dismantling the programs of the New Deal and The Great Society have controlled the debate by casting social policy issues within the context of an economic crisis. They have further established the parameters of the debate by arguing *against* any tax increases, and *for* program cuts to reduce budget deficits. These tactics have effectively cut off any discussion of the importance of social programs based on value and ethical arguments.

An environment of economic crisis (real or contrived) reduces or minimizes all policy claims to issues of economics. This one-dimensional policy agenda is not receptive to ethical, moral, social, or philosophical (bleeding liberal) claims. The one approach that offers hope for social programming in the 1990s is to address programs that serve needs. The task for proponents of programs for the aged is to recast programs issues into need-based rhetoric. Even in a cost containment, budget deficit reduction atmosphere, arguments to serve the truly needy still have salience.

The debate over who are the truly needy goes back to the Elizabethan Poor Laws of the 1500s. Regardless of shifts between more or less magnanimity, the concept of a government responsibility to address needy citizens has its roots in Anglo-Saxon colonial society and persists even in these times of self-righteous attempts to return to a glorified past of little government involvement. When all things are considered, we still must question what we will do for our needy citizens. During times of scarce resources, attempts are made to assume the best use of those resources by addressing needs. Therefore, need-based programs and need-based policy claims have a greater chance of receiving support than do policy arguments based on values, ethics, or social justice.

Although Social Security may be an income maintenance program, its political viability lies in the fact that it is contributory throughout one's work life and provides for anticipated income needs in later life. The combined features of contributory payments (taxes) and the concept of paying today for needs that are anticipated in the future make Social Security and Medicare unique among programs for the elderly. Social Security and Medicare are earned benefits, paid according to a social contract, that promise to partially address income and medical care needs in the future for those who have faithfully paid for those benefits of others during their work lives.

At a time of changing values, where "fair" is a place you take your pig, "equity" is whatever the group in power can get, and "charity" is a name given to a baby girl, it is practically and politically impractical to argue for social programs on a basis of ethics, morality, or social justice.

We must therefore cast our programs for the aged in terms of needs and clearly delineate the differences between programs that provide for the future needs through work-life contributions and programs that rely on the public largesse.

Are the Elderly Benefiting at the Expense of Younger Americans?

EDITORS' NOTE: Perhaps no question in recent times has tested so directly the integrity of relationships between older Americans and their younger counterparts than whether the economic status of the former has improved at the expense of the latter. This question extends beyond an inquiry into whether the aged are a favored constituency in the United States. Indeed, it is undeniable that older Americans as a group have faired well during the past fifteen to twenty years in terms of the response of public policy to their needs and, consequently, subsequent improvements realized in their economic status as compared with other age-groups. More precisely, questions might better be posed that inquire into whether all subgroups of the elderly have enjoyed equivalent improvements in their economic well-being in recent years and whether public funds directed toward expanding old-age benefits and entitlements would otherwise have been used to strengthen programs geared to younger age-groups. Although the returns may not yet be in regarding the outcome of the intergenerational equity debate, substantial majorities of the American public continue to believe that the health care and economic security of older Americans are legitimate priorities of the federal government.

Paul S. Hewitt, M.P.A., maintains that *YES,* the elderly are benefiting at the expense of younger Americans. He is Executive Director of the National Taxpayers Union Foundation (NTUF), where he oversees research on policy issues ranging from demographics and interest group behavior to health care and banking reform. Before joining NTUF, Mr. Hewitt served as President of Americans for Generational Equity, which he founded in 1985. In this role, Mr. Hewitt became a spokesman for the interests of younger and future generations on such long-term public policy issues as budget deficits, savings policy, and Social Security reform.

Jill Quadagno, Ph.D., says *NO*. She is Professor of Sociology at Florida State University, where she holds the Mildred and Claude Pepper Eminent Scholar's Chair in Social Gerontology. She is past Vice President of the American Sociological Association and recently served as Senior Policy Analyst on the President's Bi-Partisan Commission on Entitlement and Tax Reform. Dr. Quadagno is the author or editor of seven books, including: *The Transformation of Old Age Security; States, Labor Markets and the Future of Old Age Policy;* and, most recently, *The Color of Welfare: How Racism Undermined the War on Poverty.*

YES

Paul S. Hewitt

The question of our financial obligation to the old—and, hence, whether they are benefiting unfairly at our expense—hinges not just on our country's economic well-being now, but on how well we are likely to do in the future. Even if it were the case that today's old deserve everything we can afford, by this standard, we are doing too much. In a world where our living standards increasingly are tied to how much we save and invest, our savings rate has been the lowest in the industrialized world for more than a generation. Our average weekly wage has stagnated and stands to lose further ground unless savings rates rise. And because retirement policies lie at the root of our savings dearth, it follows, inescapably, that many of the benefits enjoyed by today's older cohorts have become unjustifiable burdens on America's future.

The Road to Ruin

In fiscal year 1995, the federal government will spend roughly $600 billion on transfers from workers to retirees. The retiree share of the budget stands at approximately 40 percent, up from approximately 26 percent as recently as 1980. Yet much more rapid growth lies just ahead. Over the next decade, spending on seniors is slated to double—growing by $590 billion over fiscal 1994–2004. To finance this growth, in 2004 we will need the equivalent of $6,000 in new taxes from every household in America. Throughout this apparent growth spurt, members of the large baby boom generation will still be in their peak earnings years, while the small cohort born during the Depression and World War II will be retiring. When the boomers retire in the following decade, costs will explode uncontrollably. Imagine the difficulty future policy makers will face trying to balance a budget in which spending increases automatically by $200 billion *each year.*

This approaching dilemma is underscored by the recent report of the President's Commission on Entitlements and Tax Reform. The Commission predicts that by 2012 entitlement spending and interest on the national debt will consume *all* of the revenues generated under current tax laws. By 2030, according to Office of Management and Budget Director Alice Rivlin's infamous leaked presidential options memo, annual budget deficits could soar to $4.1 trillion under today's tax and spending policies. Obviously, we cannot incur debt on this scale. But closing the gap with new taxes could devastate living standards. An analysis of the government's 1994 actuarial projections shows that if the economy grows henceforth at better than twice the rate of the past quarter-century, after-tax income growth will merely stagnate over the next 45 years. Under projections that more closely track recent economic trends, take-home pay for the average American in 2040 will be 59 percent below today's (Howe, 1994).

The Dependency Trap

At the root of this problem lies a system of retirement financing that is badly out of sync with our economic needs. There are two basic alternatives for financing retirement plans. Individuals can fund their own retirement through saving. Or, through taxes, they can help fund someone else's retirement, with the hope that still others will be taxed to fund theirs. The former approach emphasizes self-sufficiency and thrift. By definition, such plans cannot be insolvent, because all benefits are prefunded (saved in advance). In contrast, the latter approach—embodied in current U.S. aging policy—involves no saving whatsoever. Beneficiaries are dependent on government. And at any given tax rate, changes in the "dependency ratio" or a slowdown in economic growth can plunge an unfunded system unto insolvency.

The most important distinction between these two approaches is that one requires saving, and the other discourages it. As of the end of 1991, America's social insurance programs had racked up $15 trillion in unfunded liabilities—the equivalent of $156,000 in debt per household. Were this money at work in the economy today, our domestic incomes certainly would be higher and our social problems less vexing. Because it is not, benefits must be funded from taxes, which soak up cash that households could otherwise save, and deficits, which subtract directly from national savings.

In fact, the life-cycle theory of savings and consumption suggests that benefit promises actually discourage saving. According to this theory, the prospect of receiving cash and health benefits would have induced current retirees to consume as though they had built up savings—to save less than they would have without the benefit promises. Most people save only as much as they think they have to. In a September 1994 survey, 67 percent of respondents said they would respond to cuts in future Social Security benefits by saving more (Greenwald and Associates, 1994).

Not surprisingly, the erosion of thrift has had attendant social costs. By undermining the self-sufficiency of today's elderly, generous benefits have fostered a belligerent dependency among the aged that has pitted their powerful lobbies against the unprotected interests of America's children and grandchildren. A multi–billion dollar direct-mail industry thrives by promoting the theme that seniors are not getting (or might not get) all they are owed from the young. When this large and affluent constituency is mobilized to get more for itself, the ensuing inequities range from regressive benefit transfers and the "crowding out" of worthy programs to unsustainable Ponzi schemes that soak the young. As David Stockman once observed, in the battle for budget share, strong interests with weak claims invariably prevail over weak interests with strong claims. Needless to say, there are many underserved constituencies more deserving than perpetually vacationing retirees with $50,000 incomes and paid-off mortgages.

Correcting Course

The urgent need to correct this anti-savings bias necessarily puts limits on our obligations to today's old. Were we to learn that Earth lay in the path of a giant meteor, we would quickly dispense with quibbles over even the most contentious social issues. Similarly, the current controversy over the size and distribution of senior benefits must be seen against the backdrop of serious converging threats to our national prosperity. Our old age entitlements will soon be unaffordable. Conversely, foreign competition requires us to raise our savings rate or lose jobs and markets to high-savings competitors. Social insurance programs are a major drag on savings. To protect our prosperity and assure that there will be adequate resources to serve future older populations, we have no choice but to embrace reform.

But reform will be expensive. Eventually, we must convert the nonpoverty aspects of retirement policy into a national thrift plan. Capitalizing such a system will require sacrifices by both working Americans and current beneficiaries. Of course, not all seniors are equally deserving, and benefit cuts should reflect this. There is plenty of room to reduce spending without harming the needy or dependent. Recent studies by the Congressional Budget Office indicate that Social Security has become mildly regressive—that beneficiaries tend to be better off than the workers who finance their benefits. Not surprisingly, public opinion favors spending less on the wealthy and upper-middle classes. Early retirees who are neither poor nor unemployable are also candidates for cuts.

Defenders of the status quo will argue that we owe even the wealthiest recipients their benefits—even if it harms the economy or is regressive—because government must follow through on its promises. Yet, today's elderly receive far larger subsidies than earlier senior cohorts. And during their working years they paid much lower taxes than the working people of today. Most considerations of fairness argue that current beneficiaries should share in any sacrifice. Nor should we overlook the fact that much of what government "promised" today's beneficiaries, in effect, they promised to themselves by voting for myriad benefit increases during the 1960s and 1970s. Although government arguably has a duty to follow through on its promises, it does not have the moral right to promise people that it will finance their luxuries by taxing their children.

As for the issues raised by trust fund accounting, they are red herrings. The vaunted Social Security "surplus" consists entirely of IOUs from the Treasury that Congress has agreed to repay by raising taxes on workers in the next century. Currently this surplus is equal to only one year of Social Security outlays. Even at its peak, under highly favorable conditions, it will equal only two-and-a-half years of funding. The trust funds have a negligible impact on the system's outlook. Similarly, the claim that our budget deficits are attributable only to programs that lack trust funds and earmarked tax revenues is fallacious. Such distinctions are lost on most Americans, who simply want the taxes they now pay to be spent more wisely. These claims also overlook the fact that for the foreseeable future all of the growth in spending, taxes, and deficits will come from entitlement programs.

Wishing Won't Help

The purchasing power parity of the average annual income in the People's Republic of China is approximately $2,000; yet, China's savings rate approaches 30 percent. Taiwan has accumulated more investment capital than any other country on Earth. Chile, with its new national thrift plan, is rapidly expanding its domestic savings. It is no coincidence that their economies are among the world's fastest growing—or that the United States, with its meager 1.5 percent savings rate, is losing jobs and industry to them. In the post–Cold War world, a nation's savings pool, like its environment, is a public good, which benefits all citizens—especially the semi-skilled, whose pay depends inordinately on the productivity of plant and equipment. Social insurance programs that diminish this pool should be treated as the hazardous byproducts of an earlier era's discredited thinking.

Wish otherwise, we might. But our increasing financial commitments to today's seniors are undermining the very prosperity on which those commitments were based. In their current form, they are unaffordable, counterproductive, and grossly unfair to those who will grow old in the next century.

REFERENCES

Greenwald, M. & Associates. (1994). Survey of public attitudes of entitlements. *National Taxpayers Union Foundation Survey Report No. 7.*
Howe, N. (1994). Why the graying of the welfare state threatens to flatten the American dream—or worse. *National Taxpayers Union Foundation Policy Paper No. 10.*

Rejoinder to Mr. Hewitt

JILL QUADAGNO

Paul Hewitt argues that the United States is spending too much on the elderly and that as a consequence of this overspending, our savings rate is the lowest in the industrialized world. Some simple comparisons indicate he is wrong. The savings rate for the countries that make up the European community average 8 percent compared with less than 2 percent for the United States. But Social Security spending is not the cause. The United States currently devotes only 4.8 percent of its Gross Domestic Product (GDP) to Social Security, a rate that is low by international standards. In other nations, the percentage of GDP spent on pensions ranges from 15.03 in Austria to 11.87 in Sweden to 4.97 in Japan (OECD, 1994). Payroll taxes for pensions in these countries are also significantly higher than ours. They range from 36.6 percent of wages in France to 34.8 percent in Austria to 14.7 percent in the Netherlands (OECD, 1988). Our rate of 15.2 percent also pays for Medicare.

If international comparisons indicate that Social Security spending is not the cause of the decline in the savings rate, then why has it dropped? Social Security has been around for sixty years, and since 1975, entitlement spending (that is, spending on Social Security, Medicare, and Medicaid combined), as a share of GDP has remained stable. The big decline in savings occurred during the 1980s, when the deficit skyrocketed, the result of a large tax cut in 1981 and a big increase in defense spending. If Congress succeeds in reducing the deficit, then the savings rate will rise.

Even more misleading is Hewitt's description of the elderly as greedy geezers with wealth to spare. The elderly are neither wealthier than other Americans nor are they perpetually vacationing on $55,000-a-year incomes. The per capita income of the elderly is lower than for all households, and fewer than 6 percent have incomes above $55,000. Research by Fay Cook and Richard Settersten of Northwestern University shows that older people are not frivolous in their spending habits. Rather, spending on essentials (housing, food, transportation, health care, and clothing) accounts for 93.4 percent of total household spending among the poor elderly and 87.1 percent among the most affluent elderly. The elderly do spend more of their total household income (nearly 15 percent) on health care than do people aged forty-five to fifty-five years (about 5 percent). Higher spending on health care by older people results from poorer health and high out-of-pocket health care costs. A $200 monthly expenditure on prescription drugs can hardly be considered a luxury.

The elderly did not vote themselves myriad benefit increases in the 1960s and 1970s. Congress enacted these increases because poverty rates among older people were at record levels. And younger people do not mind paying Social Security taxes to finance these benefits. In a recent poll, 81.4 percent of respondents were satisfied paying taxes for Social Security. Only 4.8 percent were willing to cut Social Security taxes (Cook and Barrett, 1992). Social Security is one of the few examples of government spending that Americans support, because they know it benefits their own parents and grandparents and spreads the burden of caring for older family members across the entire society.

The United States does have an obligation to responsibly finance the retirement of the baby boom generation. This can be accomplished with minor restructuring of Social Security at a cost of a 2 percent growth in share of Gross Domestic Product, a price that is already exceeded by our European competitors. That is not a terribly heavy price to pay for the retirement security of a generation whose education, employment, and housing needs we have managed to meet thus far without sacrificing our nation's economic security. Let us not allow misleading evidence on savings patterns to incite a new round of elder-bashing.

REFERENCES

Cook, F. L., & Barrett, E. J. (1992). *Support for the American welfare state: The views of Congress and the public* (pp. 62–65). New York: Columbia University Press.
OECD. (1994). *New orientations for social policy* (p. 59). Paris: OECD.
OECD. (1988). *Reforming public pensions* (p. 88). Paris: OECD.

NO

JILL QUADAGNO

This country's tradition of national support for the elderly began during the Great Depression in response to reports documenting high rates of unemployment and poverty among older workers. The Social Security Act of 1935 established a program of public pensions for retired workers as well as programs of unemployment insurance, old age assistance, and aid for dependent children. In 1965, Congress passed Medicare, a program of health insurance for those older than sixty-five, and Medicaid, which covered health insurance for the poor and nursing home care for the aged and disabled (Duncan & Smith, 1989). Yet despite federal efforts to wage war on poverty, in 1967 poverty rates for people older than sixty-five years of age were at a postwar high of approximately 30 percent. In response, Congress increased Social Security benefits four times between 1968 and 1972 and in 1972 added automatic cost-of-living adjustments (COLAs). These provisions improved Social Security benefits significantly and guaranteed that inflation would not erode their value (Derthick, 1979).

These reforms of the 1960s and early 1970s can be seen partly as a response to the post–World War II decline in the economic status of the elderly, a result of rising retirement rates among elderly men and the absence of a well-developed retirement income system. The improvements in benefits increased the income of older people, and by 1984 the relative economic status of the aged had returned to postwar levels. In this context, Medicare and the Social Security reforms of 1968 to 1972 are one of the few success stories of American social policy. Yet, since the 1970s, "old people," like "welfare mothers," have been a continuing flashpoint in political debates. The predominant paradigm has become that of "generational equity," with critics charging that older people are faring better than children, because the government is more generous to them.

The generational equity debate originates in part from the different trajectory of poverty rates among children as opposed to the elderly. In 1967, when poverty among older people was at an all-time high, child poverty rates, which had been falling since the 1950s, were only 17 percent. In 1973, rates of old age poverty began declining, whereas child poverty rates began rising to 22 percent by 1994. Because rates of poverty among the elderly have declined, proponents of generational equity often blame them for the rise in poverty among children.

Why Are Children Poor?

Defining child poverty as an issue of generational equity has undeniable political appeal, but it misses the real issue: that poor children live in households run by parents with low income. Rising poverty among children is partly a result of declines in family income over time. The postwar era was a period of rapid economic growth. Between 1947 and 1973, median family income (in constant dollars) rose from $14,830 to $28,890 (or 36 percent *per decade*). This increase in living standards dramatically reduced child poverty. Since the 1970s, however, real wages have stagnated, and family incomes have scarcely shifted. Between 1973 and 1991, median family income increased by a modest $1,165 (Mishel & Bernstein, 1993), and the incomes of families with children grew more slowly than the incomes of all families (Gottschalk & Danziger, 1993).

The relative stagnation in wages and family incomes since the 1970s was accompanied by an increase in wage and income inequality. Between 1973 and 1989, the adjusted income of the poorest 20 percent of families with children declined by 22 percent, whereas that of the richest 20 percent increased by 24.7 percent (Gottschalk & Danziger, 1993; Mishel and Bernstein, 1993). Thus, the poor have been getting poorer. Contrary to the generational equity thesis, this increase in inequality was driven mainly by the market, not by increasing public generosity to the aged. Nearly all of the change was attributable to changes in the distribution of wages and salaries and other forms of market income, not to changes in social policy (Gramlich, Kasten, & Sammartino, 1993).

Child poverty has also increased because of changes in family composition, most notably a substantial increase in female-headed households, which have the highest poverty rates (Mishel & Bernstein, 1993). In just ten years, from 1979 to 1989, the proportion of never-married mothers grew by 84 percent. One reason that female-headed households are poor is that women earn lower wages than men, making it difficult for working women to support a family through their wages. A second factor is that many women heading families rely on Aid to Families with Dependent Children as their sole source of income. AFDC provides a meager benefit in most states, and since 1973 the real value of these benefits declined continuously. Furthermore, cuts in other benefits made by the Reagan administration in 1981 disproportionately hurt poor families. The Omnibus Budget Reconciliation Act of 1981 removed 400,000 individuals from the Food Stamp program, reduced or eliminated AFDC and Medicaid benefits for many of the working poor, and increased the share of income paid by residents of public housing (Edsall, 1984). Thus, child poverty increased because more poverty-prone households were formed and because many social programs that supported these households were cut.

As AFDC declined in real dollars, Social Security benefits retained their value, because the COLAs legislated in 1972 provided protection against inflation. This does not make the elderly a privileged class, however, for this protection has been eroded by rising out-of-pocket expenses for health care. Between 1987 and 1994, elderly household income increased by 28 percent but out-of-pocket health care costs increased by 112 percent (AARP/Public Policy Institute, 1994). In 1994, the average out-of-pocket health care expense for older people was $2,803, three times greater than that of younger Americans (AARP/Public Policy Institute, 1994). Furthermore, costs increased with advancing age. Among people older than eighty-five years, those with the highest poverty rates, average out-of-pocket expenses were $5,090.

What International Comparisons Demonstrate

The implicit premise behind the generational equity argument is that society must choose between children and the elderly. Yet a look at what other countries do for both children and older people shows that such trade-offs are not inevitable. If one uses an international standard for measuring poverty, then in the mid-1980s the United States had the highest poverty rate for young families with children, at 39.5 percent. By contrast, poverty among children was 29.5 percent in Canada, 23.2 percent in the United Kingdom, 18.8 percent in Germany, 31.1 percent in the

Netherlands, 9.1 percent in France, and 5.3 percent in Sweden. These countries have successfully used social programs to lift families out of poverty. The United States is a clearly an exception in this regard.

Even more ironic, the United States does least for those we revere most whenever discussion of family values take place, the two-parent household. In every industrialized country except the United States, government tax and transfer systems help a significant percentage of poor, couple-headed families with children attain minimum income levels. Sweden helps almost half of this group rise above poverty, and France helps almost six of every ten couple-headed families rise above poverty. The United States is unique in its failure to use social policy to improve the economic circumstances of families with children.

The comparative evidence is clear and conclusive. High spending for the elderly is *not* associated with low spending for children. In fact, the opposite is true. Among eighteen Western nations, those with high levels of spending on the elderly also spent more on children (Pampel, 1994). Others countries successfully protect children *and* the elderly against poverty. There is no trade-off.

Conclusion

Americans grow old in much the same way as they mature. Throughout the life course there are sharp divisions between affluence and poverty in the United States, and these divisions persist into old age. Inequality and poverty are generic features of the American distribution of income, not a generational phenomenon. Poverty in America is, however, associated with being female, having children and, more profoundly, with being a member of a minority group. Although other countries have successfully used tax and transfer policies to eliminate the risk of poverty, the United States remains a "welfare state laggard."

References

AARP/Public Policy Institute. (1994). *Coming up short: Increasing out-of-pocket health spending by older Americans.* Washington, DC: American Association of Retired Persons.

Derthick, M. (1979). *Policymaking for Social Security.* Washington, DC: The Brookings Institution.

Duncan, G. J., & Smith, K. R. (1989). The rising affluence of the elderly: How far, how fair, and how frail? *Annual Review of Sociology, 15,* 261–289.

Edsall, T. B. (1984). *The new politics of inequality.* New York: W. W. Norton.

Gottschalk, P., & Danziger, S. (1993). Family structure, family size and family income. In S. Danziger and P. Gottschalk (Eds.), *Uneven tides: Rising inequality in America* (pp. 165–194). New York: Russell Sage.

Gramlich, E., Kasten, R., & Sammartino, F. (1993). Growing inequality in the 1980s: The role of federal taxes and cash transfers. In S. Danziger and P.

Gottschalk (Eds.), *Uneven tides: Rising inequality in America* (pp. 225–250). New York: Russell Sage.

Mishel, L., & Bernstein, J. (1993). *The state of working America.* Washington, DC: Economic Policy Institute.

Pampel, F. (1994). Population aging, class context and age inequality in public spending. *American Journal of Sociology, 100*(4), 199–121.

Rejoinder to Professor Quadagno
Paul S. Hewitt

Dr. Quadagno defends the large, non–means-tested transfers that take place under Social Security and Medicare by asserting that: (1) without them, large numbers of today's elderly would fall below the poverty line; and (2) issues of generational equity should be addressed by increasing spending (presumably means-tested) on poor children and their families, rather than through old-age benefit reforms. Her argument fails to acknowledge the harm done to the economy and the well-being of working families (and the future elderly) by runaway old-age benefit spending. Nor does it address the failure of welfare programs to promote behavior that is conducive to self-sufficiency.

Dr. Quadagno appears to celebrate the overwhelming reliance of today's aged on Social Security and Medicare, pointing to this dependency as a measure of the programs' success. Yet, far from being a triumph of social engineering, dependency among the aged is a serious social problem rooted in dysfunctional behavior. When middle-class Americans save too little and retire early with the expectation of living comfortably on government subsidies to ever later ages, they become costly, demanding burdens on society. Whereas the universal model for upward mobility and self-sufficiency is hard work and sacrifice for the future, our existing old-age benefit system induces income earners to sacrifice only for the present via taxation. It has proved singularly unable to encourage Americans to sacrifice for the future. Indeed, to the extent that social insurance taxes soak up income that could be saved and create the expectation of future benefits, they systematically discourage future-oriented behavior.

Dr. Quadagno mistakenly casts generational equity as a debate among those who believe that government subsidies are the ticket to upward mobility. It is, she says, the contention that "older people are faring better than children, because government is more generous to them." In this world view, generational equity is purely a matter of which cohort gets what now. Most advocates of generational equity would disagree. Their paradigm asks whether a given policy will make future generations better or worse off. If it makes the future worse off—for example, by promoting consumption and expanding debt—it is generationally inequitable, independent of whether subsidies also flow to youth.

The achievements of Social Security and Medicare must be viewed against the backdrop of the large and growing burdens they impose on young families and economic growth. Their evaluation must take into account the cultural costs of making the old dependent on the taxation of the young. Rather than knitting together the interests of different generations in the extended family, age-based entitlements encourage each generation to perceive its interests separately and competitively.

To meet the test of generational equity, old-age policy must require that workers save and that the well-off and able-bodied get less. Such a requirement will promote individual self-sufficiency—which, after all, ought to be the end goal of any antipoverty program. More importantly, the ensuing increase in the national savings rate will help to reduce the comparative disadvantage in capital costs that has undermined United States industrial competitiveness in recent decades. Reversing the outflow of high-paying manufacturing jobs is perhaps the best long-term antipoverty policy the United States could have.

Income transfers will continue to be an important tool in our antipoverty arsenal. There should always be "safety net" programs for the unlucky. But a wise society does not seek to eliminate hunger by feasting on its seed-corn. Nor can we hope to benefit the future elderly with indiscriminate income subsidies that substitute taxing and spending for saving and investing.

Do the Elderly Really Have Political Clout?

EDITORS' NOTE: In the popular press as well as in the halls of Congress, "senior power" is an accepted reality. The "gray lobby," composed of literally hundreds of organizations and interest groups advocating on behalf of older citizens, is considered to be such a potent force in political affairs that changing popular senior programs such as Social Security and Medicare has been described as the political equivalent of "touching the third rail." Yet, reputation is not always the equivalent of reality, and questions have been raised as to whether the elderly *really* have as much political clout as has been attributed to them. Proponents point to the dramatic increase in public support for the elderly in the past thirty years, resulting in more than 30 percent of all federal dollars now being spent on behalf of senior citizens. Others, however, question the extent to which aging interest groups actually were responsible for these policies, and they argue that whatever clout the "gray lobby" once may have had is rapidly fading. How much power does the gray lobby *really* have? To what extent do aging interest groups such as the American Association of Retired Persons actually speak for elderly persons as a whole? And, are there even identifiable common interests that are shared by today's diverse population of senior citizens?

Henry J. Pratt, Ph.D. says *YES.* He is Professor of Political Science at Wayne State University. He is author of numerous articles on the politics of aging, in addition to two books: *The Gray Lobby* (1976) and *Gray Agendas* (1993). He is a Fellow in the Gerontological Society of America.

Robert H. Binstock says *NO*. He is Professor of Aging, Health, and Society at Case Western Reserve University. A former President of the Gerontological Society of America (1975–1976) and Director of a White House Task Force on Older Americans (1967–1968), he currently chairs the Gerontological Health Section of the American Public Health Association. He is the author of some 150 articles and book chapters dealing with politics and policies on aging. Among his nineteen authored and edited books are four editions of the *Handbook of Aging and the Social Sciences* (the most recent, co-edited with Linda George, published in 1996).

YES

HENRY J. PRATT

The elderly have achieved a popular reputation in Washington for political clout. In the print media, in commentaries on TV and radio, and in weekly news magazines, one finds accounts of Social Security and related age-benefit programs replete with references to "the seniors' lobby," "senior citizens organizations," and "elderly voters"—the implication being that this is a political force of the first magnitude. Without arguing the existence or nonexistence of an "elderly vote," it is clearly the case that candidates for office, whether for a seat in Congress or the Presidency, typically avoid stances that are likely to prove offensive to elderly Americans; not wishing to give offense, politicians are adept at claiming credit for their "service" to elderly voters. Although there is reason to be skeptical regarding the notion of "senior power," the evidence does, in my view, support the position that the elderly, and more particularly their representatives in government, do exercise significant political power.

A set of public policy concerns that are broadly, though not universally, shared by elderly Americans defines their core interest. Although seniors' organizations adopt public policy stands on a broad range of concerns, not all of these enjoy the same high level of membership support or are considered as equally credible among government policy makers. The case for seniors as possessing clout, therefore, rests on the occasional mobilizations of seniors on matters of central concern and on the reputation for political effectiveness that such mobilization has helped to engender. The following discussion employs two indicators of senior-group clout: (1) power potential, as indicated by the group's size, material resources, and so forth, and (2) level of political access and related reputation for political influence. Conclusions reached on this basis then can be usefully tested against findings for other countries.

Power Potential

By all of the usual measures of interest group potential, old-age organizations are advantaged relative to most other political organizations represented in Washington. In terms of size, they are enormous. The American Association of Retired Persons (AARP), with 33 million members and $300 million in 1990 revenues, is now the largest and probably wealthiest voluntary organization in this country. The National Council of Senior Citizens (NCSC), with approximately 4 million members in its chapter affiliates across the country, is also relatively large. And as Day points out, "Although many members join these organizations for purposes other than political participation, and although many may not be politically active on a regular basis, they often respond as *en masse* to calls for action by the leadership" (Day, 1990, p. 99).

Staff capacity is a second element in an interest group's power potential. Cadres of full-time professional employees can become an important element in translating the group's potential strength into terms capable of comprehension by lawmakers and officials. Thus, AARP's government relations arm, which in 1970 consisted of just two individuals, now employs approximately 150 workers.

Leadership is a third determinant. Judgments regarding old-age-group leadership must be somewhat subjective, but it does appear that present-day seniors' groups measure up reasonably well in this regard—in marked contrast to the Townsend Movement of the 1930s, in which dismal leadership performance, once the early days of widespread popular enthusiasm were past, became a liability (Holtzman, 1963). Finally, the organized elderly in Washington stand at or near the top in terms at least of one other determinant of potential, namely, legitimacy. Few groupings enjoy the deference commonly bestowed by younger adults on elderly individuals, and this in turn augments the alliance capacity of old-age groups with other interest groups in Washington (Hudson, 1978).

Political Access and Reputation for Influence

In her book, *What Older Americans Think: Interest Groups and Aging Policy,* Christine L. Day (1990) very usefully explores the matter of old-age organizational access in the current era. After first identifying the elderly as "a distinct group with common interests, needs, and legitimate demands," Day points out that such organizations enjoy two kinds of advantages—a combination atypical of interest groups elsewhere in government. Seniors' organizations combine the advantage of a narrow interest group, able to build alliances with government officials in specialized policy areas, with the broad appeal of a public interest group, whose political fortunes affect everyone, in the future if not in the present. Day's interviews in the middle 1980s among executive agencies as well as congressional committee staffs produced a near-unanimous conclusion: the level of official access is high, and the elderly, as represented by their organizations, are viewed as "their own best advocates" (Day, 1990, pp. 93, 96).

Published accounts of several aging-related Capitol Hill struggles over the past quarter-century lend empirical support to these general observations. Aging organizations were almost invariably participants in the coalitions that achieved the legislative gains of the 1970s and 1980s. On some occasions, for example, in the struggle that culminated in the Employee Retirement Income Security Act (ERISA) of 1974, their coalitional role was secondary (Day, 1990, p. 94). On other occasions, such groups played a primary role. Thus, analyses of the events surrounding the 1988 Medicare Catastrophic Coverage Act identify AARP as a leading actor (Kosterlitz 1987; Rovener, 1988). Likewise, my own previously published analysis of the 1972 Social Security Amendments—legislation that resulted in a dramatic enlargement in this program's scope and benefit structure—found the National Council of Senior Citizens (NCSC) to have played a complex and important role in its legislative history (Pratt, 1976, chapter 11).

Apart from their apparent contribution to recent age benefit expansions, the old-age organizations are at least as important, perhaps more so, as upholders of the Social Security and Medicare status quo. Nowhere was such defensive power more apparent than in connection with the 1981–1983 struggle on Capitol Hill over reform of Social Security. In a move intended to save some $45 billion of federal spending, the Reagan Administration in May 1981 submitted legislation designed to pare back the early retirement benefit that workers can receive at age sixty-two, and also to cut the basic Social Security benefit and introduce a delay of three months in the cost of living adjustment (COLA). Thirty-six million retirees would have lost benefits on the COLA delay alone. This plan was immediately met by a storm of criticism from Save Our Security (SOS), a coalition of some two dozen elderly groups, which vowed to fight the proposal to the death. The following day, cards and letters began rolling into the White House and Congress, opposing cuts in early retirement benefits. Within a week's time, the Administration plan was dead on Capitol Hill (Light, 1985, chapter 10). The National Council of Senior Citizens then played a major role in the 1983 struggle to craft legislation capable of arousing broad public support (Light, 1985). Seniors' organizations also took a leading role throughout the 1970s and 1980s in the politics surrounding Medicare and long-term care (Day, 1990).

AARP's special concern for the more able-bodied and highly skilled elderly was apparent in connection with its three-decades-long campaign to secure abolition of mandatory retirement in the United States. AARP lobbyists pointed toward the existing Age Discrimination in Employment Act as the base on which nonmandatory retirement legislation could be appropriately erected. In collaboration with friendly lawmakers on Capitol Hill, the Association eventually helped to secure enactment of legislation that first (1978) postponed the permissible age of mandatory retirement and later (1986) outlawed the practice altogether for U.S. workers (Ford, 1978–1979).

Seniors' Clout Elsewhere

Seniors' organizations exist in essentially all of the countries in the North Atlantic community, and in each case they are typically among the larger political interest groups active in that setting. Although data and interpretation relating to such organizations are less abundant than is true for the United States, published accounts make clear their fairly large role in public policy making. Such a conclusion is supported by recent accounts of Canada (Gifford, 1990; Sears, 1985), the United Kingdom (Williamson & Pampel, 1993), and Sweden (Williamson & Pampel, 1993). The United States appears to be consistent with the existing pattern among the other industrial democracies.

REFERENCES

Day, C. L. (1990). *What older Americans think: Interest groups and aging policy.* Princeton: Princeton University Press.

Ford, L. C. (1978–79). The implications of the age discrimination in employment act amendments of 1978 for colleges and universities. *Journal of College and University Law,* 161–209.

Gifford, C. G. (1990). *Canada's fighting seniors.* Toronto: James Lorimer.

Holtzman, A. (1963). *The Townsend Movement.* New York: Bookman Associates.

Hudson, R. B. (1978). The 'graying' of the federal budget and its consequences for old-age policy. *Gerontologist, 18*(5), 428–440.

Kosterlitz, J. (1987, August). Health care '88. *National Journal,* August 29.

Light, P. (1985). *Artful work: The politics of social security reform.* New York: Random House.

Pratt, H. J. (1976). *The gray lobby.* Chicago: University of Chicago Press.

Rovener, J. (1988, March 26). Catastrophic-costs conferees irked by lobby assaults. *Congressional Quarterly, 46,* 777–780.

Sears, V. (1985, June 15). Gray power: Coming of age. *Toronto Star,* p. B1.

Williamson, J. B., & Pampel, F. C. (1993). *Old age security in comparative perspective.* New York: Oxford University Press.

Rejoinder to Professor Pratt ROBERT H. BINSTOCK

Henry Pratt and I agree that the elderly have some forms of power, including the ability of their organized interest groups to participate in political and policy processes. We differ sharply, however, regarding the significance of this participation. He argues that the old-age lobby, representing a so-called core interest of older people, has played a "significant" role in shaping public policy. I argue that they have had little impact or clout in the enactment and amendment of major old-age policies.

Although I respect Henry for his years of scholarship on old-age interest groups, I find a number of flaws in the evidence, logic, and concepts he mobilizes to build his case. For example, Henry's lead example of old-age groups playing a "primary role" in policy making is the Medicare Catastrophic Coverage Act (MCCA) of 1988. Yet, the facts of this case thoroughly contradict his argument. The MCCA was conceived by the Reagan administration and worked on by Congressional leaders for two years; AARP simply endorsed the legislation before it was passed (Iglehart, 1989). Subsequently, many older persons protested against this new program, and it was repealed in 1989, despite AARP's opposition to the repeal.

Other misleading examples abound in Henry's essay. For instance, he portrays NCSC as having a "complex and important role" in the 1972 Social Security amendments; but Derthick's (1979) well-documented monograph, *Policymaking for Social Security,* suggests otherwise. Henry also asserts that NCSC played a major role in the struggles that led to the 1983 amendments to Social Security, even though the legislation rendered Social Security benefits subject to taxation—a reform that had been adamantly opposed by NCSC for some years. Henry credits AARP with a "three-decade long campaign to secure abolition of mandatory retirement" through legislation passed in 1978 and 1986, but AARP was hardly active, politically, before 1970. Moreover, AARP's role in this area simply was to endorse the legislative leadership of Congressman Claude Pepper. Henry also intimates that the old-age lobby was responsible for President Reagan backing off of his plans to cut back Social Security benefits, yet this plan had little support in Congress to begin with.

The notion that old-age groups represent highly salient and enduring core interests of their members is seriously undermined by evidence regarding the voting behavior of older people. Consider, for example, that 60 percent of older voters supported Reagan when he ran for reelection in 1984, a 6-percentage-point increase over 1980, even though major senior organizations had vigorously opposed Reagan's "villainous" proposals for Social Security cutbacks during his first term. Moreover, the very concept of core interest is vague and problematic. For instance, for the lowest-income quintile of older persons, Social Security constitutes 80 percent of income; for the highest-income quintile, it represents 16 percent (Radner, 1991).

Finally, it should be noted that Henry and I use rather different concepts to assess what constitutes significant political clout. His, as he states, is based on the criteria of "power potential" and "level of political access," dimensions of policy input. Mine is based on the criterion of actually being able to influence policy outcomes (and non-outcomes), In his classic work *Political Influence,* political scientist Edward C. Banfield defined influence as "ability to get others to act, think, or feel as one intends" (1961, p. 3). In my view the evidence clearly indicates that older Americans and their organized interest groups have far less ability to achieve such results than Henry would have us believe.

REFERENCES

Banfield, E. C. (1961). *Political influence: A new theory of urban politics.* New York: The Free Press.

Derthick, M. (1979). *Policymaking for social security.* Washington, DC: The Brookings Institution.

Iglehart, J. K. (1989). Medicare's new benefits: "Catastrophic" health insurance. *New England Journal of Medicine, 320,* 329–36.

Radner, D. R. (1991). Changes in the income of age groups, 1984–1989. *Social Security Bulletin, 54*(12), 2–18.

NO

ROBERT H. BINSTOCK

Older Americans have some political "clout" or power, but not nearly as much as the media and some academic writers would have us believe. Although older people constitute a large block of voters, they do not vote cohesively; they distribute their votes in virtually the same fashion as do younger age-groups. Some of the dozens of old-age interest groups are very well financed, have large bureaucracies, and engage actively in political lobbying. Because they purport to represent "the elderly," they have access to policy makers and public platforms. Yet, their actual impact on policy is limited and is likely to remain so in the immediate future.

Voting Behavior

Older Americans vote in large numbers, constituting between 16 percent and 21 percent of people who voted in national elections from 1980 through 1992 (New York Times/CBS News Poll, 1992). They also vote at much higher rates than do middle-aged and younger adults. But older people are as diverse in their voting patterns as any other age-group; their votes divide along the same partisan, economic, social, and other lines as those of the electorate at large. Older and middle-aged voters were rarely more than a few percentage points apart in presidential elections from 1952 through 1980 (Campbell & Strate, 1981). Voting behavior in presidential and congressional elections from 1980 through 1992 exhibited the same pattern: sharp divisions within each age-group, and very small differences between age-groups. Even in the context of a state or local referendum that presents a specific issue—such as propositions to cap local property taxes or to finance public schools—the best available studies show that old age is not a statistically significant variable associated with the distribution of votes. Overall, the weight of the evidence indicates that older people's electoral choices are rarely, if ever, based on age-group interests.

Old-Age Interest Groups

The last three decades have witnessed a tremendous expansion in the number, the memberships, the visibility, and the political activity of old-age interest groups. By far the largest of these aging-based organizations is the American Association of Retired Persons (AARP), which claims some 33 million members, 1,700 employees, and had revenues totaling $469 million in 1994. Although it is only one of some half-dozen old-age mass-membership organizations, it is by far the most important politically because of its huge membership (more than three times larger than the combined total of all the others), its vastly superior financial and staff resources, and its reputation in Washington as the most politically powerful of the age-based groups. Although AARP lobbies actively in national politics, however, its political activities appear to be less important as membership incentives than the material and associational incentives (Clark & Wilson, 1961) provided through its investment funds, insurance programs, pharmaceutical and travel discounts, credit cards, publications, local chapter educational and cultural programs, and a variety of other activities.

Despite their resources for exercising political power, AARP and the other aging-based interest groups have played only a minor role in affecting public policy. As implied by the evidence from voting behavior, there is no indication that these organizations have been able to cohere or even to shift marginally the votes of older persons, and there is plenty of evidence to the contrary. Organized demands of older persons have had little to do with the enactment and amendment of the major old-age policies such as Social Security, Medicare, the Employee Retirement Income Security Act, and the Age Discrimination in Employment Act. Rather, such actions have been largely attributable to the initiatives of public officials in the White House, Congress, and the bureaucracy, who have focused on their own agendas for social and economic policy. The impact of old-age–based interest groups has been primarily confined to relatively minor policies that have distributed benefits to professionals and practitioners in the field of aging rather than directly to older persons themselves (Binstock & Day, 1996).

Although old-age interest groups have had little impact in shaping old-age legislation, their professed role as "representatives of the elderly" enables them to have limited forms of power in other, minor aspects of policy process. In the classic pattern of American interest group politics (Lowi, 1969), public officials find it both useful and incumbent on them to invite such organizations to participate in policy activities. In this way, public officials are provided with a ready means of having been "in touch" symbolically with millions of older persons, thereby legitimizing subsequent policy actions and inactions. Moreover, their symbolic legitimacy gives old-age organizations easy informal access to public officials, the ability to obtain public platforms in the national media and congressional hearings, and what might be termed "the electoral bluff," based on politicians' concern about antagonizing unnecessarily the aged or any other latent mass constituency.

Nonetheless, these forms of power are limited. A number of legislative changes in old-age programs were enacted throughout the 1980s and early 1990s, for example, that chipped away at the long-established principle of distributing benefits and burdens primarily on the basis of old age, and replaced it with specific attention to the diverse economic circumstances of program participants. Some of these changes reduced benefits to comparatively wealthy older persons; others targeted benefits to relatively poor older persons (Binstock, 1994). Most of these changes were opposed, unsuccessfully, by AARP and other old-age organizations.

Moreover, there have been two occasions in recent years when AARP's political stances have noticeably antagonized some segments of its membership and definitely undermined some of the organization's political legitimacy as a voice that "represents older people." In 1988, AARP endorsed the Medicare Catastrophic Coverage Act, which levied a sliding-scale income surtax on relatively well-off older people to pay for new hospital insurance benefits. A great many members of the organization registered strong protests to the tax through public demonstrations, as well as through telephone calls and written communications to congressional representatives. In response, Congress immediately repealed the surtax, despite AARP's ongoing support for the legislation. Substantial dissent was also registered in 1994 when AARP announced support for the Democratic leadership's health care reform bills in the Senate and the House. On both occasions it was rumored that a small minority of members resigned.

These episodes were not major blows to the organization. Nonetheless, after the defeat of health care reform in the 103rd Congress, the president of AARP publicly acknowledged that his membership had widely divergent and strongly held views and that representing a diverse membership in public policy affairs is an ongoing struggle for the organization (Lehrman, 1995). As a result, today AARP is very cautious in its lobbying activities. The political activities of the organization are essentially membership marketing strategies and avenues through which AARP's staff and national volunteer leaders can have the gratification of being important "players" in the Washington national scene. In short, the incentive system of the organization tends to dictate that it should clearly establish a record that it is "fighting the good fight" with respect to policy proposals affecting old-age programs. But this fight, win or lose, should *not* include positions and tactics that threaten to jeopardize the stability of the organization's membership and financial resources.

A Look to the Future

Proposed changes in federal policies on aging appear to have ushered in a new era in the politics of aging, in which the fates of major programs affecting older people are much more likely to be determined by the power of organized interests that have a major economic stake in them—with respect to Medicare and Medicaid, for instance, hospitals, nursing homes, physicians, and managed care and insurance companies—than by old-age interest groups. In this political context, the viability of old-age interest groups in representing a heterogeneous population of older people in an effective fashion may become increasingly problematic. As the twentieth century comes to a close, needs within the older population might come to be represented most effectively by a new constellation of interest groups concerned with promoting the role of government in fostering the well-being of people of all ages within American society. Perhaps AARP and other old-age–based interest groups will be part of such a coalition.

REFERENCES

Binstock, R. H. (1994). Changing criteria in old-age programs: The introduction of economic status and need for services. *Gerontologist, 34,* 726–730.

Binstock, R. H., & Day, C. L. (1996). Aging and politics. In R. H. Binstock & L. K. George (Eds.), *Handbook of aging and the social sciences* (4th ed., pp. 362–387). San Diego, CA: Academic Press.

Campbell, J. C., & Strate, J. (1981). Are older people conservative? *Gerontologist, 21,* 580–591.

Clark, P. B., & Wilson, J. Q. (1961). Incentive systems: A theory of organizations. *Administrative Science Quarterly, 6,* 219–266.

Lehrman, E. I. (1995, January-February). Health-care reform at the crossroads. *Modern Maturity,* p. 12.

Lowi, T. J. (1969). *The end of liberalism.* New York: W. W. Norton.

New York Times/CBS News Poll. (1992, November 5). Portrait of the electorate. *New York Times,* p. B9.

Rejoinder to Professor Binstock   HENRY J. PRATT

What strikes me, initially, about Bob Binstock's statement is the evidence it provides of a broad area of agreement between us in regard to the political importance of elderly persons. We appear to be equally impressed by the "political activity of old-age interest groups," their "high symbolic legitimacy," "easy informal access to public officials," and "capacity to obtain public platforms in the national media," as well as by the vastness of AARP's membership, financial base, and staff resources. The two of use share the belief that, in Binstock's words, "older Americans have some political clout or power."

At a certain point, obviously, the two of us part company. For his part, Bob Binstock contends that AARP and the other aging-based interest groups "have played only a minor role in affecting public policy," and that whatever limited success they have achieved has been largely confined to matters of a narrowly self-serving character ("distributed benefits to professionals"). For my part, I find the evidence persuasive that age-group lobbyists in Washington have been fairly successful these past two decades in their repeated efforts to influence policy outcomes.

Bob implicitly acknowledges the involvement senior-group lobbyists in high-stakes, fundamental concerns such as these in his reference to AARP's endorsement of the 1988 Medicare Catastrophic Coverage Act. As he rightly points out, such endorsement ended up costing the Association dearly in terms of diminished internal support and cohesion. Yet the same struggle can be cited as evidence for AARP's capacity to influence legislation. The 1988 measure most likely would not have passed absent the legitimation provided by this Association. Its subsequent repeal, despite the AARP's strenuous objection, serves as a reminder that this group's clout, while substantial, is not without limit.

I would challenge my opponent in his contention that Social Security and Medicare provide evidence that the organized demands of older persons have little to do with the adoption of major old-age policies. Such evidence is not persuasive in my judgment. Social Security was enacted more than half a century ago, in a setting quite different from what exists presently; for example, none of today's nationally active senior citizen organizations existed in 1935, or even were contemplated. With respect to Medicare, two facts are pertinent. First, in separate writings, three observers (J. David Greenstone, Richard Harris, and James L. Sundquist) have all observed that the National Council of Senior Citizens was a participant in the events leading up to enactment of this 1965 legislation. The group's mass rallies and protests, for example, helped to rebut American Medical Association (AMA) propaganda to the effect that the pending legislation would disadvantage the elderly and that seniors were mostly opposed to its adoption. With respect to AARP, a group newly formed and of little importance in the early 1960s, the scale of political commitment has since been greatly enlarged.

In closing, I wish to return to the area of agreement that appears to unite my thinking with that of Bob Binstock. The two of us evidently perceive the same essential facts; our difference consists in how best to interpret them. Moreover, I agree with Bob's cogent observation that the existing set of old-age interest groups may encounter increasing difficulty in providing representation to the heterogeneity of older persons, and that new groups could arise to displace those currently occupying center stage.

Should Older Persons Have the Right to Commit Suicide?

EDITORS' NOTE: Among the most controversial of issues facing an aging America is the legitimacy of policy that would legalize the taking of one's own life. Some argue that suicide for older adults, particularly those who are severely and irreversibly incapacitated, enables them to exercise a degree of personal autonomy and control in the face of their impending demise. Euthanasia, or elective death, has gained increasing numbers of advocates in recent years. Such individuals tend to align themselves with the right-to-die movement and subscribe to either passive or active interpretations of the elective death decision. Others maintain that the life of the individual and his/her value to the community should be respected and that there should be some societally determined limits on autonomy. For them, euthanasia is the wrong solution to the very real problems of incapacitated elderly. Instead, they argue we should provide the necessary social support, health care, hospice care, and compassion to those who feel they face an undignified life, or an undignified painful death. Proponents for and against legalized suicide rely variously on issues of religion, personal freedom and dignity, and societal cost–benefit criteria in formulating their arguments. Social, legal, and philosophical principles permeate much of the rationale. Meanwhile, the highest rate of suicide in the United States and other industrialized nations continues to be recorded among the sixty-five years and older segment of the population, with older white men exhibiting by far the greatest propensity to take their own lives.

Margaret Pabst Battin, Ph.D., says *YES*, older persons should have the right to take their own lives if they so choose. She is Professor of Philosophy and Adjunct Professor of Internal Medicine, Division of Medical Ethics, at the University of Utah. She has authored, edited, or co-edited nine books, among them an anthology on philosophical issues in suicide, a scholarly edition of John Donne's *Biathanatos,* a collection on age-rationing in medical care, a text on professional ethics, and *Ethics in the Sanctuary,* a study of ethical issues in organized religion. Dr. Battin recently published *The Least Worst Death* and *The Death Debate.* In recent years, she has been engaged in research on active euthanasia and assisted suicide in Holland and Germany.

Lois Snyder, J.D., says *NO.* She is Ethics and Health Policy Counsel at the American College of Physicians,* the national professional society of doctors of internal medicine and the subspecialties of internal medicine. Snyder is also Faculty Associate at the University of Pennsylvania Center for Bioethics and is a member of the board of directors of the American Association of Bioethics. She is a frequent writer and speaker on health care policy, bioethical, and medical–legal issues. She is the editor of two books, *Ethical Choices: Case Studies for Medical Practice* and *Care of the Nursing Home Resident: What Physicians Need to Know.*

YES

Margaret Pabst Battin

Begin with an uncontroversial (though often ignored) thesis: An older person should have the right to shape the character of his or her own life in accord with his or her own basic values. Add to it a merely logical point: Shaping the character of one's own life includes shaping the very end of it, including the process of dying. From these two premises, we can derive a thesis that is more controversial: An older person should have the right to shape the character of the very end of his or her own life, including the process of dying. And if we redescribe this as the claim that the older person should have the right to commit suicide (suicide is, after all, one among various possible processes of dying), we get a thesis that is deeply, profoundly controversial. We should not find the conclusion problematic if we accept these uncontroversial premises—but we do. This is, I think, not merely a logical but a moral mistake. I want to argue that we should accept the conclusion: *older people should have the right to commit suicide,* though this right, like any other right, may be limited in specific respects.

But why should this conclusion be so controversial? First, look at the facts of suicide in old age.

The Realities of Suicide in Old Age

It would be nice to think that no old people ever considered suicide because the circumstances of life were so bad—because of pain, limitation, economic hard-

---

*The views expressed here are those of the author.

ship, age-prejudice, chronic illness, loss of function, loss of social roles and net-works, and so on. It would be nice; but it is not true. These things all occur; they are often part of what it is to grow old. Though some of these circumstances are avoidable or treatable, some are not, and many that could be avoided or treated are not adequately recognized or responded to. Society is often unwilling to provide resources that might help the old live their lives in easier, fuller ways.

One of the cruelest myths of aging is the "golden years" myth—it is a myth of denial, which in its insistent optimism tries to get us to think old age is a be-nign, full, rich time, the ripened fruit of life well lived, when that is not always so. But some older people are more realistic: they see what is beginning to occur and what may lie ahead: physical deterioration, economic dependency, chronic illness and pain, the loss of meaningful social roles. They recognize that old age can be a benign, full, rich time, but they also recognize that that is not likely to be the way old age is for them: what they foresee is loneliness, isolation, lack of communica-tion, lack of mobility, lack of familiar activities, and a creased, sagging face they no longer want to see in the mirror. Some of these older people commit suicide.

Do they have a right to do so? We know a lot about these suicides: they are primarily men, most often in their seventies or eighties, usually widowed; they live alone, many in rooming houses in the poorer urban areas, and they have few or no friends. They are alcoholic. They are depressed. They use guns, sometimes ropes, and sometimes they just rig up the exhaust pipes of their cars. The suicide rate for men aged eighty years and older is higher than for any other group—higher than for teenagers, higher than for men in early middle age, and many times higher than for elderly black women, who have the lowest rates of all in the United States. Do these old men have the right to commit suicide? They face a limited, dreary future through depressed and alcoholic eyes, and they do not see the point of going on.

Realism about the Future in Old Age

But the realities of elderly suicide as it is reported—the despairing acts of debili-tated old men—contrast with other views. Consider another old person, surveying her future as realistically as she can: although she is not in pain and has no chron-ic illnesses or limitations at the moment, she knows that the oldest old—people older than eighty-five—have an average of 6.2 chronic conditions; that a woman is likely to outlive her husband; that the longer she lives, the fewer of her same-age friends will be alive and the more difficult it will be to make new ones; that she has a one in four, perhaps almost a one in two, chance of contracting Alzhei-mer's disease if she lives to eighty-five; that she has a one in two chance of ending up in a nursing home. Even if she is not worried about the current political turmoil over Medicare and Social Security or the possibility that these programs will be bankrupt or gutted by the time she reaches old age (this would only make her wor-ries worse), she may still have a realistic view of the risks in growing old. Do we say that this woman has a right to commit suicide, now or in the future, if what she wants is to preclude the possibility of a bad end to an otherwise good life? If she has the right to shape her life in accord with her own basic values, including the very end of it, why cannot she choose a process of direct, self-caused dying, one that others might negatively label suicide but that she sees as a matter of prudent self-protection and culmination?

And consider yet another old person: one who is entering old old age, without serious medical problems, but who simply views his life as complete—not in a fatalistic or depressed way, but with a measure of real satisfaction. Concerned about the financial impact of extended old age and the likelihood of being a burden on family members, he is ready to die now. His motivation is partly self-regarding—he does not want to be *old*—but he also does not see the point of enduring a long process of inevitable deterioration and decline, or imposing on the family he loves an open-ended obligation to care for him for a period whose length and severity he may not be able to control. His motivation is partly self-interested, but importantly altruistic as well. Ought he not be able to act on motivations of this sort?

To be sure, the lives of the old and the old old could be far, far better than they are, if they were provided with or able to maintain richer social networks, more accepting families, better economic supports, more dedicated medical care, more physical therapy and understanding counseling, and so on. Many older people do live out full lives in circumstances that are both physically and emotionally comfortable, until death takes them swiftly and easily at the end. Some lucky people live in societies that do far more than others to try to ensure that the end of life is good. But this is not what all older people face, especially not in societies that are callous about old age and that lose interest in those no longer regarded as productive citizens, and in any case it is what no older person in any society, callous or concerned, can count on. All older people risk a series of continuing losses: of people with whom they are intimate, of physical function, of social roles, and of cognitive and perceptual capacities, whether these risks actually eventuate or not. Given that a realistic view of old age must recognize these risks and must admit that they do eventuate for at least some older people, do not older people have the right to commit suicide—or, put in less negative language, the right to shape the character of their own lives, including the very end of life and the manner in which they die? Why must old people be forced to risk the worst if, after living their long lives, they genuinely choose a way of dying that seems to them better than what they otherwise face?

Is There a Right to Suicide?

Whether there is such a thing as a basic, fundamental right to suicide for all persons is a matter of profound dispute. I myself hold, to make a long and intricate argument short, that suicide is not merely a right, but a *fundamental* right (Battin,

1995), like the right to live, to associate freely, to worship, and so on. Of course, in many cases, suicide is not conducive to human dignity—for instance, this is usually the case among lovesick teenagers, distraught young women making "cries for help," despondent men in mid-life crises, and so on; for this reason, the right to suicide, though fundamental, is not equally distributed. Nor can we speak of "rights" when people are manipulated, engineered, or coerced into suicide, whether by greedy family members, unprincipled physicians, cost-cutting health care institutions, or callous societies. But some suicide in old age, like some (though by no means all) suicide in certain other circumstances, including terminal illness, severe disability, self-sacrifice for a social or religious cause, and so on, *may* represent a considered, principled choice to bring one's life to a fitting conclusion—the conclusion that person sees as fitting—rather than risk what the alternative may bring.

In old age, the alternative is highly likely to be physical deterioration, loss of control, loss of social relationships, sometimes pain, confusion, loss of memory or other symptoms, and increasing dependence on one's family or other caregivers. Some people accept these losses with grace; others, also viewing them in realistic ways, choose not to have their lives end in this way. Where this is a free, uncoerced, considered choice, it must be recognized as constitutive of human dignity, and hence a fundamental right. Suicide in old age is not always like this— indeed, most of the reported suicide in old age involves lonely, depressed, alcoholic old men, in whom suicide is a matter of hopelessness and despair. But where the choice to end one's life does emerge from reflective, fully voluntary choice, it must be honored as a matter of fundamental right.

References

Battin, M. P. (1995). Suicide and rights. In M. P. Battin (Ed.), *Ethical issues in suicide.* Englewood Cliffs, NJ: Prentice-Hall.

Rejoinder to Professor Battin   Lois Snyder

Professor Battin asks us to accept her conclusion that older people should have the right to commit suicide. But she has not argued why there is or should be such a right—she has mostly detailed why some people may want such a right, with a brief reference to human dignity. She asks us to accept these alleged desires as evidence of a right. As a noted law professor critical of Professor Battin's book on philosophy and suicide has remarked, "Whether there *is* a 'fundamental right' is the question, not the answer" (Kamisar, 1993).

Professor Battin says that society should recognize right status for suicide for people who may believe there is a risk that old age will include discomfort and disability. Those individuals would ostensibly wish to control the manner of death before those things happen on the assumption that they will happen. Other advocates have tried to focus the need for a right on individuals with a much stronger case: the real and immediate physical and emotional suffering of the terminally ill, especially those in unbearable pain. Those advocates are more, although ultimately not fully, persuasive in stating an alleged need for a right to commit suicide.

Some have argued for a right to suicide based on a detailed analysis of the principle of respect for autonomy. Many commentators regard autonomy as the key, or sometimes only, aspect of their argument supporting suicide or assisted suicide. But they fail to consider the moral, social, and ethical heart of the matter they raise: Autonomy for what? What are the purposes and consequences of such self-determination for the individual and for society? If society has determined that we do not have the freedom to freely choose to sell ourselves into slavery, can we self-determine ourselves into the ultimate state of self-determinationlessness? Ironically, should we have the right to do so with the assistance of others, no less of the healing profession, as the current manifestation of a pro-suicide movement—physician-assisted suicide proponents—maintain?

Those thinkers who "make an ideology out of autonomy" (Kass, 1990), undervalue the role and interests of society, the necessary precondition for the exercise of autonomy. I strongly believe in individual rights, but rights have limits and corresponding responsibilities and are set in a context.

Overdosing on pills, shooting or hanging oneself, rigging a car exhaust pipe—even in a case of terminal illness, these are not "dignified" or "fitting" ends to a human life, although these words are used by Professor Battin in describing why she would support a right to commit suicide. Can we as families, communities, and members of society do a better job of caring for, meeting the needs of, and demonstrating support for the elderly who would see suicide as their best option? Yes. Should we validate a right to suicide? No.

REFERENCES

Kamisar, Y. (1993). Are laws against assisted suicide unconstitutional? *Hastings Center Report, 23*(3), 32–41.

Kass, L. R. (1990). Practicing ethics: Where's the action? *Hastings Center Report, 20*(1), 5–12.

NO

Lois Snyder

Rights and the U.S. Constitution

A right to suicide, the intentional taking of one's own life, is not a right you can find in the U.S. Constitution or in common law. The State has an interest in preserving life. But this interest is not absolute and must be balanced against the individual's right to bodily integrity.

In 1989, the U.S. Supreme Court heard the case of Nancy Cruzan, the young woman in Missouri who was languishing in a persistent vegetative state, her mind as close to death as was possible while her body was sustained through artificial feeding. I argued in an *amicus* brief then, and still believe now, that there is a constitutional right to bodily integrity that includes a right to refuse life-sustaining medical treatment, under the Due Process Clause of the Fourteenth Amendment.

How far does a right to bodily integrity go? The actual circumstances of the life being lived should be considered. In another landmark case, *In re Quinlan* (New Jersey, 1976), a court said that the State's interest weakens and the rights of the individual grow as the degree of bodily invasion by the treatment increases and the prognosis dims. The Supreme Court did not, however, agree that there is a fundamental right to bodily integrity. So, if the Supreme Court did not even hold that there was a fundamental right to refuse treatment under the Constitution, is it likely that a right to suicide will ever be found? No. In fact, every court that has heard cases in this area has specifically distinguished the refusal of life-sustaining treatment (permissible) from committing suicide (prohibited). The former is a right to protect oneself from intrusion, not a right to control the manner and time of death.

With that I agree. The refusal of treatment is one thing. I do not believe bodily integrity, as a matter of constitutional text, doctrine, history, tradition, common sense, or logic, should be expanded to include a right to suicide. In the refusal of treatment, the individual has an interest in being left alone to die a natural death from an underlying disease. A right to suicide would represent a positive right to something—to kill oneself. There are and should be some limits on individual autonomy. Just as an individual does not have the freedom and right to become a slave (doing so would undermine that very freedom), neither should there be a right to suicide. Such a right would undermine the very meaning of autonomy, which is about far more than just "control."

This does not mean I am unsympathetic to the pain and anguish of individuals (and their families) who have reached the point where they consider suicide to be an option. But what about those individuals who are reaching that conclusion because they are depressed (some studies have found that 95 percent of suicides have a diagnosable psychiatric disorder at the time of their deaths)? Or just need effective pain and symptom control and compassion from their health care providers? Or feel like a burden on their family? Or are concerned about finances? Or feel lonely? Or are otherwise vulnerable? Do they need a right to suicide, or help? Does societal expression of a right to suicide make people, especially the elderly or sick, come to question their worth and feel they have a duty to commit suicide?

Physician-Assisted Suicide: Oregon's Law as an Example

Many proponents of a right to suicide support euthanasia and physician-assisted suicide to implement that right. But no one has been clamoring for a right to suicide. What is in demand is what is called "aid in dying," and many seem to blur the line between physician-assisted suicide (a doctor provides the means for a suicide, such as a prescription for a lethal dose of drugs) and euthanasia (the doctor directly kills, through, for example, the use of a lethal injection).

On November 8, 1994, Oregon voters made that state the first place in the world to legalize physician-assisted suicide on demand with a law full of safeguards and procedures (although the law is now tied up in litigation). The Oregon "Death with Dignity Act" explicitly holds that actions taken in accordance with the act "shall not for any purpose constitute suicide, assisted suicide, mercy killing or homicide, under the law." But residents will be able to obtain prescriptions for lethal doses of drugs from doctors if they make three requests for the drugs under a very detailed set of procedures. This *is* assisted suicide. Calling it otherwise is legal sleight of hand. The Act calls this the obtaining of medication for the purpose of ending one's life in a humane and dignified manner. In fact, throughout the text of the law the word *medication* is almost never used alone. Rather, referring to those who will avail themselves of it, a new phrase is invoked—medication has been converted to the mantra "medication-to-end-his-or-her-life-in-a-humane-and-dignified-manner." Does saying it is so necessarily make it so?

Much has been written in medical ethics on why euthanasia and assisted suicide should be prohibited. It is a fundamental tenet of medicine that physicians be, and be seen as, healers and comforters, not agents of death. For thousands of years, doctors have taken an oath to do no harm and "give no deadly medicine to anyone if asked, or suggest any such counsel." Doing otherwise would compromise the physician–patient relationship and the trust that is necessary to sustain it. It would also undermine the integrity of the profession. Slippery slopes are invoked about the possibilities for misuse and abuse of power, and about cracks in our moral infrastructure that could lead to crumbling. For example, a recent report from Holland, where euthanasia is illegal but the law is not enforced, found that Dutch doctors sometimes act without patient requests in performing euthanasia, that there was a sense among some physicians that certain patients were better off dead, and a sense among some patients that they had a duty to die.

There is more than a little irony to Oregon's Death with Dignity Act. It was born and voter approved in the state that mandated rationing in health care for its poorest residents when it compiled a list of health care services that would and would not be available to Medicaid patients. Ostensibly, medication-to-end-life-in-a-humane-and-dignified-manner is available to all. Some people, the old, the poor, the young, the depressed, might feel more pressure to avail themselves of this option than others. Would older adults come to feel that they should take their lives—that they have, in the words of Hemlock Society founder Derek Humphry, "terminal old age"? Dr. Leon Kass (1991) has called Humphry's best-selling book *Final Exit: The Practicalities of Self-Deliverance and Assisted Suicide for the Dying* (1991), "humanitarian evil, evil with a smile: well-meaning, gentle, and rational..."

Rights and Responsibilities

People who want to will commit suicide. We as a society should encourage them not to and should provide the social support, medical care, and compassion to those who feel they face such an undignified life or an undignified painful death that they want to turn to suicide.

Suicide and attempted suicide are no longer illegal in this country, largely because of the role of mental illness in suicide and because punishment of the innocent family of the suicide was thought to be unjustified. But that does not confer a right to commit suicide. Is a society that takes the next step and recognizes such a right or puts its seal of approval on physician-assisted suicide an enlightened and compassionate society? Or is it one in which the single-minded focus on a narrow definition of individual autonomy and self-determination to the exclusion of other values has gone too far and undermines the whole notion of society, of values that bind individuals together, and of the value of life? In the United States, there is no general "right" to health care. Should there be a right to suicide, particularly for older persons? No.

REFERENCES

Cruzan v. *Director, Missouri Department of Health,* 110 S.Ct. 2841 (1990).
In re Quinlan, 70 N.J. 10, 355 A.2d 642, *cert. denied,* 429 U.S. 922 (1976).
Humphry, D. (1991). *Final exit: The practicalities of self-deliverance and assisted suicide for the dying.* The Hemlock Society.
Kass, L. R. (1991, December). Suicide made easy: The evil of "rational" humaneness. *Commentary,* pp. 19–24.

Rejoinder to Professor Snyder   MARGARET PABST BATTIN

I have argued that suicide is a fundamental right, though subject to limitations, and that when an older person makes a considered, principled, and uncoerced choice concerning a fitting conclusion for his or her life, this choice must be respected. My opponent in this discussion, a lawyer, raises a number of legal issues to challenge this contention. But in doing so, I think, she makes a category mistake: I have argued about what is, or is not, a matter of fundamental *moral* right; she argues about what the law actually recognizes and about practical difficulties that recognizing such a right might raise. I say there is such a right; she says the law does not see it. I say there is such a right; she says it may be abused. Thus far, we need not disagree: there can certainly be fundamental moral rights still unrecognized by law (as freedom from slavery once was) and that, because they can be abused, require scrupulous protection. I think the right to suicide—in old age, as in other circumstances—is one of these.

But, of course, my opponent believes we disagree. She thinks the rule of law is important; I agree, but I do not think fundamental moral issues can be resolved by looking at what the law currently has to say. She thinks the State's interest in preserving life must be balanced against violating bodily integrity; I think the state's interest in preserving life must be balanced against violating human dignity as well. She thinks *Quinlan, Cruzan,* and Oregon's 1994 "Death with Dignity Act" are relevant; but those are cases about young women in their twenties, not elderly people, and the Act is about the terminally ill, defined as being within six months of death. I think we must ask whether the principles explored in these legal contexts can be extended to older persons, and I think it is important to recognize that we do not yet even have a way of thinking clearly about whether the question of suicide in old age should be considered a separate, special issue, independent of the question of whether any other persons, such as the terminally ill, have such rights. Because the very old are coming to the end of their lives no matter what—death is, after all, inevitable and comparatively near—do they have a special, distinct right concerning how their lives shall end?

In any case, the law is evolving so rapidly in its treatment of right-to-die issues, both in the United States and in many other countries (especially including Canada, Australia, and the Netherlands), that what the law has to say today may not be what it has to say tomorrow. So my opponent, although a lawyer, is, I think, wrong about an appeal to the law and what the law would show. She is also wrong, I think, about the human qualities of the alternative to legalizing assistance in suicide. She favors giving patients the right of "being left alone to die a natural death for an underlying disease," but this just means that it is the disease that kills the patient, rather than the far more humane act of the physician who helps a suffering patient bring about an easier death. Some terminally ill patients do not want to be "left alone to die a natural death," because they recognize that "natural death" is a highly romanticized term cloaking often awful physiological processes; old age can sometimes compound the indignities this brings. As Mary Rose Barrington, an English jurist and administrator of a group of almshouses for the aged, puts it: "Death taken in one's own time, and with a sense of purpose, may in fact be far more bearable than the process of waiting to be arbitrarily extinguished" (Barrington, 1969).

The possibility of abuse is *never* grounds for the suppression of a fundamental right; rather, it is grounds for redoubled protection of its exercise. Of course, a choice of suicide, whether in old age, terminal illness, or another situation, cannot count as the expression of a fundamental right, rooted in human dignity, if it is manipulated, pressured, or forced; but it can also be a reflective, fully voluntary, genuine choice. The irony is that the law is often going in exactly the wrong direction—trying to evade and ignore the basic right, when it should be dedicated to careful reinforcement of protections for voluntary, uncoerced exercise of that right. This is an important right, a basic right, relevant to all of us as we contemplate the ends of our lives, regardless of whether we might ever actually choose to have them end in this way.

I think both my opponent and I would agree that it would be a very good thing for society to do more to discourage suicide by making the conditions of life in old age better, including providing social support, medical care, compassion, and respect, but we do not agree that it would be a good thing for society to try to discourage suicide by suppressing genuine, thoughtful, realistic choice about how one wishes to face the oncoming end of one's life. On the contrary, society ought to respect a wider range of options about dying, of which legally accepted, carefully protected, socially respected suicide is just one.

After all, we owe older people a crucial thing we rarely grant them: respect, indeed admiration, for their courage to face the facts of old age and the eventual occurrence of death in a forthright way, and to choose what they consider the least worst way of having their lives end. We owe equal respect to people who face the same facts, survey the same future possibilities, and choose to continue to stay alive as long as they can. What is crucial here is respect for older people's fundamental rights, including both the right to encounter death as they choose, even if it means suicide, *and* the right to continue to embrace life if—as may well be the case for most older people—that is what they prefer.

REFERENCES

Barrington, M. R. (1969). Apologia for suicide. In A. B. Downing (Ed.), *Euthanasia and the right to death* (p. 102). London: Peter Owen. Reprinted in M. P. Battin and D. J. Mayo (1980). *Suicide: The philosophical issues.* New York: St. Martin's Press.

Should Health Care Be Rationed by Age?

EDITOR'S NOTE: In an effort to curtail rapidly rising U.S. health care costs and improve cost-effectiveness, numerous philosophers, economists, and policy makers have called for rationing of existing health care resources. The elderly, who account for more than one-third of all U.S. health care expenditures, have been a natural target for such efforts. It is argued that the United States cannot afford to squander scarce health care resources on older persons who will receive limited benefit, and that chronological age should be a key consideration in determining access to expensive, life-prolonging medical technology. Some have suggested that there is a natural life span of approximately 70 years, after which individuals should be allowed to die rather than use up limited societal resources. Others, however, contend that rationing violates basic American values of human worth and equality. They maintain that proposals to ration health care based on age are inherently ageist, valuing the lives of older persons less than the lives of younger persons. Yet, America's rapidly growing elderly population and limited health care resources seem to be on a collision course that inevitably will force tough decisions by policy makers and health care providers. Is rationing health care the best solution to the impending health care crisis? Should chronological age be used to decide who will, and who will not, receive medical care?

Eric Rakowski, D. Ph., J.D., is Professor of Law at the University of California at Berkeley (Boalt Hall School of Law). He has written on a number of topics in moral philosophy, including abortion, euthanasia, and the permissibility of taking life to save more lives. *Equal Justice* (Oxford University Press, 1991) sets forth his views on distributive justice.

Stephen G. Post, Ph.D., is Associate Professor of Biomedical Ethics at Case Western Reserve University School of Medicine. His most recent book is *The Moral Challenge of Alzheimer Disease* (Johns Hopkins University Press, 1995). He is an elected Fellow of both the Hastings Center and the Kennedy Institute of Ethics.

YES

ERIC RAKOWSKI

Are we morally obligated to save a younger patient before an older one if only one can live? Should we prefer the young when conducting medical research or dispensing medical care? Other things being equal, I believe that the answer is yes.

Plainly, age should not *always* determine whom we help. We might not aid a murderer awaiting execution even if he were youngest, and many would give priority to the prime minister (or, perhaps, an outstanding surgeon or composer), notwithstanding his age. Likewise, if a rare drug could prolong the younger person's life by one painful month or keep his elder hale for thirty more years, nobody would give it to the younger. The important question is whether the number of years a person has lived should *ever* influence the rationing of publicly funded medical care if patients are alike in all other relevant respects. (I assume that people may attach importance to age in buying *private* medical insurance and that the government may not interfere with their decisions.)

I believe that we should favor younger people, other things being equal, for two independent reasons. First, as a matter of distributive justice, we ought to give people as nearly equal opportunities as we can without imposing excessive hardships on the naturally more fortunate. Preferring the younger of two people who are otherwise identical and who would benefit equally from treatment would most nearly equalize their opportunities to lead satisfying lives. Second, we should generally respect people's informed preferences regarding matters that affect their personal well-being. We should therefore allocate public medical resources according to whatever rules recipients would have selected if they were aware of the benefits of rival medical protocols and of what justice entitles them to have if they do not choose something else. If, as I believe, people who receive public health care would in these circumstances overwhelmingly choose to make age relevant to decisions about who will live or how aggressively someone will be treated, then the government should abide by their desires.

The Argument from Distributive Justice

People are born equally undeserving. Because nobody has a stronger moral claim than anyone else to the world's resources, all are equally entitled to those resources. What this principle implies for existing societies is a very complicated question, given historical contingencies and competing moral principles. Property rights were already divided up before we were born, and people arguably may transfer at least some of what they have earned to those they love without helping everyone else equally. Nevertheless, at least as an initial matter, each of us can claim an equally valuable set of possessions and prospects, stretching over a lifetime, in virtue of our common abilities to reason, feel, and act morally. What justice demands (subject to qualifications of the sort I mentioned) is that people have equal *chances* to build the lives they desire; how they use their opportunities is for them to decide.

One implication of this view is that people are obligated to share in any good or bad luck that they could not reasonably have anticipated or against which they could not have protected themselves fully by, for example, avoiding risks or buying insurance. Otherwise, their opportunities will be unequal. Those who are unlucky are therefore entitled to compensation from those who fared better, so long as the unfortunate did not voluntarily run the risk of whatever disadvantaged them and so long as others' better circumstances are not the product of their shrewd gambles.

One important respect in which people's luck may differ through no fault or merit of their own (although sometimes they *can* be held responsible) is in their health and the opportunities for enjoyment or gainful work that good health or a long life makes possible. If the view that I have defended elsewhere (Rakowski, 1991) is correct, then in these cases justice mandates (unless the unfortunate have waived their right to redress) that people hobbled by poor genes or by unforeseen illness or mishap be recompensed by their luckier peers, to restore as nearly as money and medical science can the fair plane of opportunity on which they stood before the onset of misfortune.

Years of life are the precondition to enjoying all goods and opportunities. For that reason, life-years are the most important items in the bundles of resources and opportunities to which people are entitled. To be sure, segments of time cannot be transferred from one person to another to even out everybody's share. But deciding which of two people should receive a life-saving medicine means adding time to one or the other person's bundle of resources. If justice calls for overall equality to the extent we can achieve it consistent with other moral strictures, then we should assign the medicine, other things being equal (such as prognosis and personal responsibility), to ensure that the two have as equal a chance as possible to realize life's goods, taking account of the years they have lived and the years they will live if treated or not treated. Age is one relevant factor, though certainly not the only one, in deciding whom to save.

Does helping the young first treat older people disrespectfully, because both stand to lose what they probably value most—their lives—and each wishes to go on living as much as the other (Harris, 1994)? I think not. Even were it possible to compare the intensities of two people's desires to survive, that comparison would have no bearing on the justice of favoring youth, just as somebody's coveting my car more than I do gives him no right to take it. Justice requires not that we treat people's wishes or interests equally at any single point in time; that view seems to require, unreasonably, that we choose randomly between a person who would gain a month of life from treatment and someone who would gain thirty years, so long as both wanted to live as long as they could. Rather, justice calls for coming as close as we can to providing equal opportunities to all over a lifetime. We cannot justly ignore what two people have already had in deciding what each will have in the future.

In what way should age differences shape doctors' decisions? Suppose that Ruth or June can be treated, but not both. Suppose, further, that treatment offers them exactly the same expected benefit—ten years of identical health—and that the two are alike in all morally relevant respects except their ages. If Ruth is younger than June, should the doctor invariably favor Ruth?

One answer is that Ruth may claim priority simply because she has lived less long. How old either is matters not at all. A second approach follows from what John Harris has labeled "the fair innings argument" (Harris, 1985). If June already has lived a full life (seventy years, say), then she has had a fair innings, an opportunity to enjoy what life normally offers to people; hence, Ruth should be preferred: But if neither has already crossed the age threshold, then their different ages provide no reason to favor either according to the "fair innings" approach.

Some might be attracted to the fair innings argument because it would not require doctors to favor Ruth just because she is a few years younger. Helping Ruth straightaway might seem especially offensive if she would then live *longer* than June already has. Nevertheless, if we wish to approach equality to the greatest degree possible, we must reject the fair innings argument. The disparity between the years available to two people will always be minimized if we choose strictly according to age. For example, if Ruth is twenty-five and June is thirty and we can give either ten years, helping Ruth will leave one person with thirty-five years and one with thirty, resulting in a disparity of five years; helping June instead will produce a threefold disparity of fifteen years (forty versus twenty-five). To keep the difference as small as can be, Ruth should be helped.

Compare eyes. Suppose that we have to decide whether to give a cornea (the last one there will be) to somebody who has sight in one eye or to somebody who is blind. Both fall short of the norm of binocular vision, just as neither Ruth nor Jane has already lived what the fair innings argument considers a normal life of seventy years. If we wish to equalize so far as we can the lot of the two people whose vision is impaired, should we toss a coin to decide because both lack a normal complement of two eyes? Obviously not. We should help the blind person. The same goes for years of life.

This argument holds true even if two people are close in age, though of course the closer they are, the less reason one has to help the younger first, and thus the less important age differences are relative to other differences between them. Those inclined to balk at even a tiny preference for a slightly younger person should ask why random choice would be a better rule. Choosing randomly would not raise people's average life expectancy, compared with a rule of favoring the younger. And the latter rule would give people, on average, a greater *minimum* number of years than any other—something most people would value if they were asked to select a rule in ignorance of the future when they were young. There seems no reason to depart from the default rule of putting the younger first, apart perhaps from the seeming arbitrariness of always saving the younger person when the two are nearly the same age. But because arbitrariness is precisely what those who propose to flip a coin desire, it is not clear why they should object to saving the younger first. Birth order is as random—and thus as fair—as a coin toss, and it carries the additional advantage of maximizing equality of opportunity.

The Argument from Personal Autonomy

There is a second argument for making health care rationing decisions on the basis of age. This argument from personal autonomy coheres not only with the theory of justice I offered, but also with any other theory that respects people's freedom to choose what is best for them. If personal autonomy deserves respect, the argument runs, then government officials should allocate publicly funded medical care as potential patients would prefer in making insurance decisions for themselves. If this claim is sound, the important questions become what people want, or would want if they had reasonable foresight; how to combine their disparate preferences into one or a few health insurance plans; and how strongly paternalistic the state's policies should be if people's considered choices seem myopic or irrational.

It is certainly plausible to claim that prudent individuals insuring over a lifetime would take account of age in deciding how to treat people in need and what investments to make in research, medical equipment, and physicians' skills (Battin, 1987; Daniels, 1988). Gazing forward from the vantage point of youth, they would want to maximize their life expectancies and probably also their chance of living a certain number of years. This is, to be sure, speculation; for reasons Norman Daniels recounts, lifetime insurance policies are not now sold, and it would, I think, be dangerous to infer what people would want from existing government programs in the United States, given the political clout of the elderly and the powerlessness of the poor. But Daniels's conjecture seems reasonable. If recipients would want age to affect who will survive after they had thought carefully about their health needs over a lifetime and the benefits of available treatments, then the government should assign age precisely that importance (Menzel, 1990).

This argument must be qualified in various ways, in particular with respect to the care of children, who lack the experience, intelligence, and wherewithal to make their own insurance decisions. My central point is that if the argument from autonomy is correct, adults *may* make age a relevant factor in allocating health care; morality does not force them to do so or to refrain from doing so. If, as seems likely, they would do so in many situations, there exists a second support for the principle that justice affirms as a background rule: that age ought to be one basis for rationing care.

REFERENCES

Battin, M. P. (1987). Age rationing and the just distribution of health care: Is there
a duty to die? *Ethics, 97,* 317–340.

Daniels, N. (1988). *Am I my parents' keeper? An essay on justice between the
young and the old.* New York: Oxford University Press.

Harris, J. (1985). *The value of life.* London: Routledge.

Harris, J. (1994). Does justice require that we be ageist? *Bioethics, 8,* 74–83.

Menzel, P. T. (1990). *Strong medicine: The ethical rationing of health care.* New
York: Oxford University Press.

Rakowski, E. (1991). *Equal justice.* Oxford: Oxford University Press.

Rejoinder to Professor Rakowski

STEPHEN G. POST

Eric Rakowski appeals first to the notion of equality of opportunity in defending
the use of age as a criterion for the just distribution of life-saving health care. This
concept of equality entails, he argues, that equal years of life is a moral goal, for
years of life "are the precondition to enjoying all goods and opportunities."
Health care should be allocated, it follows, so as to favor the relatively young over
the relatively old.

Although it is true that scarce medical resources ought not to be made available to the fragile elderly who are certainly at death's door, especially when
younger people might benefit for years if provided with those same resources, in
general Rakowski's argument is abstract and unworkable. The basic medical reality is that outcome predictions based on age are notoriously useless in clinical
practice. Age is in fact one of the poorer predictors of success. There is no way to
fine-tune outcome measures, which rely on often vague probabilities, to clarify
the individual case. The art of medicine is characterized by uncertainty. Any effort to make allocation decisions based on whether a thirty-five-year-old will live
a few years longer than a forty-five-year-old is futile.

Furthermore, the principle that justice involves relatively equal life spans
between persons is an unprecedented extension of equality of opportunity. We
simply do not have such powers of control over individual human destiny. Some
bodies seem to last for the long haul, and others do not. There is much genetic
luck involved. The principle of equalizing life spans ignores the extent to which
such equalization is beyond medical control.

Moreover, life span has little or nothing to do with opportunity and the desire to make the best of one's years. The poet John Keats died in his mid-twenties
of tuberculosis. But in his last five years of consumption, he responded to mortality through poetic creativity. The great Danish existentialist Soren Kierkegaard
died relatively young as well. He indicated that the sense of mortality haunted
him and allowed him to use every moment to the creative fullest. In short, it is less

the number of years of life than what the individual determines to do with even a few years that makes for an enriching life. Many people squander their lives no matter how long, never seeming to cultivate virtue or generativity.

I agree with Rakowski that any age-based rationing of health care ought to be autonomous, that is, emergent from the society through some sort of communitarian dialogue. But in reality, consensus is unlikely on a matter so laden with cross-cultural particularities. In our highly pluralistic society, many cultural groups would value the aged as much as or even more than the young.

NO

STEPHEN G. POST

Age-based cutoffs of life-extending medical treatments would be simple but wrong. Cutoffs would categorically deny such treatments purely on the basis of some arbitrary age such as eighty or perhaps eighty-five. This is an approach that eliminates all of the complexity of considering the elderly person in his or her uniqueness. Geriatricians have largely rejected age-based cutoffs because they are keenly aware of the remarkable physical heterogeneity in even the oldest old. Age alone is not a good predictor of treatment outcome, even if it would allow for neat and simple implementation.

Many very old people have lived generative lives in their eighties and nineties. Among musicians, guitarist Andre Segovia performed into his early nineties, as did cellist Pablo Cassals. Artists from Picasso to Grandma Moses were also creatively robust in their eighties and nineties. Along the way, many such individuals benefited from life-extending treatments that returned them to a good quality of life.

Some highly creative octogenarians lived prodigal lives, squandering opportunities while young. Many of us look back on the first several decades of life and ask why we were so wasteful of our talents and opportunities. We seem captivated by rites of passage, from fast driving and six-packs of beer to gang violence and spur posse. Hopefully, as we mature in wisdom, life becomes more meaningful and prodigality fades.

Maturity and accumulated wisdom ought to be appreciated rather than discriminated against. All age-based cutoff plans imply that a young life is more worthy of saving than an old one. Thus, all such plans are at bottom "ageist" in assuming that the young, perhaps because of bodily strength, are somehow more worthy of life. Our images of human perfection are excessively youthful and unappreciative of wisdom.

The roots of ageism may lie in the loss of the three-generation family, in which grandparents lived in the family home and served as mentors for the children. Grandparents can perform a role that parents often cannot. For example, they have classically passed on spiritual traditions. They serve as nonparent men-

tors, and their absence leaves a void. Since World War II, our single-family houses leave no room for grandparents, who either live independently or in a nursing
home. In contrast to classic wisdom cultures of the past, the young do not enjoy
the teaching function of the elderly. For wisdom, they turn to the latest software.
The social protection of elderly people has always been in part based on reciproc-
ity, that is, their teaching roles were valued by the younger. But once this function
is removed as the culture is stripped of traditions, elderly people become vulnerable to negative stereotypes and rhetoric. So the first reason against age-based cutoffs is that the contributions of elderly people are lost to society and the young.

Second, age-based rationing threatens to fragment the covenant between
the old and the young, because it builds on an adversarial construct of intergenerational relations. Instead of pursuing fairness in treatment decisions for people of
all ages on an individual basis, whether a premature neonate, a twenty-year-old
with terminal acquired immune deficiency syndrome (AIDS), or a ninety-year-
old with advanced dementia, age-based rationing throws a whole demographic
group in the wastebasket purely because of age. Alternatively, we need a health
care system that attends to the individual regardless of age, perhaps imposing rationing based on extremely poor quality of life or imminence of inevitable death.
Old age may be relevant to either of these bases, but only in an individualized way.

Third, age-based cutoffs convey the threatening message to old people that
they are no longer "equal" in value and therefore can be disposed of. Rationing
systems that harp on elderly people alone are inherently discriminatory. Proponents of such systems contend that there really is no discrimination because
everyone gets old eventually, and therefore we will all live under the specter of
age-based cutoffs. But this amounts to claiming that a discriminatory practice,
because imposed universally, becomes fair. The human brain begins to deterio-
rate by age thirty. Were we to discriminate against all people older than thirty
years on this basis, generation after generation, our consistency would not justify
the imposition.

Fourth, age-based cutoffs make a mockery of individual freedom. Old people do not have a right to request "futile" medical treatments, nor do the young.
But with regard to beneficial treatments, it is more respectful of individual values
and capacities to leave the monumental decisions of treatment refusal and withdrawal to the person. Let the individual decide when the flame is no longer worth
the candle. If ration we must, then restrict the freedom of all rather than of the elderly alone. For example, if society decides to limit life-extending treatment to
people with a diagnosis of early Alzheimer's disease, then such restrictions must
also be applied to younger patients with AIDS-related dementia. It is morally
wrong to suspend freedom in one age-group while it runs amok in another.

Fifth, age-based cutoffs are likely to encourage preemptive suicide among
elderly people. No longer allowed access to interventions that may restore them
to a reasonably good quality of life, they would be condemned to an otherwise
avoidable downward course that makes assisted suicide or voluntary mercy kill-

ing look attractive. Abstract theories of age-based cutoffs obscure the brutal fact: this individual person, simply because he or she is old, must face the needless relegation to hospice-like care and death.

Finally, age-based cutoffs are deeply sexist. There are approximately thirty-seven men for every one hundred women who are aged eighty-five years and older. Women outlive men. This gap may narrow as women assume traditionally male labor patterns. But for now, age-based cutoffs limit treatment for many more women than men. I am aware of no woman who has proposed such cutoffs, although a number have raised feminist counterpoints.

In summary, rationing of life-extending treatments, if necessary, should be done in an age-neutral manner. Categorical age-based cutoffs would be relatively simple to implement and are in this sense appealing. However, although resources might be saved, much would be lost with respect to the reasonable honor that good societies owe those who grow old. It will always be the case that, in old age, people use more medical resources, for they become more frail. But this is not unjust, because all of us, when we are old, will draw on these resources to a much greater extent than is ordinarily the case for those who are still young.

What is the alternative to age-based rationing? Increasingly, public programs such as Medicare and Medicaid, and private managed care systems, will need to develop priority lists that preclude some treatments. Americans of all ages will need to realize that there is no unlimited right to health care, although there is a limited one.

Specifically, there is a right to nonfutile health care consistent with need rather than want, with efficacy, and with affordability. As for the distinction between needs and wants, there is no "right" to many cosmetically enhancing surgeries, to repeated efforts at artificial insemination, to futile or scientifically nonvalidated treatments, and to genetic enhancement. There is a right to treatment that responds to disease conditions; this is classically consistent with the goal of medicine. It would be shameful to deny clearly beneficial treatment to an older person to ensure that all middle-aged people have access to at least several tummy-tucks, and all adolescents to at least one nose job.

Older people do not have a right to genetic testing when the results are too vague to be clinically useful, or when there is no preventive treatment or lifestyle modification possible. They may of course want this testing, but it is not an obvious need. Nor do older people have a right to any treatment that does not restore health, assist in the endurance of chronic illness, or provide relief from pain. It is these classic goals of the art of medicine that should help distinguish wants from needs. Physiologically futile treatments are of no medical benefit and therefore do not constitute need.

As for efficacy, some treatments will be successful one time in ten, or perhaps one time in fifty. As with a baseball hitter, we must ask whether such a low batting average is worth supporting. For each success, dozens of failures must be paid for. For example, in the population of elderly people with mild dementia, the drug tacrine may very rarely have clear benefits in slowing the loss of memory. Such slowing is clearly a desirable goal. However, it is an expensive drug that would be hugely expensive if provided to all patients, even if there is the occasional success. We need to emphasize the high failure rates of many medical treatments and consider cutoffs based on these rates, rather than on age. It is possible, of course, that people who are frail and elderly will show higher failure rates than other populations, although age alone is a poor indicator of treatment outcome.

As for affordability, some treatments work consistently. However, they are extremely costly. An example is liver transplantation. Can such a treatment be made available to every person in need? Even the most successful treatments, such as kidney dialysis, are extremely costly when provided to everyone.

In the final analysis, many societal values and goods are at least as important as health care. Included would be education, redeveloping the industrial–manufacturing base that has eroded and left inner-city populations and whole towns in dire poverty, the war against drugs, and housing. We have too many tertiary care settings surrounded by ghettos. I am reminded of Vienna, where the immense St. Stephen's Cathedral was built 1,500 years ago amid huts and desperation. Rationing may be a necessary last resort, but the burden should not be placed on the shoulders of the old alone (Binstock & Post, 1991; Post, 1993).

REFERENCES

Binstock, R. H., & Post, S. G. (Eds.). (1991). *Too old for health care? Controversies in medicine, law, economics, and ethics.* Baltimore: Johns Hopkins University Press.

Post, S. G. (1993). *Inquiries in bioethics.* Washington, DC: Georgetown University Press.

Rejoinder to Professor Post   ERIC RAKOWSKI

Stephen Post's essay addresses two distinct issues. We plainly disagree about the first, though we may not be too far apart on the second. The first issue is whether age is relevant to the rationing of publicly owned, life-extending medical resources. Post says that these resources should be rationed "in an age-neutral manner," so that a ninety-year-old and a twenty-year-old should have the same chance of receiving a scarce drug if they will benefit similarly from treatment. I reject this claim, for reasons I have given. Treating people as equals, in my view, requires looking not only at whether they would be helped to the same extent by some life-extending drug that only one can have, but at how that drug will affect the opportunities they enjoy over the course of their lives. If two people will benefit equally from treatment but one has had less of a chance to lead a full and meaningful life, then there is reason to help that person first. That reason might be outweighed by other considerations, but it at least tips an even balance. Furthermore, potential recipients of public medical assistance, deciding in ignorance of their station which patients to treat, would predictably endorse age-sensitive rules. Post must either claim that people would not in fact embrace an age-sensitive rationing rule, or that a principle of justice other than the one I defended is correct and for some reason takes precedence over what people would overwhelmingly want. I am not sure which of these claims he would defend, or why.

The second issue Post discusses is whether people ought to be denied various medical treatments once they reach a certain age. I did not address this question explicitly, but an answer is implicit in my argument from patient autonomy. When people buy private health insurance, they inevitably make certain bets. They buy in advance the right to a range of treatments should they need them, and they forgo other possibly beneficial treatments because of their expected cost. Public health care, I suggest, should be thought of in a parallel way. From the standpoint of those receiving public assistance, a fixed sum of money is available for all of the medical treatments that members of that pool will receive. That amount may be more or less than justice requires. The important point is that funds are limited and that each person has the same right to determine how they are used. The problem, then, is ascertaining what plan of distribution these people favor, or which they would favor if they thought carefully about the costs and benefits of rival treatments, and combining their possibly divergent preferences into a single insurance scheme for the group (Rakowski, 1994).

The choice they face is not a moral choice, but a decision about what is in their self-interest. There would be nothing reprehensible in deciding to end life-sustaining treatment for patients older than eighty. But it seems to me unlikely that people would actually favor such a scheme. They might reasonably reduce the entitlements of older patients, either because the elderly generally have already had opportunities that the young still only hope to enjoy, or because it would be prudent of people to favor the young when choosing in ignorance of their own identities. But strict age-based cutoffs would likely attract little support. Thus, I am inclined to think that Post is right in condemning across-the-board denials of treatment to geriatric patients. I agree with his conclusion, however, not because some old people are great artists or wise teachers, nor because discriminating against the elderly would spur suicide or violate some make-believe covenant between generations. I agree because inflexible age-based cutoffs are incompatible with the model of rational insurance I conjecture most people would favor.

Reference

Rakowski, E. (1994, July-August). The aggregation problem. *Hastings Center Report, 24,* 33–36.

Is Managed Care Good for Older Persons?

EDITORS' NOTE: Escalating health care costs for older persons have been attributed in part to America's fee-for-service health care reimbursement system, in which financial incentives favor increased rather than decreased use of health care services. In response, insurance companies, health maintenance organizations (HMOs), and even the government increasingly are turning to managed care to increase efficiency and limit unnecessary use of high-cost services. Managed care can be observed in a variety of forms, including Medicare's capitated reimbursement system for acute inpatient care, pretreatment authorization before surgeries and other expensive procedures, preadmission screening before admission to a long-term care facility, and coordination of benefits for acute care, residential care, and community-based long-term care. Supporters point to the potential for a more efficient and effective use of limited health care resources as well as better care than is possible under the individually managed, poorly coordinated fee-for-service system. Critics raise concerns about whether efforts to contain costs might be at the expense of quality care, particularly for the most vulnerable individuals. Is managed care the solution to America's health care crisis? Will managed care result in improved care, or will some segments of the population find themselves worse off than before? In particular, will managed care be good for older persons?

Jennie Chin Hansen, R.N., M.S., says *YES.* She is Executive Director of On Lok, Inc., the San Francisco nonprofit organization that pioneered the managed care organization known as PACE, the Program for All-Inclusive Care for the Elderly. PACE provides total medical and long-term care in the community for the frail elderly. Ms. Hansen is President of the American Society on Aging and was a California delegate to the 1995 White House Conference on Aging.

Marty Lynch, Ph.D, and Carroll L. Estes, Ph.D., say *NO*. Dr. Lynch is Executive Director of the Over 60 Health Center in Berkeley, California. He co-chairs the Elderly Task Force of the National Association of Community Health Centers as well as the Public Policy Committee of the American Society on Aging. Dr. Estes is Director of the Institute for Health & Aging, Professor of Sociology, and former Chair of the Department of Social & Behavioral Sciences at the University of California, San Francisco. She is President of the Gerontological Society of America, Vice President of the National Older Women's League, and a past President of the American Society on Aging and the Association for Gerontology in Higher Education. Her most recent co-authored books are *The Nation's Health* (4th Edition), *Health Policy and Nursing,* and *The Political Economy of Health and Aging.*

YES

JENNIE CHIN HANSEN

The Benefits of Managed Care for Older Adults

Managed care can offer enormous advantages for older people in care delivery, in ease of access to resources and in cost of care. We define "managed care" as a health care delivery approach that is complemented by a financing system. In this care delivery approach, an interdisciplinary team of professionals shares responsibility for managing and integrating all of the care needed by an enrollee in a health plan. The financing system—fixed per-person payment—encourages flexible use of resources and the prevention of conditions that require expensive treatment (e.g., acute hospital care).

The alternative to *managed* care is *ad hoc* care, discrete health care services acquired on a piecemeal basis. Individuals "manage" their own care by seeing specialists and often using high-cost, sometimes unnecessary, services. If one's care needs are intermittent and simple, and one has the knowledge and financial resources (e.g., insurance coverage) to access the treatment necessary to solve the problem, then *ad hoc* care may work fine for both the individual and the health care provider. Conversely, *ad hoc* care does *not* work well for the older person whose care needs are complex and ongoing, or who lacks the resources to identify, obtain, and coordinate the many particular services required to ameliorate these problems.

Managed care avoids three dangers inherent in *ad hoc* care for the older person: (1) personal financial insecurity, (2) the burden of shopping for and patching together increasingly complex care as needs increase, and (3) social costs (financial and other).

First, managed care can operate more efficiently, enabling the provider to offer the enrollee a greater range of services without additional private expense. For good reason, older persons served through the *ad hoc* "system" fear that their health care costs may impoverish them, or that one day they will have to choose between food and medicine. Currently, the elderly now pay more than half of the cost of their care from their private resources. Despite Medicare efforts to exert controls to slow cost escalation, the consumer's copayments, cost of insurance to supplement Medicare, and deductibles all keep going up. Moreover, coverage of long-term care services by Medicare and "Medigap" policies is extremely limited, meaning that either personal dollars must pay for additional long-term care insurance or one must pay out-of-pocket for the supportive care essential for multiple chronic diseases and functional impairments. In managed care, the fixed, all-inclusive premium and low—or no—copayments for service reduce the enrollee's personal financial risk. Services that might otherwise be unavailable or uncovered can be offered, including preventive care that may avoid catastrophic incidents and costs. Thus, managed care can provide greater assurance of affordability in the short and long run.

Second, managed care's ability to reduce the burden of finding and coordinating services is a valuable benefit. As an older person's health needs become more complex and energy flags, the importance of coordination increases. Searching out specialists for diagnosis and treatment, communicating the same information repeatedly to them, and keeping track of multiple bills and appointments exhaust both the patient and the family caregiver. Often in a managed care program, the primary care provider serves as a gatekeeper helping to access and manage specialty care and other services. Because the full range of health service providers may be included within a single managed care organization, referral and communication among health care and ancillary service professionals can be accomplished more readily.

Third, managed care has the capacity to reduce costs to the health care system and society. Because the managed care provider is at financial risk, the incentive is to keep enrollees as healthy as possible. It has been demonstrated that the timely use of preventive care can decrease the need for costly health care services such as hospitalization. Well-managed care can thus have a positive impact simultaneously for the individual, the family bank account, the provider, and society.

On Lok (PACE): An Example of the Benefits of Managed Care

Our positive stance on managed care grows from experience with On Lok, which in the early 1970s created a consumer-oriented health care model for older people who require long-term care but do not want to go into a nursing home. The On Lok approach is being replicated throughout the United States as the Program of All-inclusive Care for the Elderly (PACE), a fully integrated managed care system for the frail elderly that meets complex medical and social needs by putting together, in one place, all medical, restorative, social, and supportive care. In PACE, an interdisciplinary team assesses each participant's needs systematically, recognizing the interactions of social, emotional, and physical factors. Their treatment plan addresses the whole person (not just disease manifestations) and incorporates all care settings—home, community, and institutional facility. The team monitors the participant's progress over time and adjusts the care plan to fit ever-changing needs. This same interdisciplinary team gives care, usually in a day health center or at home, for the balance of the participant's life. Contracts with hospitals and nursing homes enable PACE to manage inpatient care, as well.

On Lok and PACE have an *integrated reimbursement system* in which Medicare and Medicaid both provide per capita payments each month, based on the program's census of entitled enrollees. These funds are pooled and used without regard to traditional restrictions, eliminating unproductive paperwork and providing built-in incentives for providers to control cost. For a fixed monthly rate, PACE gives as much care as long as is needed, regardless of how costly this becomes. With no "out" and no place to shift costs. PACE manages its financial risk by keeping the participant as healthy as possible.

Our experience with On Lok and PACE shows that a managed care system can enable 95 percent of the persons normally expected to be in a nursing home to stay in the community. Moreover, we have experienced consistently lower hospital utilization among our frail enrollees than occurs in the general sixty-five-plus population. A system such as On Lok/PACE allows money to be diverted from acute care or nursing home care to the community-based services consumers prefer, such as day care and home care.

On Lok's experience in providing total health care for a fixed capitation payment shows that providers can be motivated to control costs while delivering effective, high-quality care. An all-inclusive system stimulates creativity among care providers and takes away red tape, enabling health care professionals to take care of people, instead of maximizing a revenue stream. While savings accrue to payers, frail PACE enrollees experience quality, convenience, continuity, and the availability of every service and treatment needed, without confusing copayments or deductibles!

Lessons Learned: How Managed Care Can Be Most Beneficial for Older Adults

Caring for people who have chronic, debilitating illnesses means cutting across traditional boundaries—primary, specialty, acute, and long-term care; "high tech" intervention and "low tech" maintenance; institutional and community-based care; and medical and social approaches. The skills of health care professionals from many disciplines must be pooled, and the health care team must have the time and opportunity to focus on *care* as much as, or more than, on *cure*. Key ingredients of On Lok's success that pertain to managed health care for everyone are:

- Inclusion of primary care physicians in the planning, coordination, and delivery of care
- Comprehensiveness of services, ranging from social support to acute medical care
- Continuity of care with emphasis on prevention (even among the very old and very frail)

Fundamental to our argument supporting managed care for older persons is the integration of acute and long-term care. Any managed care program that enrolls the elderly must integrate these components or the incentive will be to shift costs—to disenroll the older person at the very time need is greatest and one is least able to handle the burden of managing care for oneself. With such integration, care can be continuous, and savings can be realized.

The managed care model practiced by PACE is a proven way to meet the complex, changeable health care needs of the older population. With a managed care program such as PACE generally available, fewer nursing home beds would be needed to meet the projected growth in the numbers of frail elderly, and better outcomes could result for participants, their families, and payers.

Rejoinder to Ms. Chin Hansen

MARTY LYNCH
CARROLL L. ESTES

If every managed care plan for the elderly was like On Lok, or like the Over 60 Health Center (the Gray Panther–founded center where one of us works), we would have little trouble supporting managed care. These programs integrate medical, home, and community care and control costs at the same time. Unfortunately, the managed care plans faced by most of the 3 million older people enrolled in Medicare-sponsored HMOs are nothing like the small number of pacesetter national models.

For most elderly, managed care means enrollment in a Medicare Risk HMO, most often owned by a for-profit insurance company. The pro argument is correct in suggesting that these plans help eliminate some paperwork and may lower out-of-pocket costs for older consumers; they certainly provide incentives to eliminate unnecessary procedures and hospital days. However, an older person would be naive to enter one of the large Medicare HMOs expecting to have his or her care coordinated by an interdisciplinary team. Certainly, for most HMOs, the elderly consumer will find no direct link to home and community care beyond the limited amount of skilled home health covered in the Medicare benefit. It will also be unusual for an elderly stroke victim (for example) to find even all of the Medicare-covered services provided by any single managed care entity. It is much more likely that the HMO has contracted with a physician group and a hospital to assume the risk of providing care within the capitated payment. Physicians in the group are probably located in different offices with about the same amount of coordination as there would be in fee-for-service Medicare. Skilled home health, in so far as any is covered, is probably contracted out by the hospital to a home health agency. If the elder requires personal care because of functional disabilities, he or she must buy it separately or apply for publicly supported services.

For most elders in managed care, no matter how disabled, there simply are not comprehensive services, well-coordinated care, and interdisciplinary teams to care for them. If managed care programs offered all of the services of an On Lok, we would be much more optimistic, even enthusiastic. Medicare cost containment is theoretically possible, but doubtful in reality. Medicare HMOs now serving the elderly are mostly tremendously successful investor-owned business ventures that do control hospital use, sometimes offer additional benefits such as limited pharmacy or dental coverage, but have not saved the Medicare program a dime (Brown, Clement, Hill, Retchin, & Bergeron, 1993). Nor do they offer the integrated chronic illness care or social services of the national models. Significantly, also, HMOs do not provide any opportunity, like On Lok does, for consumers to be involved either in planning their own care or in governing their health plans to assure appropriate care and good quality.

Because current policy initiatives favor the managed care approach, we must watch carefully, and somewhat fearfully, as elders with disabilities and complex health problems get pushed into managed care systems that are not equipped to handle them. Low-income elders, especially, are vulnerable. As out-of-pocket costs rise in fee-for-service Medicare, elders will have little (free) choice and will be forced into managed care for economic reasons. We know the insurance plans will do well financially. We have little faith that their disabled patients will do as well in terms of care.

REFERENCES

Brown, R., Clement, D., Hill, J. Retchin, S., & Bergeron, J. (1993). Do health maintenance organizations work for Medicare? *Health Care Financing Review, 15*(1), 7–23.

NO

MARTY LYNCH
CARROLL ESTES

As the United States health care system rushes headlong into managed care, we cannot help but stop and think whether this is really a good thing for our most disabled elders with complex health conditions? Is managed care simply the velvet glove of rationing? Managed care provides the rationale for policy makers to shift billions of dollars to insurance companies and open up new avenues for the medical industry to profit while the elderly pay more for less care.

Managed care can have many different definitions. We focus on health maintenance organizations (HMOs), particularly on the Medicare risk HMOs, which receive a set dollar amount per member per month to provide all Medicare-covered benefits. The Health Care Financing Administration (HCFA) reports that, although enrollment in Medicare risk HMOs now is only approximately 10 percent of the Medicare population, it is growing by as much as 2 percent per month. In many large urban market areas, these HMOs also offer non-Medicare benefits such as limited pharmaceuticals, dental benefits, and eyeglasses, at no premium cost to the beneficiary.

Managed Money Not Care

In the absence of meaningful health reform, policy makers and legislators have turned to managed care as the solution to our health care woes. The promise of managed care is more appropriate care at the right price, and substitution of primary and preventive care for high-cost hospital and specialty care. The managed care organization ideally receives less dollars than were being spent in the fee-for-service system (typically 95 percent) (Brown & Hill, 1994) and is expected to provide all covered benefits as well as make a profit and cover the cost of all the full-page ads and free meals used to market the plan. The primary doctor takes on a new job, that of gatekeeper; he or she is responsible for deciding when hospital, specialty care, or some special test is appropriate for an older user. Often the decision made about the patient's care will affect eventual incentives paid to the physician or group of physicians. Consumers might feel more comfortable if the physician could help them make the best decision without worrying that it might cost the individual doctor or his or her colleagues in the incentive pool at the end of the year. (Of course, in fee-for-service medicine, the physician makes more for every procedure performed—also a perverse incentive as far as the patient is concerned.)

HMOs also charge to manage money for Medicare. Typically an HMO takes 12 percent to 20 percent off the top before paying providers. In fact, HMOs and the competitive system cost much more than the 2 percent to 3 percent that it costs to administer the existing fee-for-service Medicare program. Research on Medicare HMOs also shows that HMOs typically enroll a more healthy population than the average. The government pays them 95 percent of average cost for patients who would only cost 89 percent to 90 percent of average under fee-for-service care (Brown, Clement, Hill, Retchin, & Bergeron, 1993).

Certain Groups of Elderly and Disabled Fare Worst in HMOs

Healthy elders and younger adults may fare well in HMOs, especially if they only need routine family care and are able to advocate for themselves when necessary. Older people with complex problems and disabilities are most likely to have problems in HMOs. We remember the case of the older woman with a broken hip who was assigned a physician in another town when she joined a large HMO. She had no relatives to drive her, but the HMO was only of minimal help in finding her a doctor close to home.

Elders with chronic diseases and disabilities are most likely to require specialty care and special testing and procedures. HMOs limit access to specialists, and unusual tests and procedures often are more difficult to access. Family members of persons with Alzheimer's disease have reported to us how they found it difficult to gain access to special Alzheimer diagnostic and treatment centers when they joined a Medicare HMO, despite the fact that most private internists are not experts in the medical management of dementias. Younger disabled people who wish to see specialists with expertise in their particular disability face the same obstacles.

Little research has been done that looks at how elders with multiple chronic problems and disabilities fare in the HMO world. One study examining adults with chronic problems (Safran, Tarlov, & Rogers, 1994) found that financial satisfaction and coordination were highest in HMOs, whereas access, continuity, and accountability were highest in the fee-for-service sector. Comprehensiveness was lowest in HMOs. If these findings hold true in future research, disabled elders rightfully have some very legitimate fears about being able to gain access to the best care.

The Tradeoff: Lower Out-of-Pocket Costs versus Quality and Satisfaction

Low-income elders, more often women, minorities, and the very old, may be more vulnerable in the face of the utilization controls practiced by HMOs. Given limited available income, low-income elders face stronger pressure to choose the plan that will minimize their costs for deductibles, copayments, and noncovered items such as prescription drugs. This pressure will grow as Medicare premiums increase and copayments for services in the traditional Medicare system are also raised. At the same time, poor elders, those older than eighty-five years of age, and minority elders face more health problems and disability than do those who are sixty-five and white. Those with limited means must accept the trade-off of being served by the HMO's panel of physicians and accepting utilization review by the plan to limit their costs.

Quality Assurance

Many (not all) disabled elders and their families are unable to protect themselves against overzealous utilization review processes. The physician has been our agent in a complex technical medical system; now the physician must be the gatekeeper as well. Although the large HMOs and government are discussing the development of "report cards" to judge their performance and educate consumers, these report cards are aimed at basic medical processes and outcomes. We need a special "report card for the disabled." Medicare HMOs may provide excellent acute care and still miss the boat on the broader needs of the disabled.

Recent Health Care Financing Administration (HCFA) studies (Brown et al., 1993) found that recipients in Medicare risk HMOs received 50 percent less home health care than those in fee-for-service Medicare. Can we cut 50 percent of such care and hope to be adequately serving those who return home after an early discharge from the hospital? HMOs significantly reduce the number of hospital days used by their enrollees. There are questions that must be examined carefully when an HMO both reduces hospital days dramatically and at the same time reduces home health visits. There are no adequate standards available to assure that the disabled get high-quality long-term care especially attuned to their needs. Deregulation will mean even fewer standards. We are hesitant to leave it up to the HMO industry to make the decisions about appropriate levels of care when they have large financial interests at stake.

There Is No Real Incentive to Provide Preventive Care in the Current Market

One of the promises of the HMO approach is that lower-cost and more appropriate primary and preventive care may be substituted for high-cost hospital and specialty care. The HMO industry has done an excellent job of reducing unneeded hospital days. There is little question that they are willing to creatively substitute a brief stay in a skilled nursing facility, intense home care, outpatient surgery, or primary physician care to prevent hospital use. The promise of primary prevention and health promotion may, however, be little more than industry myth in the current market. Prevention in health care pays off only in the long run. In a system in which pension plans as well as individuals are shopping and changing plans quickly, there is little incentive for HMOs to spend dollars on prevention, the benefits of which may only be reaped by some other HMO down the line. A clearer incentive is to save on high-cost care now; someone else can worry about long-term effects later. The elderly (as well as the young) can benefit from preventive health activities; unfortunately, they may never see those activities in the existing HMO market.

The Majority of HMO's Are For-Profit Insurance Companies. Is There Room for Consumer Involvement?

Medicare changes will shift billions of dollars of public funds to this industry with few strings attached. Consumers have a right to be involved in decisions about care as well as in decisions about overall policies of a delivery organization that serves them, yet very few for-profit insurance companies (if any) appear willing to offer consumers a say. Elders and their families as well as younger disabled people are well able to understand options related to their care. They are also able to take limited amounts of dollars into account and know that health costs are rising. The Independent Living movement as well as several community-based long-term care projects have begun to develop a concept of self-case management.

Until HMOs design services that meet the special needs of frail and disabled elders, we cannot believe that for the most vulnerable of the elderly they remain anything but an unknown and perhaps exploitative phenomenon. Until consumer involvement, improved quality measures, and integrated services for the disabled elderly are incorporated into HMOs, we cannot, in good conscience, trust care of the most vulnerable elderly to them.

REFERENCES

Brown, R., Clement, D., Hill, J., Retchin, S., & Bergeron, J. (1993). Do health maintenance organizations work for Medicare? *Health Care Financing Review, 15*(1), 7–23.

Brown, R., & Hill, J. (1994). The effects of Medicare risk HMO's on Medicare costs and service utilization. In H. Luft (Ed.), *HMO's and the elderly.* Ann Arbor, MI: Health Administration Press.

Safran, D., Tarlov, A., & Rogers, W. (1994). Primary care performance in fee-for-service and prepaid health care systems. *Journal of the American Medical Association, 271*(20), 1579–1586.

Rejoinder to Dr. Lynch and Professor Estes

JENNIE CHIN HANSEN

My opponents suggest that pitfalls abound as managed care plans now proliferate. However, given the need to spend health care dollars wisely in today's financial climate and the historical incentives of the fee-for-service model, it is entire appropriate to review current utilization patterns to bring about a reduction in unnecessary services. To obviate the possibility that service reductions based on the goal of financial profit could prevail at the expense of appropriate quality, financial incentives and risks can be structured in a manner that links outcomes and enrollee satisfaction. The system can be designed so that only if enrollees fare well as a result of getting the right service at the right time will the financial consequences be positive. Oversight can be provided through the public sector or by means of accrediting bodies.

Tradeoffs

The opposing authors argue that poorer persons will inevitably have fewer choices as a result of managed care. But the system can be structured to include full financial risk to the risk provider, so that insufficient or inadequate care would result in losses instead of profits. If there are established oversight systems, managed care's strengths can be captured for the consumer and payers. The implication that poor persons now have adequate access to care can certainly be questioned, because many providers do not accept coverage paid for by Medicaid, the current safety net for the poor.

Quality Assurance

Concern is expressed over the absolute reduction of services such as home care in some HMOs. Yet, the more salient question is whether there is more appropriate use of resources than in the fee-for-service system, which provides incentives to generate volume because reimbursement. What is more important to measure is the actual outcome of care rather than strictly equating volume with quality.

Finally, whether we are ready or not, managed care is becoming a reality for the well-off elderly as well as for those whose health care services are financed by public funds. My opponents point to legitimate pitfalls and caveats that are yet to be fully addressed in these rapidly growing businesses. Special divisions or "carve-outs" should be designed to assure that consumer input, accountability, and quality and cost oversight do occur. Moreover, managed care is most likely to benefit the elderly if programs are governed and run by not-for-profit entities, so that the accountability is to the enrollee and community rather than the shareholder or financial investor of a for-profit system.

Is Aging More Problematic for Women Than Men?

EDITORS' NOTE: Reviews of the literature that focus on the problems of aging are likely to conclude that particular subgroups of the older adult population can be separated out as facing greater difficulties during the course of aging, relatively speaking, than others. For instance, African American elders are said to face double jeopardy, challenged by being both old and of minority status. It is undeniable that older women are more likely than older men to be included among those who are argued to be at greater risk on a number of measures of well-being. Indeed, it has been suggested that to be old, black, and female places one in a state of triple jeopardy. Is the case closed on this matter? Are men immune to the vicissitudes of growing old? Is their experience less arduous on all counts compared with women?

Nancy R. Hooyman, Ph.D., says *YES.* She is Professor and Dean at the School of Social Work at the University of Washington in Seattle. In addition to *Social Gerontology: A Multidisciplinary Perspective,* she is the co-author of *Taking Care of Aging Family Members,* and *Feminist Perspectives on Family Care: Policies for Gender Justice,* and has edited *Feminist Social Work Practice in Clinical Settings.* Her research interests are in family caregiving of persons with chronic disabilities, home-based services, feminist practice models, and older women's issues.

Robert L. Rubinstein, Ph.D., says *NO.* He is Director of Research and Senior Research Scientist at the Polisher Research Institute of the Philadelphia Geriatric Center. He has conducted research in the United States and in Vanuatu (southwest Pacific). His research interests include gender and aging, the home environments of older people, and childlessness in later life.

YES

Nancy R. Hooyman

Yes, in every aspect of their lives! Older women have been discriminated against both for being old and for being female, yet until recently, they have largely been ignored both by the women's movement and by gerontology. They form the fastest-growing segment of our population, constituting 56 percent of the population aged sixty-five to seventy-four years and 72 percent of those older than age eighty-five, and making the aging society primarily female (Hess, 1990). Their predominance reflects differences in life expectancy, with women outliving men by an average of seven years. Although some might argue that women's greater likelihood of surviving to old age makes them more fortunate than men, living longer does not necessarily equate with living better. Instead, the processes of aging and the quality of life in old age are profoundly different for men and women, with old women more vulnerable than men to poverty, poor health, widowhood, divorce, and living alone. Accordingly, the problems of aging, such as inadequate retirement benefits, social isolation, and caregiver burden, are typically women's problems. Because gender structures an individual's chances across the life course, gender and age interact to affect the distribution of power, privilege, and social well-being. As a result, inequities in society's resources experienced earlier in life are exacerbated in old age.

Older Women's Socioeconomic Status

The greatest problem is poverty, with old women constituting more than 70 percent of the older poor population. In fact, older women's risk of poverty is about twice that of men's, a risk that increases with age and race (U.S. Senate Special Committee on Aging, 1992). Unmarried women living alone, ethnic minority women, and those age seventy-five and older are especially likely to be poor. Older women's median annual income is only approximately 58 percent that of older men. Even when older women are employed and have educational backgrounds comparable to those of men, they are still less likely to be financially well-off. Accordingly, older women are more likely to depend on Supplemental Security Income (SSI), but this does not necessarily allow them to escape from poverty.

Gender differences in employment and earnings history, career interruptions—typically to provide care to family members—and retirement circumstances all contribute to old women's higher rate of poverty. For example, women's total average retirement benefits are only about 73 percent of those of their male counterparts (Older Women's League, 1990). Although women form the majority of Social Security beneficiaries, they are three times more likely than their male peers to receive only the minimum benefits. As a result, Social Security is less effective at lifting women out of poverty than men. Women are also less likely to receive private pensions. Although not all older women are poor, as a whole they have fewer assets such as savings, have accumulated lower lifetime earnings, depend on Social Security as their sole source of income, and receive low retirement or disability benefits. For many women, poverty in old age represents a lifelong pattern, because women at all ages are twice as likely be poor compared with men. For others, the experiences and consequences of poverty are new, typically because of widowhood or divorce.

A primary reason for their economic vulnerability is that most women of this current cohort older than age sixty-five years did not work consistently for pay, largely because of societal expectations to marry, have children, care for relatives, and depend on husbands for economic support. As an illustration of the effects of these gender norms, the average women spends nearly half of her life caring for dependents, leaving the paid labor force to provide care for 11 years compared with 1.3 years for her male counterparts (Older Women's League, 1990). These interruptions carry severe economic costs, reducing both current income as well as retirement benefits in old age. Women who in young and middle adulthood followed society's rules by marrying and fulfilling household obligations frequently find themselves alone in old age with less than subsistence income, inadequate health care, substandard housing, and little chance for employment to supplement their limited resources. As noted by the late Tish Sommers, former President of the Older Women's League, "Motherhood and apple pie may be sacred, but neither guarantees economic security in old age" (1975, p. 11).

Generally dependent on men for both their income and their retirement benefits, most women of previous generations lacked the means to build up their economic security for old age. A deleterious consequence of such dependency is that if older women become widowed or divorced, they frequently lose their primary source of income. This vulnerability, resulting from the close interconnections between marital status and income level, has been described as being "only one man away from poverty" (Minkler & Stone, 1985). If a women has cared for an ill husband, her resources may be even further depleted by his sickness. On his death, she may not receive benefits from a private pension, unless he has been willing to reduce his monthly benefits to provide her with a survivor annuity. Even among women who are eligible for survivors benefits, most do not receive them in full, often because of misinformation about how to access these funds.

Another illustration of the poverty that emerges from the interconnections between women's status as unpaid family caregivers and underpaid employees is that, when employed, women are typically paid substantially less than men, generally in low-status service, clerical, and retail sales jobs without adequate pensions or benefits such as life or health insurance and with limited or no career advancement opportunities. Low wages translate into low retirement income, with the average Social Security benefit for retired women workers being less than the minimum wage. Moreover, the minority of women with private pensions receive approximately half the benefit income of men because of salary differentials during their shorter work careers. Because of lower retirement benefits, older women may find themselves forced to continue working well beyond the age at which they would choose to retire.

In summary, women's traditional family roles result in discontinuous employment histories. This pattern, combined with limited pension options and lower Social Security benefits, produces a double jeopardy for women's economic status in old age. Older women's poverty also adversely affects their health status. In turn, the costs associated with their higher incidence of chronic disease combined with lower access to health insurance can deplete the already limited resources of low-income old women.

Older Women's Health Status

Women's family responsibilities and limited economic opportunities adversely affect their physical and mental health in old age. Some might argue that the higher incidence of chronic disease among women is a side effect of the "benefit" of women living longer than men. However, when such additional years are characterized by arthritis, hypertension, strokes, diabetes, digestive and urinary problems, orthopedic problems, and visual impairments, the quality of women's lives is reduced. These chronic diseases interfere with women's daily functioning and require frequent physician contacts and hospitalization. Contrary to common perceptions that men are at higher risk for heart attacks than are women, cardiovascular disease is the number one killer for both. Women also face health problems specifically associated with their reproductive functions, such as breast, cervical, and uterine cancers—all of which have increased in recent years—as well as high-risk complications from hysterectomies. Of those older people with osteoporosis, a substantial majority are women. Women begin losing bone mass between thirty and thirty-five years of age; because this increases with age, the risk of bone fracture grows dramatically, resulting in a greater number of injuries and more days of restricted activity and bed disability compared with their male counterparts. Accordingly, women are more likely than men to die of postoperative complications associated with hip fracture. The threat of hip fractures can create numerous fears—of additional falls, further fractures, hospitalization, institutionalization, loss of independence, and death. As a result, an older woman's social world may become increasingly circumscribed, with accompanying feelings of loneliness and isolation.

Gender differences in patterns of illness and social support are particularly striking among the oldest old, where women form the majority of nursing home residents. As an illustration of how social rather than medical factors influence nursing home placement, older men are more likely to be married, with wives to care for them at home, instead of being institutionalized. Women older than seventy-five years of age, however, few available resources for home-based care and often are unable to afford private home health services. The nursing home industry is increasingly a women's industry, with low-income women as both residents and attendants.

Previous employment and family care patterns affect older women's access to adequate health care and health maintenance or promotion information. Specifically, the workplace determines such access through opportunities to enroll in group insurance plans. Most insurance systems exclude the occupation of homemaker, except as a dependent. As a result, older women who are never or sporadically employed generally have inadequate health insurance. Low-income divorced or widowed women, unable to rely on their husband's insurance, are especially disadvantaged. Some uninsured women gamble on staying healthy until qualifying for Medicare coverage at age sixty-five. Because the incidence of chronic disease is higher among older women than among men, many women do not win this gamble. Yet they may fall just above the income eligibility line for Medicaid and thus not have access to any insurance.

Because of their lower socioeconomic status, older women are more likely than men to depend on Medicaid. An insidious negative effect of this dependency is that health care providers are often unwilling to accept Medicaid patients, making it difficult for older women to obtain adequate care. In addition, with Medicaid cutbacks and the shifting of costs to the patient through copayments and deductibles, more low-income women are unable to afford adequate health care. Because public funding for home- and community-based care is limited, many women who depend on Medicaid are faced with the difficult choice between moving into a nursing home or getting little or no care.

Older Women's Social Status

Older women's physical and mental health problems as well as their lower socioeconomic status are frequently intensified by the greater likelihood of their living alone. Nearly 50 percent of older women (compared with 16 percent of older men) live alone for approximately one-third of their adult lives, primary because of widowhood or divorce (Schwenk, 1992). Because 85 percent of all wives outlive their husbands, and most do not remarry, widowhood is a more common status for women than for men. The expected years of widowhood are far greater than the difference in life expectancy between women and men at these ages. The rates of widowhood and consequently of women living alone increase with age, although there are some exceptions to this pattern among older ethnic minority women, who are more likely to live in an extended family setting than their Caucasian counterparts. As noted above, the primary negative consequence of widowhood and divorce is low socioeconomic status, with rates of poverty higher among divorced and widowed women than for their married counterparts. These economic conditions have numerous social implications: low-income women have fewer options to interact with others, fewer affordable and safe accommodations, and fewer resources to purchase in-home support services.

Projections over the next four decades suggest that succeeding cohorts will continue the pattern of women outliving men, resulting in a large population of oldest-old women from the baby boom cohort. At the same time, older women's economic and health concerns are expected to increase, in part because of public health and long-term care policies that perpetuate gender inequities along with current cutbacks in Medicare, Medicaid, and Supplemental Security Income (SSI), which are lifelines for older women. Public policies need to be redesigned to reflect the double jeopardy faced by many older women and to foster economic and income equity.

REFERENCES

Hess, B. (1990). Gender and aging: The demographic parameters. *Generations, 14*(3), 12-5.

Minkler, M., & Stone, R. (1985). The feminization of poverty and older women. *The Gerontologist, 24*(4), 351–357.

Older Women's League. (1990). *Heading for hardship: Retirement Income for American women in the next century.* Washington D.C.: Older Women's League.

Schwenk, F. N. (1992). Income and expenditures of older widowed, divorced, and never-married women who live alone. *Family Economics Review, 5*(1), 2–8.

Sommers, T. (1975). On growing old female: An interview with Tish Sommers, *Aging,* Nov–Dec, 11.

U.S. Senate Special Committee on Aging. (1992). *Aging America: Trends and Projections.* Washington, D.C.: U.S. Department of Health and Human Services.

Rejoinder to Professor Hooyman
ROBERT L. RUBINSTEIN

Dr. Hooyman's excellent account concentrates primarily on economic differentials between men and women, certainly an important issue. But, it is difficult to extend the relative economic deprivation of older women to all domains of experience. In the domain of health, for example, although some age-based illnesses primarily affect women, men do not live as long, approximately seven years less on average than women. This difference is acknowledged by Dr. Hooyman, but she suggests that it is offset by the low quality of life that older women have (Men may have less life, but it is substantially better in quality, she suggests.). Most studies of the well-being of elders, however, suggest that levels of life satisfaction are generally positive for all elders.

Dr. Hooyman is less able, I believe, to argue her points with reference to older men's health. Women live longer but experience more chronic health problems because of their longevity. But even with a shorter life span, older men still experience lengthy periods of poor health and reduced function. A recent issue of AARP's *Perspectives in Health Promotion and Aging* notes that men are less likely to seek out or use either health information or health professionals; older men are more reluctant to acknowledge or respond to health problems; diseases that disproportionately affect older men receive less public attention than diseases that affect older women; and diseases that affect older men are often only viewed as "symptoms" of old age. These certainly act together negatively to artificially create less apparent need for older men's health services.

Finally, with regard to the social and psychological aspects of being an older man, men are clearly emotionally and interpersonally challenged. The generally smaller social networks of older men (which are often mediated and maintained by their spouses) and men's psychological brittleness argue for a process of socialization that emphasizes the use of only a very limited range of life's possibilities for men. Traditionally, men's attachments have been viewed as primarily to work rather than to people. A recent issue of the *Philadelphia Inquirer* reported an analysis of the last five recessions, in which men lost more than nine times as many jobs as women and took significantly longer to regain the number of jobs lost. The changing and uncertain employment profile for men (and women) suggests both the reality of hardship as well as the need for older men to develop cognitive and emotional capacities broader than mere attachments to work.

NO

ROBERT L. RUBINSTEIN

This is certainly an unpopular position to support, but I believe careful examination will show that aging is at least as problematic for men as for women. To begin to explore the problems aging has for men, however, we must first acknowledge certain realities about gender and aging in the United States. Clearly, there are profound negatives about being old and female in America. Literature from gerontology suggests deepened suffering for older women in the form of single, double, or triple jeopardy. Being old and female, or old, female, and of a minority status, or old, female, and sick have been identified as multiple negative possibilities for women. We know, too, that most older men and women were brought up in times that emphasized the skill limitations of women and provided a "natural logic" to explain this: skills for each gender were said to be largely "natural" or "innate" and therefore unavailable to the other gender. Yet social developments in the last few decades have enlarged the sphere of what is both "natural" and possible in society for women as well as for men. Women are now engaging in modes of behavior that until recently were widely believed to be at best unladylike and at worst unobtainable.

Regardless of these changes, the reality is that both men and women suffer from profound, subtle, and not-so-subtle forms of age discrimination or ageism. Indeed, culturally, it is impossible to talk about old age without implying decline and illness. The three, aging, decline, and illness, go together in our cultural model of the life course. How this triad affects men can be seen not only in the social worthlessness attributed to most elders regardless of gender, but also for men in the experience of superannuation of life and skills within a rapidly changing technology, and for many a sense of worthlessness and an inability to express oneself. These can lead to early mortality, hopelessness, and increased frequencies of suicide, alcohol abuse, and a profound inability to relate to other people.

Unfortunately, it is not yet fully possible to suggest that men, as women, are also victims of a structurally dehumanizing system, one that actively prevents both men and women from achieving their fullest potential. Even so, that men are so often out of touch with their feelings and must relate narcissistically or aggressively to others suggests their profound systemic victimization and dehumanization.

It is true that poverty disproportionately affects older women, particularly, but not exclusively, minority women, widows, and the very old (Barusch, 1994). Changes that accompany aging and affect physical appearance seem to be socially evaluated more negatively in women than in men. And, educational and professional opportunities for women of the sixty-five and older cohort have been severely limited. Older women have clearly suffered from a colossal amount of discrimination in society and from an inability to pursue interests and abilities.

Once we leave these specific domains, however, findings on gender differences in late life are more difficult to interpret simply. Concerning mental health, for example, the rate of depression is significantly higher for women than for men in later life; however, the rate of suicide for older men, particularly older white men, is many times that of older women.

Findings about residence and gender are also difficult to interpret. Women are significantly more likely to live alone than are men, because women outlive their spouses and then "age in place." However, there seem to be no systematic differences with regard to well-being and loneliness experienced on the basis of coresidence. Living alone is often viewed as a desired expression of independence, as a symbol of viability, and as indicative of a lack of need to rely on children.

In many ways, the crux of the debate on aging and gender is that older women live longer than men. There are seventy-eight men per one hundred women aged sixty-five to seventy-four years; sixty men per one hundred women aged seventy-five to eighty-four years; and thirty-eight men per one hundred women aged eighty-five years and older. These figures are at the center of any debate about gender and age. Men suffer both from periods of terminal illness and from earlier deaths. For whatever reason, men get less of life.

Certainly, differences in longevity based on gender can be entered into the debate at some risk of oversimplifying complexities to an absurd degree. If life is valued innately or axiomatically (life is better than no life), is it better to have more of it or less of it, regardless of quality? Yet the sheer, basic arithmetic of life cannot be negated: men get less of it.

Because of greater longevity and survival, women experience more chronic disease and disability then men. Stated another way, all of the men *not* surviving will have experienced chronic or acute conditions *and* death. Yet the picture is complex. The major causes of death in later life are heart disease, cancer, stroke, pulmonary disease, diabetes, and influenza and pneumonia. The death rate for heart disease for older men is approximately 1.6 times that of women; the cancer death rate for older men is approximately 1.7 times that of older women; the rates for other disorders such as diabetes and stroke are more similar. Of course, no one is sure whether differential mortality is based on "wired-in" genetic predispositions or the cumulative effects of stress and the profound biological and psychological degradation experienced by men. As far as I am aware, however, no one has suggested that the "longevity gap" experienced by men be the specific object of programmatic intervention or special attention.

Men and women of the current age sixty-five and older population were brought up and socialized to live in a world that offered a greater contrast and specificity in gender roles. Although it is hard to generalize about people, it seems that women have larger social networks than men and have greater interpersonal skills than do men. Married men often rely on their spouses for interpersonal tasks, organizing social relationships, and family "kin keeping." Older men, it may be argued, suffer because they have been socialized insufficiently and inappropriately. As social products, men are emotionally and socially challenged and have been victims of a system that has often made access to interpersonal skills, nurturance, and caring abilities difficult.

When the issue of gender and age is placed in a larger, cross-cultural context, literature suggests the widespread existence of male-centered societies, but with an age and gender rebound effect so that middle-aged and older women in many societies tend to gain a degree of independence, freedom, control, and power beyond that of their reproductive years. There does not seem to be, for men, any phenomenon that may be similar to "postmenopausal zest." For many women, a change of life, beginning in one's fifties and extending decades, may bring a new energy and vitality to living (Kerns & Brown, 1992), even in Western societies. Similarly, even in the most male-centered societies, patterns of resistance to dominant ideologies about women, the body, and aging (such as those described by Lock [1993] even for the highly male-centered culture of Japan) suggest a creative vitality for mature women, despite limiting circumstances, that is unparalleled by men, who lack such opportunities. Such mature creative or expressive phenomena have not been described for men, although it is instructive to note an upswing in nontraditional caring roles for men (Kaye & Applegate, 1990).

In sum, it is difficult to argue that aging is entirely more problematic for women than for men. And, regardless, there is the very serious problem that men just do not survive as long as women. The reality is that, although there are many difficulties for older women, there are some benefits and rewards to being old that men just do not have. And the cumulative lifetime suffering of older men is quite often great and unaddressed.

REFERENCES

Barusch, A. S. (1994). *Older women in poverty: Private lives and public policies.* New York: Springer.

Kaye, L. W., & Applegate, J. W. (1990). *Men as caregivers to the elderly.* Lexington, MA: Lexington Books.

Kerns, V., & Brown, J. K. (1992). *In her prime: New views of middle-aged women.* Urbana: University of Illinois Press.

Lock, M. (1993). *Encounters with aging: Mythologies of menopause in Japan and North America.* Berkeley: University of California Press.

Rejoinder to Dr. Rubinstein
NANCY R. HOOYMAN

The difficulty of arguing that aging is more problematic for men than for women is, in fact, illustrated by Dr. Rubinstein's article, in which he acknowledges that women face greater problems than men in old age. In fact, he states that women experience a "colossal amount of discrimination in society and from an inability to pursue interests and abilities." Not only is Dr. Rubinstein's position "unpopular to support" (as he states in his opening paragraph), it cannot be supported empirically. No matter what problem is identified, with the exception of suicide, it is likely to be experienced more frequently by women than by men.

Admittedly, a fundamental difference is that women live longer than men. I would agree with Dr. Rubinstein that "the sheer, basic arithmetic of life cannot be negated; men get less of life." Yet when men and women of the same age cohort are compared, old women are more likely to experience negative consequences from their earlier behaviors, such as lower income, fewer retirement benefits, and less access to health care as a result of caregiving demands during young and middle adulthood. Although Dr. Rubinstein attempts to argue that men have been deprived access to such caring and nurturing roles, he overlooks how these caregiving roles have deprived women of other options in the workplace and educational arena. When opportunities for caring have existed, as with the growing number of families in which both parents are employed, men consistently and currently assume less child care responsibility, for example. Similarly, when men in old age do assume care responsibilities for ill wives, they are more likely to receive formal services and assistance from family and friends than do women caregivers. Therefore, although Dr. Rubinstein argues that men are "victims of a system that has made access to interpersonal skills, nurturance and caring abilities difficult," men have not necessarily seized such opportunities when available; or if they have, they have tended to receive more support for doing so than their female counterparts.

Dr. Rubinstein also points to the "superannuation of men's life and skills within a rapidly changing technology" as creating a sense of worthlessness among older men. If this is the case, however, the pattern is likely to be even more problematic for women than for men, because women have consistently had less access to labor market skills, whether technological or not; and for women who are in the labor force, they are more likely to be in low-paying, part-time jobs often made expendable by technology.

Women's predominance within both caregiving roles and poorly paid jobs has created the fundamental daily reality that women experience higher rates of poverty than men across the life span and particularly in old age. Since the 1960s, older men have enjoyed a fourfold reduction in poverty; older women, a twofold reduction. The poverty rate for women who are not married increases four times; for men in the same situation, two times. And older women's poverty is often intensified by current public policies. This is because the norm for the development of U.S. policies has been a male-headed household and male labor force participation patterns. This gender-based difference in the effects of public policies is clearly illustrated by Social Security, which is founded on marriage as an economic partnership in which the husband is the breadwinner. As another example, SSI benefits to couples (which benefit older men) are greater than benefits to individuals (80% of which are older women). Because of the underlying biases of many public policies, women who violate the norm of being married (e.g., are divorced or widowed) pay a much greater price than men. In fact, the effectiveness of Social Security in helping older individuals escape poverty declines as age increases for all groups except for white men, who disproportionately benefit from Social Security. Because gender structures an individual's chances across the life course, the gender-based inequities experienced in the labor market are not only maintained in the postretirement years but are actually amplified in retirement.

Dr. Rubinstein's is not a winnable argument. Instead, I would argue that this debate is not one to pursue. Instead, our energies as practitioners and researchers should be focused on identifying ways to improve the lives of both women and men who fall below the poverty line, face loneliness and physical and mental health problems, and are denied access to adequate health and long-term care.

Does the Provision of Formal Services Lead to Families Relinquishing Their Caregiving for Relatives?

EDITORS' NOTE: Most families take responsibility for the care of their frail elderly relatives. Furthermore, families, rather than formal service personnel, predominate as providers of health care and other services to the burgeoning ranks of America's impaired older population. Even when formal services are available, many families appear reluctant to use them, expressing an attitude that derives in part from Americans' long-standing commitment to self-sufficiency, fierce independence, and the centrality of the family as the primary caregiving group. Although the tradition of family elder care apparently endures, the growing number of older persons exhibiting functional incapacity has led to increased concerns about the plight of the overburdened family caregiver. Research has repeatedly documented the substantial levels of financial, physical, social, and emotional stress absorbed by spouses, daughters, sons, grandchildren, and other relatives who have committed substantial time and energy to caring for elderly members of their families. In light of the obvious and potentially escalating burdens and liabilities associated with elder caregiving, what is the likely consequence of making available service interventions able to meet the needs of functionally impaired family members who are otherwise receiving help from their relatives? Are these formal services more likely to fulfill a substitutive rather than a supplemental function?

Vernon L. Greene, Ph.D., says *YES*. He is Professor of Public Administration in the Maxwell School of Citizenship and Public Affairs at Syracuse University. His primary field of work concerns public policy responses to population aging, with particular interest in long-term care policy. He is a Fellow of the Gerontological Society of America and serves on the editorial boards of the principal journals in the field.

Sharon L. Tennstedt, Ph.D., says *NO*. She is Director of the Institute for Studies on Aging at the New England Research Institutes, Watertown, MA. Her research interests include caregiving patterns for disabled elders, health promotion, and community intervention trials. She holds faculty appointments at Boston University and Harvard University.

YES

Vernon L. Greene

I have been asked by the editors of this volume to argue the rather unpopular position that families reduce their efforts on behalf of frail, older relatives when professional services are available that can functionally substitute for direct family caregiving, a notion often referred to as the "substitution hypothesis." That is, I am to argue the affirmative case, and I do so in the conviction that it should prevail in many cases on the existing evidence, notwithstanding that arguments and evidence for the existence of such substitution have in the past frequently met a very stony reception in important sectors of the gerontological community.

As I read the literature of the last ten years, a careful perusal of the empirical evidence reported, or what can be reasonably inferred from it, leads me to conclude that a preponderance of results either favors the substitution hypothesis, or at least is no less consistent with it than the usual other findings (e.g., "complementary" use of formal services, or no relationship at all). Yet the abstracts and discussion sections of many of these same papers largely give the impression that substitution was not a major part of the process generating the data being reported. Why is this?

In general, what seems to me to be, on the whole, a surprisingly weak body of scholarly work for a field in which interest has been so intense for more than a decade, springs from two basic sources: (1) a failure to clearly identify just what is meant by "substitution" and thus what is to be taken as definitive evidence of its measurable effects, and (2) a distortion of work in the field by a strong normative presumption against finding substitution in caregiver behavior, a presumption that has become part of the dominant ideology regarding the family relations of older people in both the policy and scholarly arenas. These two factors interact in the research process and have had an unfortunate reinforcing effect on one another over the years. I will briefly consider each of these, starting with the first.

Just what do we mean, in the present context, by "substitution"? I would say, unremarkably, that we mean a behavioral response by a family caregiver in which their own in-kind caregiving is by choice reduced from what it otherwise would have been in response to increased availability or relative attractiveness of professional services. This would encompass situations in which, with other factors held constant, the perceived opportunity costs to caregivers of using professional services decrease, the opportunity costs of in-kind caregiving increase, or perhaps both. This might, for example, be because the price of professional services is reduced through public or charitable subsidy (producing the so-called woodwork effect), or because of an increase in the market wage that the caregiver could earn applying some of the time or energy previously given over to caregiving. Simple economic logic, not to mention common sense, would predict in such circumstances that there would be a tendency to substitute professional for family care. To those (many) who have objected (strenuously) that this is a crass imposition of a cash/market nexus in a social situation driven by love and commitment, I would point out that love and commitment also apply to other people whose welfare may require the caregiver's income or the time and energy made available by substituting professional services.

While the nature of this presentation precludes my usual impulse to review the literature, I think it fair to say that the empirical evidence that has usually been advanced in support of the substitution hypothesis is a finding of negative association (correlation), cross-sectionally or longitudinally, between levels of family and professional care. Evidence against substitution, and sometimes in favor of a contrary "complementary use" hypothesis, is typically a finding of weak or positive correlation, respectively (see, for example, Tennstedt et al., 1993). Unfortunately, things are not so simple.

Consider the following scenarios: A caregiver providing care to a frail older relative herself experiences a decline in functional health, finds herself unable to provide the amount of care she once did, and decides to make greater use of professional services. Or consider a situation in which the health of the person being cared for declines, so that more care than the caregiver can or is willing to give is required, and so professional care is sought or increased. And what of a caregiver whose family experiences financial difficulties, requiring her to seek work that competes with caregiving (Wolf and Soldo, 1994), or a caregiver one of whose children becomes chronically ill, thereby requiring more of her time that was previously given over to the care of an older relative? All of these cases will produce a statistical tendency toward a negative association between levels of professional and family care. But are any of them what we mean or worry about under the epithet of "substitution?" Are they things we wish to discourage through public policy? Probably not.

Consider now the case of findings that family and professional services increase together. Does this establish, as typically claim, the absence of substitution (much less the presence of "complementarity")? Not at all. How do we know, for example, that family caregiving would not have increased still more in the absence of increased use of professional services? On the basis on any scholarly evidence published of which I am aware, including that of my learned opponent, we do not.

The logical complexities of defining, much less empirically modeling, "substitution" in the sense usually meant have not really been addressed very successfully in the literature, despite a now extended period of intense interest. We really should be further along than we are. My own view is that the behavior involved is simply too complex and full of endogenous effects and unobservable influences to be understood in detail outside of carefully controlled experimental investigation.

I believe there is yet another set of reasons why progress on the substitution question has been so slow, and it has to do not with its analytical complexity, but with the fact that the questions have become so freighted with normative baggage that it has compromised, however subtly and unconsciously, the scientific objectivity of work in the area. These influences arise in both the policy arena and in that of the scholarly research.

It is clear enough what is thought to be at stake in the public policy debate on this issue. The expansion of home- and community-based long-term care services has been a long and fervently sought policy goal of most social gerontologists. It is feared that policy makers will view findings of substitution effects when professional services are made more available as evidence of a mere substitution of public for private resources, leaving the elderly needful of such services with little net gain and public expenditures imprudently increased. There is also sometimes an articulated fear, of uncertain sincerity if not accuracy, that such substitution would reduce the contact of disabled elderly people with caring relatives, and might erode the underlying family values that encourage people to privately provide care to their elderly disabled kin.

These concerns strike me as poorly thought out in logic and largely unfounded in fact. First, those voluntarily providing extensive care to disabled kin to begin with seem unlikely to be in the main people who would use available professional services to merely freeload at public expense. More likely they will substitute other labor that provides both private and public benefits, such as care for adolescent children, attention to other pressing family needs, increased workforce and household productivity, and perhaps attention to their own stress-related problems that otherwise might undermine their ability to function as a caregiver in any context, thereby throwing their responsibilities even more fully onto the public sector. When "substitution" is considered in its full range of consequences, it is by no means clear that it is inefficient from either a public or a private standpoint. And as for substitution undermining "family values," one should bear in mind that families with sufficient economic resources are already at liberty to substitute professional efforts for their own, yet one does not hear demands that they be discouraged by public policy from doing so. As usual, public policy in support of "family values" is here again largely a cynical disguise for denying public help to the less affluent.

Finally, from the standpoint of scholarly research, the seminal event influencing objective investigation of the substitution issue was Ethel Shanas's famous Kleemeir Award lecture, *Social Myth as Hypothesis,* delivered at the Gerontological Society meetings in 1978 and subsequently published in *The Gerontologist* (Shanas, 1979). In this brilliant polemic, Professor Shanas attacks what she calls the dominant "social myth" that older people are increasingly alienated from their families, and identifies the notion idea that families may be prone to allowing professional social services to replace their own efforts as being a noxious derivative variant that must be firmly stamped out. Shanas compares the myth with its many variants to the Hydra of Greek mythology, whose many heads defied decapitation by substituting for any struck off multiple replacements. In the same vein, she complains that "new adherents of the myth rise up" to raise these issues anew each time they are "refuted." She compares the effort to refute the "myth" to the labor of Hercules in slaying the Hydra. The views expressed in this address were promptly and resoundingly endorsed by a number of other distinguished members of the field. The "social myth" thesis and its normative apparatus became almost overnight a touchstone for work in the area of family relations of older people.

Somehow, though, all of this strikes me as not entirely in the proper scientific spirit. Hypotheses competing with one's own findings or beliefs are characterized as "social myth." Efforts by colleagues to press forward with research on how families do in fact adjust their caregiving behavior in light of availability of professional services are characterized as a "rising up" of "adherents of the myth" if their findings suggest evidence of alienation (including "substitution"). Indeed, I remember my astonishment several years ago when an academic researcher of particularly close acquaintance, still fairly fresh out of graduate school, received the peer reviews for a paper he had submitted to the field's flagship journal and whose results lent some qualified support to the hypothesis of substitution of publicly subsidized professional home care for family care. The paper was rejected, and the reviews were quite remarkable. Rather than criticize the research itself, they denounced the findings as "completely wrongheaded," opining that their publication would be "dangerous," that they were "insulting" to the families of older people, and indeed represented the very "Hydra-headed monster" of which Shanas had warned us to beware. These reviews illustrate, in a remarkably egregious form, the usually more subtle intrusion of advocacy into science that has hindered the study of the family relations of older people in general, and the study of substitution effects in particular. In my view, progress on these questions has been significantly hindered by the chilling effect of what I would call the myth of The Myth. I would conclude by concurring that there is indeed a Herculean labor needed to strengthen research in this area, but it is a labor of a more Augean sort than the slaying of the Hydra.

REFERENCES

Shanas, E. (1979). Social myth as hypothesis: The case of the family relations of old people. *The Gerontologist, 19*(1), 3–9.

Tennstedt, S. L., Crawford, S. L., & McKinlay, J. B. (1993). Is family care on the decline? A longitudinal investigation of the substitution of formal long-term care services for informal care. *The Milbank Quarterly, 71*(4), 601–624.

Wolf, D. A., & Soldo, B. J. (1994, Fall). Married women's allocation of time to employment and care of elderly parents. *Journal of Human Resources, 29,* 1259–1276.

Rejoinder to Professor Greene
SHARON L. TENNSTEDT

My colleague, Dr. Greene, has done little to dissuade me from the conclusions drawn from my empirical work on the substitution of formal services for family care of disabled elders. The stance he has taken is that the issue has been influenced more by subjective factors than by empirical evidence. That is, that many are not open to the fact that service substitution might occur because the premise is so contrary to the widely accepted norm of family responsibility. In my experience, norms derive from empirical evidence, and there is more evidence to support family responsibility and care of disabled elders than to negate it. In fact, there is not one shred of empirical data in Dr. Greene's argument to support family relinquishment of caregiving responsibilities. Instead, his argument itself falls prey to that of which he is most critical—subjectivity.

Turning to what empirical data are available, I offer the results of a recent study conducted by my colleagues and myself (Tennstedt, Crawford, & McKinley, 1993), in which there *is* evidence of service substitution. However, what is most important for public policy consideration is that any substitution of formal services for informal care was found to be temporary. With the benefit of longitudinal data on a representative sample of older people, the results indicate that service substitution typically occurred when there was a change in the informal care arrangement. However, not only did it occur in a small proportion of cases, the situation was also reversed by the next contact. That is, disabled older persons were using formal services as a temporary stopgap measure while the family care arrangement was reconstituted. Not only is this an appropriate use—or substitution—of formal services, it is the intent of publicly funded long-term care.

The call for better definitions or experimental investigations is always legitimate. However, here it is a smoke screen. The type of rigorous experimental trial necessary to detect all potential forms of service substitution is not likely to be conducted. Furthermore, an experimental trial that comes close—the National

Long-Term Care Channeling Demonstration—showed no evidence of widespread family withdrawal when publicly funded services were provided.

To summarize, I maintain that there is no evidence that families have relinquished or will relinquish their caregiving responsibilities. What we see is judicious use of formal services to maintain disabled elders in the community. Instead, and I think Dr. Greene would concur, concern with "service substitution" has been a convenient and sometimes deliberate obstacle to the development of a comprehensive long-term care policy in this country.

REFERENCES

Tennstedt, S. L., Crawford, S. L., & McKinlay, J. B. (1993). Is family care on the decline? A longitudinal investigation of the substitution of formal long-term care services for informal care. *The Milbank Quarterly, 71*(4), 601–624.

NO

SHARON L. TENNSTEDT

More than 16 years ago, Ethel Shanas (1979) argued that families were *not* abandoning their own—that family care of disabled elders was not diminishing. Since then, many others have echoed her point, and many studies have produced results to argue against family withdrawal from elder care. Yet the question continues to be asked, and, although unfounded, frequently the assumption that families will be unavailable or unwilling to provide care is made.

What is fueling this fire that should be cold embers by now? The source of the concern regarding family withdrawal from elder care is a good place to start. It is all a matter of numbers—the increasing number of older people and the number of dollars it will cost to care for them. The rapidly increasing size of the older population, coupled with increasing longevity, means that many more people will be living to advanced ages, when they are likely to need help with daily living activities. Looking at the rapid increase in health care costs over the past two decades, policy makers assume similar increases in long-term care costs. And here is where the family comes in.

It has been well documented that families provide upwards of 80 percent of the help with personal and household activities needed by older people. This help, generally referred to as informal care, is provided at no public cost. However, there are changes occurring in the family structure that call into question the availability and the willingness of families to continue providing this informal care. Decreasing fertility rates mean that fewer adult children will be available to provide care for elderly parents. Rising rates of marital disruption create situations, and possibly altered family structures, that could interfere with an adult child's ability to provide care. Increasing geographic mobility might result in substantial distance from an older parent that makes regular hands-on help difficult, if not impossible. And finally, increased participation of women—the majority of caregivers—in the workforce makes them less available to provide care. Certainly, given these trends, it is understandable that policy makers would think that families would relinquish their caregiving role if more long-term care services were available to take their place.

Even if less than half of all informal care now provided was replaced by formal services, public costs would skyrocket. When considering further development or expansion of long-term services, or even public financing of the services currently available, policy makers worry about the "woodwork effect." That is, how many people currently not using services would begin to do so? Faced with projections of a much larger population of older people, they wonder just how many persons will use these services—and how much more will it cost?

I would agree that expansion of long-term care services or public financing of these services is likely to result in their increased use, but this will not be because of widespread withdrawal of families from their caregiving activities. If one assumes the latter, then one has disregarded the older person's role in decision making and assumes that families make service decisions on their behalf. In reality, most older persons, while functionally disabled, are quite capable of making sound decisions regarding such issues. Many disabled elders decide to use services because they see this as a way to remain independent, that is, independent of help from their offspring. This is not to say that they prefer formal services to family help, but that some equate family help with dependence and see formal service use as an intermediate step. If more community long-term care services were made available, these elders would likely use them.

However, although some elders decide to use services *instead* of asking family for help, many more receive help from *both* family and formal services. Several studies have shown that this mixed pattern of care is more likely to occur when an elder is more disabled, and particularly when personal care is required (Chappell & Blandford, 1991; Noelker & Bass, 1989). When families are involved in care and the decision is made to use formal services, I would argue that this should not necessarily be considered family withdrawal from care, or substitution of formal services for informal care, as it is sometimes called. At levels of greater disability, family care might not be sufficient or appropriate to meet all needs. Certain types of personal care (for example, care to a parent of the opposite sex) might best be provided by a formal provider and should not be seen as family withdrawing their help.

Admission of the elder to a nursing home, however, is often seen as the ultimate withdrawal of family from care. However, one should avoid drawing too hasty a conclusion here as well. Most families do all that they can to avoid nursing home placement. When the decision to admit is made, it is often at the encouragement of a health care provider in the midst of an acute health care crisis—often when the situation seems overwhelming. And after all, does not "the doctor know best"? Usually, the decision for nursing home admission is given much greater consideration and made only when all other options for adequately meeting the elder's needs for care have been exhausted.

But getting back to those undeniable social trends—yes, they do influence the family structure, but structure might not be the critical factor in determining continuity of family, or informal, care. Data from many studies can be used to argue against the projected negative impact of changing family structure on the provision of care to disabled elders. Consider decreasing fertility rates. If recent projections materialize (Zedlewski & McBride, 1992), the average number of children will decrease from 2.9 in 1990 to 1.9 in 2030—when most of the "baby boomers" will be old. This means we will have a very large group of older people with fewer offspring. Although this decline technically might decrease the probability of each person's having a caregiver, it does not mean that care will not be available. Most studies have reported that most care is provided by one person (Stoller & Earl, 1983; Tennstedt, McKinlay, & Sullivan, 1989). This suggests that having at least one child ensures that an older person will receive care. Furthermore, we also know that in many cases, other persons or secondary caregivers are also involved (Tennstedt et al, 1989). These persons become more involved if the primary caregiver is no longer able or available to provide care (Jette, Tennstedt, & Branch, 1992).

But what about older persons who live at great distances from their children—perhaps the children have moved for career reasons or perhaps the parents had moved away to a warmer climate? Clearly this distance interferes with or prevents hands-on assistance. However, these elders often develop mutual-help relationships with their peers. In fact, in the longitudinal Massachusetts Elder Health Project (Tennstedt & McKinlay, 1989), at least 10 percent of elder participants have reported receiving help primarily from friends and neighbors. And this does not necessarily mean that families are not involved or have withdrawn from the caregiving role. In response to the difficulties of long-distance caregiving, several model programs of case management or information and referral services have been developed across the country. These services are often offered through employers. Yes, in these cases, particularly when an older person lives alone, formal services are more likely to be used than when a family caregiver lives in close proximity. However, the use of services is *not* the result of family relinquishing their role. In most cases, family remain involved to the greatest extent possible.

Then there is the contention that families will not provide care because of competing demands. Elaine Brody coined the phrase "women-in-the-middle" to refer to women who were caught between child care and elder care responsibilities (Brody, Johnsen, Fulcomer, & Lang, 1983). I would argue that this concept of the "sandwich generation" is no longer relevant in most cases of elder care. Because most people are experiencing functional decline and need for assistance later in life, their adult children are often in their sixties when faced with this responsibility. Competing demands for their time are likely to come from role activities other than parenting of young children. Employment is a likely one. However, in most studies (Horowitz, 1985; Stone, Cafferata, & Sangl, 1987) approximately one-half of all caregivers are employed. Therefore, employment does not mean that families do not provide care, although it might influence what and how much they do. However, there are no consistent findings across studies that employed caregivers provide substantially less help than unemployed caregivers. In sum, competing demands might interfere with or complicate caregiving but do not result in stopping this help.

So, if provision of elder care is not influenced greatly by structural factors, what does influence it? The answer to this question, I think, is the reason that families do not and will not relinquish their caregiving role to formal services: Family members provide care because they want to do so. Almost all studies investigating the reasons for providing care (Horowitz, 1985) provide strikingly consistent results—families provide care because of love and strong kinship ties. Two excerpts from respondents in the Massachusetts Elder Health Project illustrate this (Noonan, Tennstedt, & Rebelsky, 1996). Mrs. A., a fifty-four-year-old woman living with her eighty-year-old severely disabled mother, describes caring for her as a "labor of love." She said, "I'm doing the best I can, and if I can give her the care that she needs, as long as I can, I'll be glad to do it... I don't mind it. You only get one mother."

Even in the absence of a close relationship, the sense of filial obligation to provide care is strong. As Mr. B., a forty-eight-year-old man who has put his "life on hold" to care for his eighty-one-year-old mother says, "It has to be done. Somebody has to do it. It's my mother. So I don't mind doing it... She gave me the best years of her life."

In the face of obstacles and competing demands on time, families will find a way to provide care—and to provide as much as they can for as long as they can. The changing social trends just described would have to result in an erosion of this familial obligation before any widespread abandonment of the caregiving role will be seen. Looking to the future, the older population in this country will be increasingly ethnically diverse. Minority populations are projected to represent 25 percent of the older population in 2030, compared with 13 percent in 1990 (AARP, 1993). The largest increases will occur among Asians and Hispanics. If anything, the sense of family responsibility among these groups is stronger than among the older white population. This argues for continued prominence of familial obligation underlying provision of care to older family members.

Families care and will continue to care. Formal services are used and will continue to be used. So should policy makers be concerned about creating the "Long-Term Care Field of Dreams"—"build it and they will come"? Some will come, and some will use services. Most will stay home and be cared for by their families.

REFERENCES

AARP. (1993). *A profile of older Americans: 1993.* Washington, DC: American Association of Retired Persons.

Brody, E. M., Johnsen, P. T., Fulcomer, M. C., & Lang, A. M. (1983). Women's changing roles and help to elderly parents: Attitudes of three generations of women. *Journal of Gerontology, 38*(5), 597–607.

Chappell, N., & Blandford, A. (1991). Informal and formal care: Exploring the complementarity. *Aging and Society, 11,* 299–317.

Horowitz, A. (1985). Family caregiving to the frail elderly. *Annual Review of Gerontology and Geriatrics, 5,* 194–246.

Jette, A., Tennstedt, S., & Branch, L. (1992). The stability of informal support provided to the frail elderly. *Journal of Aging and Health, 4,* 193–211.

Noelker, L. S., & Bass, D. M. (1989). Home care for elderly persons: Linkages between formal and informal caregivers. *The Journals of Gerontology, 44*(2), S63–70.

Noonan, A., Tennstedt, S., & Rebelsky, F. (1996). Making the best of it: Themes of meaning among informal caregivers to the elderly. *Journal of Aging Studies* (in press).

Shanas, E. (1979). Social myth as hypothesis: The case of the family relations of old people. *The Gerontologist, 19,* 3–9.

Stoller, E. P., & Earl, L. L. (1983). Help with activities of everyday life: Sources of support for the noninstitutionalized elderly. *The Gerontologist, 23,* 64–70.

Stone, R., Cafferata, G. L., & Sangl, J. (1987). Caregivers of the frail elderly: A national profile. *The Gerontologist, 27*(5), 616–626.

Tennstedt, S., & McKinlay, J. (1989). Informal care for frail older persons. In M. Ory and K. Bond (Eds.), *Aging and health care.* London: Routledge.

Tennstedt, S., McKinlay, J., & Sullivan, L. (1989). Informal care for frail elders: The role of secondary caregivers. *The Gerontologist, 29,* 677–683.

Zedlewski, S. R., & McBride, T. D. (1992). The changing profile of the elderly: Effects on future long-term care needs and financing. *Milbank Quarterly, 70,* 247–275.

Rejoinder to Dr. Tennstedt VERNON L. GREENE

Needless to say, it was a pleasure to read Dr. Tennstedt's thoughtful and articulate essay *contra* the idea that families substitute professional care for their own in support of frail older kin. It seems to me that her essential points come down to these: (1) whether, and the degree to which, substitution occurs depends on specific circumstances; (2) in any case, its occurrence is infrequent, small in magnitude, and benign in effect; (3) the idea of a "woodwork effect" is misguided in that it implies an opportunism on the part of caregivers that would belie the fact that their caregiving arises from their love for their kin; and, (4) it is time we got on with the study of caregiving and the development of community care systems without worrying about, or spending so much time studying, substitution effects.

On the first point, it would be hard to disagree. But I think the point is largely an empty one in that it is precisely the conditions on which substitution behavior depends that are the subject of its scientific investigation. In this sense, everything, after all, "depends." Moreover, in making the first point, I think that Dr. Tennstedt actually had in mind more the second claim, that substitution is atypical and inconsequential in magnitude. Here I would simply refer back to my original essay in saying that any such confident conclusion is unwarranted by the body of existing findings.

On the third matter, contrary to Dr. Tennstedt's view, I would predict, for reasons given in my initial essay, that in response to any large-scale expansion of heavily subsidized home care services, one would observe a significant alteration in caregiver behavior, including diversion of effort to other areas of responsibility, as formal services become more readily available and the opportunity costs of their use decline in relation to those in other arenas of family and work life where caregivers face competing responsibilities. The problem is not that such substitution will occur—it will and should. The real difficulty here is the dim-bulb view of many policy makers that this is a net loss in terms of economic efficiency or the scope of public sector budgetary exposure. As I said in my original essay, I would strongly expect that a full analysis of the consequences of "substitution" (e.g., caregiver respite and functioning, increased commitment of effort to other areas of family and workforce productivity, and so on) would show net gains to both the economy and the public welfare.

And so, in closing, I think that Dr. Tennstedt is correct to say that we are worrying too much about substitution effects. But the reason she is right is not that they are inconsequential, but that they are not the unmitigated problem that both advocates and opponents of expanded home care seem to think. Adamant denial of the existence of substitution by home care advocates, in the face of evidence that does not clearly support such a position, merely deepens the skepticism, and indirectly strengthens the hand, of those who are determined to prevent it by opposing the expansion of home-based long-term care. And failing to develop an effective system of home care under public auspice is an error that we would all come to regret as our population ages rapidly in the decades soon to come.

Should Family Members Be Paid to Provide Care to Elderly Relatives?

EDITORS' NOTE: Family members are the linchpin in America's long-term care system, providing more than 70 percent of the care received by disabled elderly persons. However, increased female labor force participation and other social and demographic changes have led some to question whether families can continue to provide care for their elderly members without additional supports and incentives. In an effort to sustain and encourage family caregiving, many states and localities offer some form of financial compensation for family members who assist a disabled elderly relative. However, some critics have questioned the wisdom of paying family members to provide care. They argue that family compensation undermines basic family values, turning normal family love and devotion into a commodity to be purchased, while simultaneously adding unnecessarily to government outlays. Discussion of compensation for family caregiving ultimately raises fundamental questions regarding the nature and extent of family responsibility, as well as the proper role of government in assisting families. Does compensating family members for providing care enhance or undermine family bonds? Can it improve the quality of care received by older persons while reducing public long-term care costs? Is it beneficial to families and society?

Sharon M. Keigher, Ph.D., and Nathan L. Linsk, Ph.D., say *YES.* Sharon M. Keigher is Professor of Social Welfare and a Fellow in the Center for 20th Century Studies at the University of Wisconsin-Milwaukee. Nathan L. Linsk is Associate Professor at the Jane Addams College of Social Work at the University of

Illinois at Chicago, and Executive Director of the Midwest AIDS Training and Education Center. Drs. Keigher and Linsk have been studying state programs' financial supports for family caregivers for more than ten years, and they have co-authored (with Lori Simon-Rusinowitz and Suzanne England) *Wages for Caring: Compensating Family Care of the Elderly.* Dr. Linsk also is author of *Care of the Elderly: A Family Approach.*

John Amson Capitman, Ph.D., and Donna L. Yee, Ph.D., say *NO*. Dr. Capitman is Director of Long-Term Care Studies at the Institute for Health Policy and Research Professor at the Heller School at Brandeis University. He is Director of the National Resource Center: Diversity and Long-Term Care and Co-Principal Investigator of a Commonwealth Fund project to develop resident-centered standards for Assisted Living programs. Capitman also leads a Health Care Financing Administration study of quality in-home care and an evaluation of the Robert Wood Johnson Foundation's Dementia Care and Respite Services demonstration. Dr. Yee is a Senior Research Associate with the Institute for Health Policy, where she has participated in several quantitative and qualitative studies conducted by the Long-Term Care Studies Division. She is Principal Investigator of the Commonwealth Fund study of Assisted Living programs and Co-Principal Investigator of the National Resource Center: Diversity and Long-Term Care.

YES

Sharon M. Keigher
Nathan L. Linsk

Although other advanced industrialized countries have socialized the costs and provisions of long-term care, the United States continues to rely on family members to provide the bulk of hands-on care. Because such care is so vital, family members should be included among persons eligible to be paid providers of services to elders.

Provisions to Compensate Informal Caregivers Can Expand the Caregiving Capacity of the Whole Society

As the U.S. population becomes gradually older and a steadily larger share of persons require care, caregiving resources need to expand. The fastest-growing cohort among the aged, those older than eighty-five years living in their own homes, will require the greatest amount of daily care and surveillance. Policies therefore will be preferred that extend care to more individuals, provide more hours of care per dollar, and provide more flexible and responsive care to those served.

Providing consumers allowances to purchase care from any providers of their choice (including family and friends) assures that limited dollars are spent to maximize consumers' own preferences in the amount and type of care (Grana & Yamashiro, 1987). With increased choice, consumers assume more risk for hiring and managing their care, and they can hire persons not necessarily employable by agency standards, such as a deaf daughter or a mentally retarded uncle. Such individuals are typically not hired by agencies because of work requirements and bureaucratic routines, particularly in a context of increasing reliance on "qualified" agencies and home care companies.

Paying Family Caregivers Is a Matter of Gender Justice and Family Equity

The opportunity costs of family care are incurred mainly by women in the household who sacrifice employment and other opportunities (Stone & Kemper, 1989). Family caregiving is a major cause of poverty in old age among women who reduce labor force participation during middle age to provide care at home. Because women provide nearly all hands-on care now, both paid and unpaid, and government simply ignores the costs they incur, compensation for informal care is an issue of gender justice (Osterbusch Keigher, Miller, & Linsk, 1987). Eligibility for formal services often "discounts" family care, assumes that it will be provided "for free," or worse, requires that family care continue for the client to receive other services. The costs to families never appear in national budgets or calculations of gross national product (GNP). Poor women who provide the bulk of paid care have families of their own and, given the low pay scale in most care employment, often need assistance in caring for their own family members as well.

A disability allowance system of care provision based on assessment of the functional impairment of consumers would equate the work required to provide care with the compensation provided. The amount of compensation provided would realistically address the market cost of obtaining and providing such care. Including informal care in this market for appropriate tasks will level the playing field for families and consumers, who may choose whichever approach is best for them.

Administrative Requirements Can Be Simple, and Bureaucratic Barriers Can Be Low

Consumer-directed care can help alleviate the rationing of government service that will otherwise be necessary as increasing numbers of elders need care. Government's role can be streamlined and simplified if limited to managing eligibility determination and per capita spending. Use of cash vouchers or direct payment mechanisms can minimize administrative costs as well. Because families and other informal care providers are already in place or selected by the consumer, costly and extensive recruitment and screening by home care agencies is avoided. Resource pools can be maintained by consumer cooperatives and caregiver associations, which can advise families on purchasing good outside help, either as respite, backup, or full-time aides.

A simplified case management system can monitor service plans and performance if necessary for selected clients. Because services are in fact home based, overhead costs such as transportation, management, office facilities, and some benefits to home care staff are also avoided. Turnover will be minimized, although it will be necessary to have backup services available from the family network or elsewhere to provide respite and vacations from caregiving. Payments also must be sufficient to cover caregivers' contributions to health care, retirement income, and disability insurance. Obviously it would be helpful if government guaranteed the latter entitlements to all citizens.

Payment for Family Caregiving Maximizes Equity among Consumers by Broadening the Lifestyle Choices Open to Them

Elders clearly prefer kin over formal service systems. Bureaucratic procedures that agencies require in delivering care, rigid time schedules and appointments, imposition of routines, and mandatory visits of a certain length of time disrupt, discourage, and control disabled elders most unnecessarily, whereas increased coverage of informal care can protect individuals from coercion of all sorts. In Europe, where worker protections are paramount, administrative rigidity seems to be emerging as the most salient argument in favor of more flexible and consumer-directed options (Evers & Leichsenring, 1994; Evers, Ungerson, & Pijl, 1994). In comparison with Europe, research literature in the United States is remarkably silent about the deleterious effects of routinized, standardized care provisions.

Opportunity Costs and Benefits

Compensation for family caregivers is especially valuable to low-income people. When people have financial compensation, it allows them to expend personal efforts to generate more care than was provided before; it frees them up to do what is needed, and more, facilitating families to hold out longer. As one forty-five-year-old Michigan woman said of her state's Adult Home Help program, which pays her $300 per month to care for her ninety-year-old aunt, "it allows people the opportunity to make their best effort in keeping their relative at home" (Keigher & Murphy, 1992, p. 267).

Although the goal of family compensation is not to be a workfare program, it does "reward" domestic work that is now undervalued and usually not considered employment. For unemployed and underemployed family members, such payments can have positive effects similar to employment. It is, in fact, a partnership allowing extension of family care at the margins. Families are not fully compensated for their time, because emotional, instrumental, and household help are all provided. This is less costly than agency-provided care, which must compensate workers fully plus overtime to sustain care arrangements.

Capitalizing on Existing and Evolving Care Arrangements

A social work practice value is to begin where the client is. When embedded in existing informal structures and family care networks, it makes sense to build on the strengths of that system. Following this principle, family compensation simply extends current care arrangements both socially and financially, honoring the unique adaptations families develop before appealing to the formal service network for help.

Our exploratory research has found that when poor disabled elders prefer family care and their caregivers are receiving state support, both client and caregiver readily see a logic to the state's paying them. Although elders do not wish to impose on their children, exchange theory suggests that they feel better about doing so if some reciprocal way exists to offset the imposition. Cash payments can do this by extending material and human resources to support and sustain the care-givers. Although many policy options are too insensitive or inflexible to support such diversity of care, fair systems of cash payments can meet individual and community needs while simultaneously respecting the cultural and personal contexts within which care is given.

Finally, as the demands on caregiving families continue to evolve, technology may yet change the nature of caring itself. Already computer applications can track care information, and personal reminder systems can cue individuals about medications, appointments, and daily living tasks. Long-distance machines already exist that can monitor or provide care through "telemedicine." On-line discussion groups are already providing socialization, and checking services are monitoring day-to-day functioning. How can improvements even like these, which all have inevitable costs, be accessible unless families are engaged in their selection and management, and unless consumers have the means to pay for them? Family caregiving and consumer discretion will continue to need more support, not less.

Conclusions

Whatever systems of long-term care develop in this country for the twenty-first century need to be responsive to changing policy contexts and technology, while preserving the individuality of care. The first value should be to preserve what is already working, to maintain its norms, to respect it culturally, and to support personal relationships and fragile social support. All of this currently exists in America within the context of existing family care arrangements and values.

Policy and provisions must include flexible mechanisms adapted to individual needs without usurping the proper roles and abilities of families and elders to choose for themselves. Simple compensation for disabled individuals that can be shared with family caregivers offers this advantage, making home- and community-based care for all who need it the first line of government provision instead of the last. Furthermore, it places the savings (the excess revenues or "profits" that might accrue from family care) back in the hands of consumers, in effect reinvesting savings in sustaining continuing care.

REFERENCES

Evers, A., & Leichsenring, K. (1994, March). Paying for informal care: An issue of growing importance. *Ageing International, 21*(1), 29–40.

Evers, A., Ungerson, C., & Pijl, M. (1994). *Payments for care.* United Kingdom: Avebury/Aldershot.

Grana, J., & Yamashiro, S. (1987). *An evaluation of the Veterans Administration Housebound Aid and Attendant Allowance program.* Project HOPE, prepared for the Office of the Assistant Secretary for Planning and Evaluation, Department of Health and Human Services: Washington, DC.

Keigher, S., & Murphy, C. (1992). A consumer view of a family care compensation program for the elderly. *Social Service Review, 66*(2), 256–277.

Osterbusch, S., Keigher, S., Miller, B., & Linsk, N. (1987). Community care policies and gender justice. *International Journal of Health Services, 17*(2), 217–232.

Stone, R., & Kemper, P. (1989). Spouses and children of disabled elders: How large a constituency for long-term care reform? *Milbank Quarterly, 67*(3–4), 485–506.

Rejoinder to Professor Keigher and Professor Linsk

JOHN AMSON CAPITMAN
DONNA L. YEE

Family care payments should be one option in a comprehensive health and long-term care program that includes universal coverage, a broad range of benefits, consumer-centered care management, and proactive quality enhancement. But family care payments removed from the context of system reforms and political redirection solve few important policy or programmatic issues in long-term care for the aged. Because Keigher and Linsk have failed to acknowledge the need for broader changes in our nation's approaches to eldercare and income security for the aged and disabled, their arguments for family care payments are less than convincing.

Moreover, Keigher and Linsk fail to specify which of a broad set of possible family care payment options they are advocating, whether a disability allowance, a voucher to purchase agency services, fee-for-service reimbursement of family members, or other potential models. These represent different policy and program options that have different impacts, depending on the larger programs in which they are embedded.

Concerns also can be raised about each of the six broad arguments for family care payments advanced by Keigher and Linsk: First, Keigher and Linsk argue that paying informal caregivers will respond to current and future shortages in paraprofessional home care labor supply. However, home care labor supply shortages are caused primarily by inadequate reimbursement and exploitative labor practices. Moreover, because informal caregiving decisions are largely unrelated to labor market decisions, family care payments are just as likely to have no effect or a deleterious effect on informal care availability in most communities. Second, in spite of the claim by Keigher and Linsk that family care payments would increase gender justice, family care payments would largely be aimed at male care recipients and would tend to disadvantage female care recipients who have less access to family caregivers, because women outlive men, and spouses are the principal providers of family care for the aged. Third, although administrative costs in long-term care are rarely viewed as a major policy challenge, states that have introduced family care payments have not demonstrated a reduction in administrative burdens. Moreover, Keigher and Linsk describe several new bureaucratic systems that would need to be developed to support recipients of family care payments. Fourth, Keigher and Linsk appropriately point out that disability allowance or voucher programs might give low-income elders the capacity to purchase service now enjoyed by the affluent, thereby increasing equity among consumers. Yet family care payments would be unavailable to elders without the family resources to provide such care; these include elders who are alone or without strong informal care availability who form the vast majority of current users of publicly and privately financed formal care. Fifth, although Keigher and Linsk decry the use of family care payments as "workfare," they suggest that low-income families would benefit from these programs. But family care payments risk hurting elders by creating incentives for them to remain in inappropriate home settings with inadequate care. Furthermore, family care payments would need to be set unreasonably high if they were to serve as an alternative approach to achieving a living wage. Sixth, and finally, Keigher and Linsk seem to believe that family payments would extend informal care and encourage innovations in caregiving strategies. However, research on intrinsic and extrinsic motivations and prosocial behavior suggests that reimbursing family care is likely to reduce rather than increase informal care hours.

NO

JOHN AMSON CAPITMAN
DONNA L. YEE

Public payments to family caregivers of frail and disabled elders, although justifiable in some situations, must be viewed in the context of larger questions about equity in family life. Family care payments also may result in less appropriate and less responsive care. Furthermore, a focus on increased availability of family care payments as an important component of long-term care reform may reduce the potential for meaningful coalitions and successful political strategies among the disabled.

Family Care Payments in the Context of Family Care

Most care that elders receive from family members is offered in the context of ongoing, bidirectional, mutually beneficial exchange within and across households and generations. Elders provide practical assistance with the challenges of daily life experienced by their family members, they provide financial support and housing in a growing proportion of families, and they provide emotional support, loving concern, and wisdom to others. Elders in turn receive similar kinds of help from their families, and the personal satisfactions of family and community building. For some elders and their families, acute and chronic illnesses and associated limitations in daily living activities alter these exchange relationships. As the elder's needs for assistance with daily activities increases, the elder increasingly becomes a recipient of care and less and less a provider of help to others. Even in these cases, elders may continue to provide financial, housing, and affective support as well as opportunities for personal satisfaction to other family members.

Family exchanges with disabled or frail elders, although often inequitable, are not the only inequity for which external financial rewards might be considered. In most families, the relative contributions of men and women to household maintenance and child-rearing continue to be notably unequal: even as women from middle and upper income families join their working-class sisters in the paid labor market, they continue to bear the lion's share of these responsibilities. Although the idea of paying women (and in some families, men) for their roles in sustaining homes and families has been advanced, most current analysts would rather see public policies and popular culture foster greater equity in access to family resources and power rather than the introduction of market concepts into the domestic economy.

Studies of caregiving for the aged and disabled have repeatedly underscored three important aspects of these exchanges that reduce the appropriateness of family care payments as public long-term care policy. First, most caregiving to disabled elders is performed by spouses, whose nonparticipation in the paid labor market is by choice rather than as a response to caregiving. The roles of children and others are far less central, and even adult children caregivers rarely report giving up labor market participation for caregiving. Second, regardless of gender or generation, caregivers are troubled by watching a loved one decline, anticipating their death, regretting lost time together, and feeling powerless in relationship to the health care system. For most who actually serve as caregivers, the major burden is not giving care but slowly losing a loved one. Not surprisingly, neither respite care programs in the community nor institutionalization reduce the stress and strain experienced by many family caregivers. For most caregivers, the availability of family care payments would neither increase their willingness to serve nor alleviate their emotional burdens. Third, patterns of family exchange and the meanings of exchanges vary enormously by race/ethnicity and culture. Family care payments may primarily make sense in European-centered cultures with weak commitments to filial and spousal responsibility and less strict concepts of gender roles and privacy. Given the needs of elders likely to be served by public long-term care programs, family care payments may be offensive or require people to engage in culturally inappropriate behaviors in many other cultures.

As a component of a community long-term care program for the poor and disabled, family care payments may address the economic plight of individuals who have to abandon or curtail labor market participation because of their inability to find adequate, affordable care. But we do not have sufficient information to assess how the availability of such benefits would alter the behavior of potential caregivers when these programs also offer the alternative of adequate levels of purchased services delivered by non–family members. Moreover, some family members may be unable to find or maintain labor market jobs, and thus view family care payments as an opportunity. In such cases, elders may feel compelled to request family care to bring new resources into the household, and caregivers may be no better suited to this demanding work than are other options. Family care payments to members without other options seem like an inadequate alternative to appropriate education, employment, and income distribution policies.

Family Care Payments and Responsive Community Long-Term Care

Like other consumer-directed care innovations (e.g., the personal assistance model associated with the independent living centers, the Connecticut self-care-management approach, or the Colorado eldercare vouchers), family care payments are intended to shift the balance of decision-making power in long-term care from the provider system to the individual care recipient. This shift in power is a desirable goal, but it cannot be achieved simply by changing the financial or personal relationships between the care recipient and the individual providing personal care and household help. Achieving this goal requires a rethinking of the long-term care system in terms of areas of choice. The availability of family care payments—and by extension, personal assistant models of service delivery—only alters the choice over daily routines. How, when, how long, and for what reasons care is to be purchased through public programs remains unaddressed by this model. Family care payments may be a desirable benefit in a program that truly maximizes the opportunities for meaningful choices by care recipients, but by themselves they do not alter the fundamental power relationships in community care.

Furthermore, it is essential to understand community long-term care for the aged as an activity with fundamental differences from most programs for the working aged disabled. Unlike their younger peers, elders with disabilities most often have functional limitations as the result of chronic illnesses and their acute exacerbations. Unlike their younger peers, elders with disabilities experience change in needs and preferences rather than stability as the norm. As a result, long-term care for the aged is best viewed as first and foremost an extension of the health care system. Monitoring of medications, implementation of other therapeutic regimens, and nursing procedures form essential components of care. Family care payments should clearly be available as one option for provision of the paraprofessional aspects of community long-term care, if they are offered in the context of policies and programs that seek to maximize the health, functioning, and community participation of elders. Without this context of professional health care, however, family care payments, like other efforts to expand the paraprofessional aspects of community care at the expense of professional services, seem ill-suited to the actual needs of elders.

Family Care Payments and the Politics of Reform

There is a pressing need for reform in health and long-term care systems in this country. For poor and middle-class persons, the availability of appropriate, coordinated, and responsive services is distributed inequitably. Some states and communities have developed impressive systems of care, whereas others have viewed care for the frail aged as a family responsibility and not an appropriate target of public action. Because of recent and proposed changes in Medicare and Medicaid, we are moving farther and farther from a system of fair health care, in which long-term care is covered on a similar basis as acute care, and persons in communities nationwide have equal access to appropriate and quality services. In this context, coalitions of the aged disabled, working-aged disabled, parents of disabled children, and the providers of care to each of these population groups need to form. These coalitions need to focus on the need for comprehensive and inclusive policies, and not on specific benefits. By focusing too strongly on family care payments, eldercare advocates can cut off coalition building with other groups who specifically need support for non–family-provided services. And by focusing too strongly on family care payments, eldercare advocates can reduce the appeal of their efforts to the bulk of current and potential long-term care users who do not wish to receive care from their families.

Family care payments ought to be available as one part of comprehensive health and long-term care reform. But by focusing too heavily on this issue, we can distract attention from the broader concerns with our nation's commitment to protecting the well-being of the least able whatever their age or source of disability. The prize that we need to focus on is not family care payments, but an overall system of health and long-term care benefits and delivery systems that recognize the diverse and changing needs of elders and others with disabilities.

REFERENCES

Capitman, J. A., & Sciegaj, M. (1995). A contextual approach for understanding individual autonomy in managed community long-term care. *The Gerontologist, 35*(4), 533–540.

Capitman, J. A. (1994, October). Targeting community care. *The Gerontologist, 34*(5), 580–581.

DeJong, G., Batavia, A., & McKnew, L. B. (1992). The independent living model of personal assistance in national long-term care policy. *Generations, 16*(1), 89–95.

Rejoinder to Professor Capitman and Professor Yee

SHARON M. KEIGHER
NATHAN L. LINSK

Our opponents have done a nice job of outlining the weaknesses of the nation's currently inadequate health and long-term care systems. In the process they have conceded that family payments for care "should be available as one option . . ." in several specific instances and helped clarify where family payments seem particularly appropriate. We certainly concur with them and take issue with only a few of their basic arguments that introducing family care payments is problematic.

Capitman and Yee argue that, because most caregivers are spouses and only a few spouses go so far as to give up employment, the economic burden of caregiving is limited. However, the opportunity costs incurred by the relatively small number of women (and some men) who provide the highest levels of care to the low-income disabled elderly are unfairly high. In addition, some caregivers give up employment or reduce work from full- to part-time to accommodate caregiving, compromising their own current and future financial well-being. Although money cannot alleviate emotional burden, it can offset both the temporal and economic resources required for relatives to give care, especially in the poorest of families.

In contrast to our opponents' concern that cash payments may induce minority individuals to engage in culturally inappropriate behavior, evidence indicates that it is precisely poor people who have benefitted the most when family payments have been legitimized in the United States, especially cultural groups with strong family networks. Our investigation of coresiding families in Michigan confirmed that the preferred provider was one who spoke the elder's language, prepared ethnic foods properly, was familiar, and could be trusted. Family providers had pride that the state recognized the value of their work, and care receivers felt empowered in many cases, because they were offering income opportunities to their caregivers.

Capitman and Yee cast caring families as the enemies of a reputedly benevolent social care system run by government and corporate interests. Because offsetting caregiving costs has the side effect of redistribution of resources, they perceive care compensation as undesirable. This argument, in effect, suggests that it is all right for families to become unbalanced because of unreasonable care demands, as long as the market economy of home- and community-based care remains undisturbed; this certainly smacks of victim blaming. Rather, empowering family caregivers by offsetting income loss or out-of-pocket expenses may enhance their participation in coalitions, enabling them to act as effective advocates from their base as vital stakeholders in the care unit.

Gerontologists should learn from the child welfare system, where kinship care has evolved so families are seen as the first alternative for foster care (Gleeson & Craig, 1994); and from the disability field, where family payments have been seen as desirable for decades as a way of providing personalized care at low cost based on consumer choice. There is no evidence whatsoever that providing family payments at levels high enough to provide significant support to caregivers, but not high enough to replace income lost from other employment, has negative consequences. Nowhere have families created unrealistic demand (coming "out of the woodwork" to "abuse" this option). Nor is there any evidence that providing care for a fee damages the psychosocial or economic fabric of family life. Instead, all studies indicate that compensated family care is a useful adjunct to other forms of community care and that states have innovated with various mechanisms to frame this policy option.

REFERENCES

Gleeson, J. P., & Craig, L. (1994). Kinship care in child welfare: An analysis of states policies. *Child and Youth Services Review, 16*(½), 7–31.

Should Older Persons Be Able to Give Assets to Family Members without Affecting Medicaid Eligibility?

EDITORS' NOTE: Established as a companion program to Medicare in 1965, Medicaid is a joint federal and state program designed to pay for the health care of poor persons, including certain older persons. It was enacted through Title XIX of the Social Security Act. The Medicaid program covers, primarily, care of persons in institutions such as hospitals and nursing homes rather than in their own homes or community-based settings. Eligibility for Medicaid is means-tested—that is, to be eligible, individuals must have low incomes and few assets. Not surprisingly, Medicaid's status as a means-tested program has resulted in the development of strategies to increase the likelihood of acceptance as a program beneficiary for those with income or assets in excess of caps. Both those who are potentially eligible for its benefits as well as those who advocate on behalf of such individuals have participated in such activities. Proponents of the right to transfer assets point to the fact that Medicare benefits, which are not similarly means-tested, could well include the comprehensive long-term-care coverage now limited to Medicaid recipients, were it not for an arbitrary decision of government policy makers. Those taking the opposing viewpoint suggest that government's primary role is to provide a safety net of last resort, not to assist in the retention of assets for individuals and their beneficiaries, a job better down through private forms of financial planning. What is government's legitimate function in this arena? And what should be the responsibility of the individual with regard to both comprehensive long-term care coverage and the protection of personal income and assets?

Allan D. Bogutz, J.D., says *YES,* older persons should be able to give assets to relatives without affecting Medicaid eligibility. He is a Principal in the Tucson, Arizona, law firm of Bogutz & Gordon, P.C., which concentrates its practice in elder law, estate planning, and fiduciary relations. He is certified as an Elder Law Specialist by the National Elder Law Foundation under the auspices of the American Bar Association. Bogutz is an Adjunct Professor of Law at the University of Arizona College of Law, a Judge pro tempore of the Superior Court of Arizona, and is past President, Fellow, and a member of the board of directors of the National Academy of Elder Law Attorneys. In addition to other publications, he is co-author of *Elder Law: Advocacy for the Aging* (2nd edition).

Marshall B. Kapp, J.D., M.P.H., says *NO.* He is Professor of Community Health and Professor of Psychiatry, Department of Community Health, School of Medicine, Wright State University. He is also Director of the University's Office of Geriatric Medicine and Gerontology and holds an adjunct faculty appointment at the University of Dayton School of Law. Kapp has published extensively, including seven books on topics in geriatrics and the law, ethical and legal issues in health care, and patient self-determination in long-term care. He is the founding editor of the *Journal of Ethics, Law and Aging.*

YES

ALLAN D. BOGUTZ

People have a right to apply existing law to their personal situations. We have long acknowledged that everyone should pay a fair share of taxes but also have acknowledged that people are not obligated to pay more than is due. Everyone has a right to take whatever deductions the law allows. The same applies in Medicaid matters; the laws that define the Medicaid system set limits on when someone is eligible and give clear definitions about the assets that an individual can own and still be eligible to have his or her long-term care expenses paid for by the Medicaid system.

The nub of this issue is that lines must be drawn somewhere. By the very nature of the process involving qualification for eligibility for Medicaid for payment of long-term care expenses, there will be some persons who will be able to take steps to protect their assets from the costs of such care. One such step toward eligibility is to give away assets so that they are no longer "available" to pay for the costs of long-term care expenses. Public policy must permit such divestiture in part because it is impossible for it to be completely prevented. People do give away their resources; they make gifts to family and others, and they may set up a trust to manage their affairs. They may do so for reasons wholly independent of any consideration of applying for Medicaid. Public policy has determined that it is not acceptable for persons to give away their resources *for the purposes of qualifying for Medicaid.* This is because Medicaid is a program to provide care to the needy, not to those who have made themselves needy to qualify. The law and regulations must, therefore, draw lines as to when transfers will be permitted (i.e., considered to have been made for other purposes) and when such transfers will be considered to have been made for the purposes of becoming eligible for Medicaid. This is a hard distinction to draw because the Medicaid system will not be able to define the intent of the applicant in making such transfers. The system has therefore attempted to create an objective test to determine when transfers will be *presumed* to have been made for the purpose of becoming eligible. Logistically, the setting of such "objective" standards will be arbitrary and result in unfairness to some applicants.

Regardless of the logistics of implementing public policy, however, there are compelling reasons for permitting persons to plan for long-term care expenses and to utilize techniques for the preservation of assets. In other words, even if the test could be fairly applied, such a test for eligibility may not in itself be good public policy and may not reflect what the public wants and expects from the national system of health care as it now exists.

Medicaid pays for long-term care expenses in nursing homes for people who do not have the assets to pay for such care themselves. For those who have assets when they entered such care facilities, costs of $3,000 to $8,000 per month will rapidly deplete those assets, and Medicaid will have to assume the costs of their care in most cases. Congress has established the eligibility levels for Medicaid; for individuals, the level is $2,000 in available resources. Until the individual's assets are spent down to that level, the costs of long-term care must be borne individually. Congress has determined that certain assets will be exempt from inclusion in resources; these items include a burial plot, headstone, casket, and burial fund of up to $1,500, a car of reasonable value, and personal possessions. The rules are different for married individuals and allow for the spouse remaining at home to have half of the family resources up to a specific value, a home of any value, contents of the home and certain other resources; the balance is attributed to the institutionalized spouse and must be spent down to the $2,000 maximum before eligibility for Medicaid. These special rules for married couples are relatively recent (1989) and were implemented by Congress in response to divorces that were occurring to assure the financial independence of the spouse at home; before 1989, the *family's* resources had to be spent down before either spouse would be eligible for Medicaid—divorce was the only method available to protect the well spouse from becoming destitute. The rules are currently under attack from Congress, which would prefer to leave the matter to the individual states.

People do not wish to spend their life savings on nursing home care. Many are shocked to find out that Medicare (the federal program of medical insurance for persons older than sixty-five years of age and certain disabled persons regardless of income or assets) covers only a minuscule portion of most nursing home bills and that their private medical insurance does not provide any coverage for long-term care insurance. People have saved to assure a comfortable retirement with an expectation that they will be able to pass their savings on to their children. These goals are totally frustrated by having to pay for long-term care in a nursing facility. Furthermore, Medicaid only provides payment for basic long-term care expenses; there is no coverage for such "amenities" as dental care, eyeglasses, private rooms, private attendant care, or anything else other than room, board, and care. Indeed, any income that a Medicaid recipient gets (less a modest personal needs allowance) must be paid to the nursing home as a "share of cost" each month. Spending all of one's money before applying for Medicaid cuts off the individual's options, leaves nothing for the next generation, and leaves nothing for reestablishing oneself in the community if discharged from the facility.

Older persons facing long-term care have been forced to deal with an ethical issue that Congress has created: Should they follow what they perceive as the spirit of the law and spend virtually all that they have before asking for help with their long-term care bills, or should they seek to protect as much of their assets as possible? Philosophically, many may agree that Medicaid should be for the poor while still believing that long-term care coverage should be available for all, regardless of assets. In other words, many people disagree with the basic tenets of the existing system and want to protect their life savings in any way possible rather than spend them down for long-term care.

People have tried to circumvent the spend-down requirement in several ways. First, they have tried to put their assets into trusts and then claim that they have no resources; they have argued that the money was handled by a trustee (named by them) who refused to pay the nursing home expenses. Congress responded by passing Medicaid Qualifying Trust legislation to essentially prohibit such arrangements. Spouses at home have "just said no" and refused to pay for the ill spouse's nursing home expenses, leaving Medicaid as the only resource; Congress has liberalized the allocation of resources to the well spouse. People have converted "available resources" (such as savings) into "excluded resources" (such as homes or cars); Congress has responded by enacting asset recovery programs that seek to recover the costs of care from such resources after the death of the Medicaid recipient. Lastly, people have simply given their assets away to make themselves poor and thus eligible for Medicaid. In response to this tactic, Congress has created a "look-back period" that includes any such transferred resources as available resources for purposes of determining eligibility. The look-back period has gone, over the years, from twenty-four months to thirty months to thirty-six months. In addition, Congress has created an essentially indefinite period of ineligibility for such transfers; the applicant will be ineligible for a period of months equal to the amount transferred divided by the average costs of nursing home care in the applicant's locality.

These are the lines that Congress has drawn: Trusts will be ineffective, spouses will be protected, excluded assets will be subject to recovery of costs on death, and transfers occurring less than thirty-six months before applying will be disregarded in calculation of available resources. But if a person can give away his or her assets and wait thirty-six months and a day before applying for eligibility, the transfer—no matter what the amount—will not affect his or her eligibility.

As an example, assume that a person for whom the average cost of nursing home care is $2,500 per month with $300,000 in savings gives her children the full $300,000, no strings attached. If she applies for Medicaid during the next 36 months, she will be ineligible for 120 months (300,000/2,500) or ten years. If, however, she waits until the thirty-sixth month to apply, she will be immediately eligible. To assure that she has 36 months of financial ability to pay, her advisor may suggest that she transfer only $210,000 to her children. This will leave her with the $90,000 in her own account to pay for the 36 months of care before application. More often, however, the parent gives everything away and relies on the children to pay for her care from the transferred funds.

The line as to how far back Medicaid will go in looking at transfers of assets for less than fair value has to be drawn somewhere, and the government has decided to draw it (for the moment) at thirty-six months. If an individual can afford to wait the thirty-six months and is willing to transfer his or her assets, *he or she must be allowed to do so*. The reasons the line has to be drawn are that it becomes impossible to trace back beyond a certain amount of time for lack of records and because it is not likely that persons will make gratuitous transfers much farther in advance of a debilitating illness requiring long-term care. The amount that could be transferred is, of course, unlimited. There does, of course, come a certain point of wealth where such planning and transfer of assets is simply unnecessary. The current system simply allows those of moderate assets to protect some or all of such assets with adequate planning.

Because the wealthy can pay their own long-term care bills and the truly poor have no planning required to become eligible for Medicaid, the real impact of the eligibility tests are on those of truly moderate means. They may very well believe they are penalized for saving.

The question is whether this is good public policy. It is impossible to prevent all transfers of assets; people have a right to dispose of their resources as they see fit. People make gifts for many reasons. Once the government draws its line-setting limit on how far back it will go in considering transfers in determining eligibility, those who can afford to do so and who are willing to bear the risks associated with such transfers have an absolute right to do so. Such persons (and the persons who advise them) are acting in full compliance with the law. When people believe that the system is unfair or unjust, they will take steps (such as this type of divestiture) so that the law, as it exists, will penalize them in the least amount possible. Such transfers in compliance with the law cannot be prohibited.

The solution, of course, is to provide people with what they want: a system that allows those who need long-term care to receive it without having to first deplete their life savings and thereby risk the economic security of themselves, their spouses, and their children or others dependent on them. Such a system would make long-term care a covered expense under Medicare or develop some other program to pay for those horrendous expenses. Until that time, everyone has a right to use the terms of the law as they apply.

Rejoinder to Professor Bogutz   MARSHALL B. KAPP

Allan Bogutz appears to hinge his whole position on the argument that the Medicaid law now permits individuals to game the system by strategically giving away assets to qualify for the public long-term care program, and that people have a right to take advantage of the law as written. No disagreement from me! The problem, of course, is that Bogutz's argument begs the very question being debated here, namely, whether the law—as a matter of sound public policy—*ought* to permit individuals to game the system in this manner.

Bogutz also places critical emphasis on his supposition that "people believe the [present] system is unfair or unjust." I would suggest that most individuals who transfer assets for Medicaid eligibility purposes do not engage in this conduct as a matter of moral protest or civil disobedience. Instead, they hire Medicaid estate planners (and handsomely remunerate them) for the much more prosaic and pragmatic purpose of trying to get something (i.e., long-term care coverage) for nothing—an understandable but unrealistic goal, at least in the long run.

Finally, Bogutz assails restrictions on asset transfers because, "Spending all of your money before applying for Medicaid cuts off the individual's options, leaves nothing for the next generation, and leaves nothing for reestablishing oneself in the community if discharged from the facility." I agree that these are all undesirable consequences, to be resisted by older persons. However, merely stating the laudable objective of trying to avoid those outcomes provides no persuasive explanation for why individuals should not be encouraged through financial incentives, or even compelled, to pursue that objective through private forms of planning and action, such as the purchase of private long-term care insurance. Put differently, if the sorts of values enumerated by Bogutz are important for particular persons, why should it therefore be the responsibility of government (and the taxpaying public that constantly feeds it), rather than that of the person himself or herself, to guarantee the realization of those private values? Government's legitimate function in the long-term care arena ought to be that of social safety net of last resort, not that of fairy godmother who exists to keep individuals from ever having to confront difficult choices.

NO

MARSHALL B. KAPP

The current system (using the term *system* in a very loose sense) in the United States for financing long-term care (LTC) services for frail older, as well as younger disabled, individuals is faulty and badly in need of change. Currently, the costs of LTC—meaning here both home- and community-based care and nursing facility care—are paid by a variety of sources: private income or savings of the individual or family, Medicare (the federal social insurance health program for the elderly), private LTC insurance, and Medicaid. Medicaid is a joint state–federal program for the poor enacted in 1965 that bears the coverage of nursing facility costs for more than half of all nursing facility residents nationally. In fiscal year 1990, Medicaid paid more than $15 billion for nursing facility care for over 1.3 million older persons. Today, nearly one-quarter of all Medicaid funds are spent on nursing facility costs (Burwell, 1991).

Because Medicaid is a general tax-financed program intended to assist poor people to obtain otherwise inaccessible health services, eligibility for benefits is means-tested. In other words, an applicant for Medicaid coverage must demonstrate sufficient financial need by showing personal income and assets falling below a threshold poverty amount. For many older individuals contemplating applying for Medicaid benefits (especially for nursing facility services) in the foreseeable future, eligibility for government benefits based on poverty is achieved by transferring away legal ownership of the bulk of one's material assets to one's spouse, children, or grandchildren before the time of filing the Medicaid application. This process of taking advantage of, or legally "gaming," the system has generated a large-scale, highly profitable industry for attorneys and financial planners under the banner of Medicaid Estate Planning.

Medicaid Estate Planning

This recent cottage industry, whose enterprise is helping individuals and families to avoid personal financial responsibility for LTC services by maximizing reliance on taxpayers, relies on three chief strategies. These are: (1) spending the client's assets now; (2) changing the type of assets owned, for example, investing money in the family house or automobile because the value of those assets are exempt from Medicaid eligibility calculation; and (3) changing the nature of the ownership of assets by, for example, establishing certain kinds of trust arrangements that appear to distance the client from control of his or her money.

Lawmakers have attempted to restrict the gaming of the Medicaid eligibility process by enacting provisions such as those contained in the Omnibus Budget Reconciliation Act (OBRA) of 1993, which requires a three-year look-back for assets given away and five years for assets placed in a trust (42 U.S.C.

§ 1396p(c)(1)(B)(I)). Under these provisions, asset divestitures or trust transfers taking place within the suspect period before application for Medicaid eligibility are presumed to have been done only for Medicaid eligibility purposes, and those assets thus are presumed still to be available to the client to pay for LTC services. For the most part, however, the actual impact of these legislative provisions has been more to inspire ever-creative Medicaid Estate Planning tactics to feign client poverty than to really enforce personal financial responsibility.

Subversion of a Public Program, Role of Private Responsibility

The upshot of the highly lucrative Medicaid Estate Planning exercise (Beck, 1992; Quinn, 1989) has been the complete subversion of Medicaid LTC coverage from its original, laudable Congressional purpose as a financial welfare safety net for individuals who would otherwise be precluded from obtaining needed services into its current incarnation as a universal middle-class social insurance political sacred cow (Soltermann, 1993), where recipients resent contributing any dollars that function as the equivalent of deductibles and co-payments. As such, it is part of the selfish, rights-obsessed, entitlement mentality that has all but destroyed the traditional commitment to personal responsibility and community solidarity that in earlier times had formed the backbone of American society (Etzioni, 1993; Glendon, 1991; Howard, 1994). Sound public policy ought not condone this sort of subversion.

Especially in the LTC arena, the primary rationale for emphasizing personal responsibility of service consumers and their families is straightforward. Put bluntly, should not the main reason for society encouraging people to save money and other assets during their lives be to empower those persons to pay for the satisfaction of their own and their loved ones' needs when they grow old? If public policy permits older persons to receive good-quality LTC services, without discrimination, at public expense without footing at least part of the bill personally, it is not the consumer directly who benefits (he or she would have received the services in any event) but rather the middle-class, middle-aged heirs of that person. Is enabling children and grandchildren to inherit houses from parents or grandparents whose LTC has been financed through Medicaid, regardless of the real financial capacity of the consumer (and, incidentally, regardless of the heir's devotion to the Medicaid recipient or contribution to his or her care while he or she was living), a legitimate objective and result of public policy?

I would respond in the negative. Unlike Medicare and Social Security retirement and disability insurance, Medicaid was neither originally envisioned nor constructed by our elected representatives as an earned benefit or social insurance program, but rather as a form of welfare. Having been subverted *de facto* into a social insurance program for the middle class, but without a corresponding public acknowledgment or stable funding mechanism, the Medicaid LTC program now hemorrhages vast quantities of dollars that become unavailable to spend on other deserving but competing social purposes.

Public policy makers thus confront a crisis compelling a choice among clear alternatives. We must either fundamentally and expressly transform the nature of the Medicaid LTC program into one of social insurance instead of welfare, with funding collected either beforehand from everyone or after-the-fact from service users, or we must (as I prefer) implement effective strategies to encourage and enhance the role of private responsibility for the costs of LTC services in the home, community, and institutions.

Public Policy Alternatives

If policy makers decide to rectify the current paradoxes and inequities in the Medicaid LTC system by explicitly transforming it into social insurance rather than a welfare safety net of last resort, one funding option would be through taxes collected beforehand, perhaps dedicated specifically to this use. Settling on a specific type of fair tax (income versus property versus sales) would be problematic, as would maintaining any semblance of cost containment once the public trough was opened even wider. Furthermore, this approach does nothing to answer the basic moral question of why I as a taxpayer should serve not only as my own parents' keeper, but as the financier for your middle-class parents as well, and with my "contribution" enforced by state coercion at that. Conscientious and community-minded persons would, in effect, be taxed doubly.

Another financing possibility for the social insurance alternative is taxing Medicaid LTC benefits after the services have been provided, through a Medicaid estate recovery process (Miller, 1994). As part of OBRA 1993, all states are mandated to seek recovery of Medicaid benefits from the estates of LTC consumers and certain others (42 U.S.C. § 1396p(b)). The law requires recovery, where available, from the estate for nursing facility, home- and community-based, and related hospital and prescription drug services for individuals fifty-five years of age and older. States can also choose to recover for other services. The states have implemented these federal mandates with highly varying degrees of vigor and success.

This financing approach is not "picking the bones of the poor," as some have claimed (Schwartz and Sabatino, 1994). Indeed, it is less objectionable than a universal income, property, or sales tax, because it attempts to target for some degree of personal responsibility the families of individuals who have actually been the beneficiaries of public largesse, and in a manner that does not interfere with access to services at the time that they are needed. Nonetheless, political weaknesses that may ultimately scuttle this strategy include the fact that many consumers of LTC services or their families find this form of enforcing personal obligations offensive and upsetting, as well as unpredictable.

Perhaps more importantly, it is quite unclear pragmatically whether an after-the-fact Medicaid estate recovery program conducted by a government bureaucracy can function as an efficient, cost-effective means of financing a significant enough portion of the nation's LTC bill. Besides the usual inefficiencies and shortcomings to be expected, states must contend with OBRA 1993's requirement that they establish procedures for foregoing estate recovery if it would work an "undue hardship" on the heirs. Whether this provision becomes the exception that swallows the rule will bear close scrutiny. Also, the potential for litigation conducted in activist federal courts striking down key provisions of estate recovery statutes and regulations is substantial (Miller, 1994).

The better policy approach is to encourage greater personal responsibility for the costs of LTC services, without causing individuals or families to suffer the perceived indignities of financial impoverishment, by enhancing the role of private LTC insurance. Private LTC insurance, which is growing in importance but is still grossly underutilized, should be promoted as a means to fulfill one's moral and social responsibilities for one's own LTC while simultaneously and legitimately sheltering one's assets for future distribution to family members or others (including charitable beneficiaries) of the individual's choosing (Radke, 1993). With private insurance policies as the first source of payment for most individuals, government then could afford to provide an effective safety net to protect the limited number of people who could not afford to purchase private protection.

In addition to private LTC insurance, other nongovernmental devices could encourage individuals to anticipate and plan for future LTC expenses. Individuals could accumulate tax-free reserves, for example, Individual Medical Accounts similar to Individual Retirement Accounts (IRAs), that would be dedicated to pay LTC expenses later in life. Another approach focuses on the development of methods such as "reverse annuity mortgages," or "reverse equity mortgages" (REMs), to convert home equity accumulated by the elderly over their lives to cash to pay for LTC expenses, without forcing the older person to sell the house outright or the taxpayer to compensate for the individual's lack of planning. Other alternatives include further development of comprehensive, capitated (i.e., financed on a per-person basis) LTC delivery models such as social health maintenance organizations (SHMOs) and continuing care retirement communities (CCRCs) or life care communities.

Conclusion

American society needs a heavy re-inculcation of personal and social responsibility. Popular attitudes and public policy regarding the financing of LTC today nicely illustrate the problems of divorcing an insatiable demand for individual entitlements, on one side, from corresponding obligations owed to the community, on the other. Now, we virtually guarantee public financing of LTC services for individuals who, regardless of their wealth, are permitted to evade personal responsibility by transferring unlimited assets to family members or otherwise gaming the system, based on an elaborate, degrading, inefficient charade of determining economic need. By doing so, we have evolved a *de facto* system of middle class welfare that can only be characterized as immoral, excessively expensive, frustratingly complex, and ultimately unsatisfying to all concerned. We surely deserve better.

REFERENCES

Beck, M. (1992, November 30). Planning to be poor. *Newsweek,* p. 66.

Burwell, B. (1991). *Middle class welfare: Medicaid estate planning for long-term care coverage.* Lexington, MA: SysteMetrics/McGraw-Hill.

Etzioni, A. (1993). *The spirit of community: Rights, responsibilities, and the communitarian agenda.* New York: Crown Publishers.

Glendon, M. A. (1991). *Rights talk: The impoverishment of political discourse.* New York: Free Press.

Howard, P. K. (1994). *The death of common sense: How law is suffocating America.* New York: Random House.

Miller, M. A. (1994). Your money for your life: A survey and analysis of Medicaid estate recovery programs. *Cooley Law Review, 11,* 585–611.

Quinn, J. B. (1989, December 18). Do only the suckers pay? *Newsweek,* p. 52.

Radke, B. A. (1993). Meeting the needs of elderly consumers: Proposed reforms for the National Association of Insurance Commissioners' Long-Term Care Insurance Model Act. *Elder Law Journal, 1,* 227–250.

Schwartz, R., & Sabatino. C. P. (1994). *Medicaid estate recovery: Picking the bones of the poor.* Washington, DC: American Bar Association Commission on Legal Problems of the Elderly.

Soltermann, J. L. (1993). Medicaid and the middle class: Should the government pay for everyone's long-term health care? *Elder Law Journal, 1,* 251–290.

Rejoinder to Professor Kapp
ALLAN D. BOGUTZ

My opponent's statement on this topic begs the question in favor of a polemic on the current state of society. Professor Kapp finds fault with the preferences of the American public for what it believes the government should provide. His claim is that there exists a "selfish, rights-obsessed, entitlement mentality that has all but destroyed the traditional commitment to personal responsibility and community solidarity...." This is a strong accusation of the public when the truth is that the public strenuously objects to an arbitrary decision made by the federal government not to include long-term care as a benefit under the Medicare program. My opponent makes no claim that those of the public who receive medical benefits under Medicare are leeches avoiding their civic responsibility by subterfuge; why is there no acknowledgment that Medicare could well have included long-term care in its benefit package?

Some long-term care is actually provided for by Medicare, provided that there is a likelihood of a recovery, such as in the case of an individual receiving long-term physical and occupational therapy benefits after a stroke. Yet if the same individual has Alzheimer's disease, he or she is treated differently! The stroke patient receives care under his Medicare *insurance,* regardless of assets or income; the Alzheimer's patient has to deplete his or her assets and be poor before the government assists him or her with "welfare." The public not only does not understand this distinction, it opposes it. This is not "selfish," "rights-obsessed," or "the result of an entitlements mentality"; it is a rejection of the arbitrary decision made at the inception of the Medicare program.

Yet, despite the characterization of those who make use of the provisions of the law to plan for protection of their assets as "gamers," the truth is that no games are being played, and no one is violating any law. There is characterization of those who assist families facing destitution because of illness as a "cottage industry" encouraging avoidance of responsibility. This is unfair to those who make their living assisting persons to protect their futures. An apt analogy exists with regard to income taxes: Is it selfish or an avoidance of responsibility to deduct one's children on an income tax return? Certainly not; the law provides for this deduction, and we have long recognized that everyone has a duty to pay taxes but no one has a duty to pay more than is owed under the law. Are tax preparers and CPAs a cottage industry encouraging "avoidance of responsibility" by telling their clients about deductions that may be available on their individual returns? Certainly not; everyone is entitled to have assistance in determining the law that applies to them.

As a "solution" to the problem, my opponent suggests that taxation should be involved, either before the need for long-term care or after benefits have been received. Although this is clearly beyond the scope of this debate, there is again a clear parallel relationship here to Medicare, which is the solution the public apparently desires: could not a new Medicare Part C provide benefits for long-term care? Extending Medicare insurance to long-term care, that is, providing the benefit as insurance regardless of assets or income, would assuredly moot the debate in which we are engaged. As another alternative, my opponent suggests recovering the costs of care paid from those who have received benefits. However, we do not charge back to Medicare beneficiaries the costs of the care that they received; it is insurance. How is it rational to treat one type of medical care differently from another? It is not.

A significant problem that has not been addressed by my opponent is that of the impossibility of drawing a line that will prevent people from giving away assets. There is, as stated, *a presumed intent to transfer to become eligible* if assets are transferred for less than fair value within thirty-six months before application for eligibility. This line could be moved (indeed, it has been: from twenty-four months to thirty months to the current thirty-six months), but *there has to be a line*. People do transfer assets for reasons other than to qualify for Medicaid; they make gifts to family members for holidays and other occasions, they transfer assets to children to help them with family needs or education or to help them deal with emergencies, and transfers are made for estate tax planning purposes. It may very well occur that a person who has made such transfers may need long-term care. How far back can we possibly look—indeed, how far back are such records generally kept or reasonably available? How far back is it likely to presume such an intent? The thirty-six-month rule probably pushes the limits because most persons are not able to plan ahead so far in advance of an illness or do not have the resources to both support themselves during the look-back period and have assets remaining to protect.

In summary, we must allow persons to be able to get information about the existing law concerning long-term care and benefits available, we must allow persons to use the provisions of that law to *legally* establish eligibility for such benefits, and we must do so because it is a reasonable use of the law and because of the preferences of the public to use the law in such a manner. At a more important level, what is needed is to examine the basic premises of the distinctions we have made as to how we provide benefits for different types of illnesses and reassess whether the system itself needs to be modified.

Should Grandparents Assume Full Parental Responsibility?

Editors' Note: Historically, grandparents have been of marginal concern, rarely considered a particularly influential feature of American family life. Indeed, the literature on the family reflects scant attention given to examining the roles, functions, and experiences of grandparenthood. However, continuing increases in life expectancy have not only meant greater numbers of people surviving into extended old age, but greater numbers of men and women assuming the status of grandparents for extended periods, and, consequently, having the opportunity to get to know their grandchildren. Some have advocated for closer ties between grandparents and grandchildren—ties that reflect strengthened emotional and compassionate bonds and long-term commitment across the generations as well as the assumption of substantial amounts of authority by grandmothers and grandfathers over their grandchildren. Others believe grandparenthood should be a time, when financial resources and health status allow, for older adults to lead independent lives reflecting substantial measures of self-reliance and autonomy. To what extent, then, should grandparents be expected to assume parentlike roles for substantial periods? Should older adults, if willing, necessarily bear responsibility for nurturing stronger intergenerational ties during times of family crises such as divorce, low income, incapacity, and instability in the middle generation?

Joan F. Robertson, Ph.D., says *YES.* She is Professor at the School of Social Work of the University of Wisconsin, Madison, and is an Affiliate of the University's McBeath Institute for Aging and the Center for Family Excellence. Dr.

Robertson is a Fellow of the Gerontological Society of America and has been an editor for the *Journal of Marriage and the Family, Family Relations,* and for numerous journals in the field of substance abuse pertaining to family dynamics and substance use and abuse. Her research focuses on family life and intergenerational phenomena.

Colleen L. Johnson, Ph.D., gives a qualified *NO.* She is Professor of Medical Anthropology at the University of California, San Francisco. She has conducted research on ethnic families, inner-city families, and family supports to older people. She also spent five years following the divorce process in Northern California suburbs, mapping grandparents' roles in the changing family system. Currently she has a MERIT Award from the National Institute on Aging to study adaptation of the oldest old.

YES

JOAN F. ROBERTSON

My response to the issue of whether grandparents should assume full parental responsibilities for grandchildren is, if grandparents are willing and able, why not? I assume this position for a number of separate but interrelated reasons. These reflect my views on the value of intergenerational relationships and the changes, strengths, and resilience of the family over time.

First, I think stereotypical views that many grandparents are meddlesome in family life and are eager to raise grandchildren should be put to rest. Over the years, my experiences, real and read, lead me to conclude that most grandparents want nothing more than to be grandparents and leave full-time parenting roles to their grandchildren's parents. Unfortunately, there are some parents who are unable or unwilling to adequately care for their children. In a number of these situations, grandparents step in and assume full-time custodial care of grandchildren to rescue the children from parental neglect or abuse and to prevent foster home placement in the impersonal and complicated child welfare system. Many of these grandparents assume parental surrogate functions with no physical or legal custody of the children.

Second, because we have no information to suggest that children being raised by grandparents is detrimental to the well-being of children or grandparents, we should allow grandparents to assume full responsibilities for grandchildren whose parents are unable or unwilling to provide for them. This assumes that grandparents are able and want to assume this responsibility. Grandparents of color and grandparents from various ethnic groups have informally adopted and cared for grandchildren with and without public assistance for centuries. The old adages that "blood is thicker than water" and "family is better than strangers" are not without merit. This is especially the case when the alternative for children without parents may be years of placement in and out of nonrelative foster homes with little opportunity for permanence nor the chance to bond with stable surrogate parents.

Third, the growth in grandparent care should encourage those who are concerned about children and family life to move beyond stereotypical views of the American family (Robertson, 1995a; 1995b). Contemporary conservative rhetoric and nostalgia that fosters an idealized "traditional" family form is inconsistent with reality (Walsh, 1993). In fact, historians tell us that the "traditional family" has never been a norm in American society (Hareven, 1982).

Fourth, gerontologists of the family consistently remind us that generational interdependence and interconnectedness have been evident in American society for centuries (Bengston & Robertson, 1985). Grandparents and extended family members have "informally adopted" and raised "parentless" children in African American, Hispanic, Native American, and in ethnically diverse families for years (Wilson, 1994), in spite of the economic or other hardships that such arrangements imposed on them. Limited descriptive research also indicates that most grandparents will provide custodial care for grandchildren when the child's parents fail to do so. Grandparents do this out of love and a deep sense of family responsibility, even in spite of detriment to their well-being, economic vulnerability, and a desire to be free from parenting.

Black low-income grandparents interviewed in a recent caregiver study minimized the stresses they endured as full-time custodians of grandchildren for fear that their grandchildren would be removed from their home. These grandparents assumed the caregiving role with full awareness of their vulnerabilities. What most hoped for was the provision of formal supports to buffer the stresses associated with the caregiving situation. Most downplayed health limitations and focused on the rewards of the caregiving situation, particularly the love they received from their grandchildren (Burton, 1992; Minkler, Rose, & Price, 1992).

I have been actively involved with many grandparent caregivers across the county, because I am a grandparent who provided full-time custodial care of a preschool grandchild without any type of public support or guardianship. My aims were personal and professional: personal because I soon realized the immense amount of informal support that I received from other grandparents who were living with similar experiences; professional because I had been engaging in grandparent and intergenerational research as a gerontologist since my graduate student years and, on some level, was comforted by the thought that I might be able to channel the emotionally charged stressful aspect of these experiences into my work to enhance practice and policy emphases in family life. Most of the grandparents appeared to be very good parental surrogates. Some were questionable. Many received foster care or Aid for Families with Dependent Children (AFDC) support for parenting their grandchildren. Many, like myself, did not. Our stories were often similar. Often, they were different. Some of our similarities were: (1) we could not easily get health insurance for the children because we were not the children's parents; (2) we had no legal right to request medical help, and many doctors refused to release medical information; (3) because of confidentiality rules, child welfare workers refused to provide us with necessary information regarding the child or the child's parents; (4) some grandparents found that schools were reluctant to talk with them because they were not legal guardians of the children; (5) grandparents could not afford legal fees to seek guardianship; and (6) some grandparents lived in fear that the children's chemically dependent parent(s) would remove the children if the grandparents made any demands or requests of the parents; hence, a number of grandparents feared for the safety and security of the grandchildren. Most striking to me was one similarity: all of the grandparents, whether poor or middle class, exhibited considerable resiliency and strength of love for grandchildren who would have been at serious risk had grandparents not been willing to put their personal or professional lives on hold and bravely step in to protect children from parents who loved them no less, but were simply unable or unwilling to provide for them.

I was also often struck by the many stories about the much too impersonal and complicated legal and child welfare systems. Most of the grandparents who were involved in the child welfare system reported that child welfare workers assumed that, because the child's parent was dysfunctional, they and the kinship system were also dysfunctional. These experiences lead me to comfortably suggest that most custodial grandparents are not eager to assume custody of grandchildren. Most see the children as family. Hence, custody is not a primary concern. This view was also affirmed in a recent study of relative foster care study in California (Barth et al, 1994). What grandparents need is to receive some formal supportive services to buffer the impact of caregiving. Many also seek guardianship to guarantee access to medical care, to include grandchildren as a dependent in their medical insurance, and the right to access school records. Others want some respite care, assistance with child care, and advice and consultation for ways to deal with the child's parents or problems that the parents may present: visitation, interference with child care, removing the children in and out of their homes, and so forth.

Fifth, it is important to stress that the situation of grandparents assuming custodial care of grandchildren when parents are neglectful or abusive is protected by public legislation. The "reasonable efforts requirement" of Public Law 96-272, the Adoption Assistance and Child Welfare Act, requires that if children are not properly cared for in their own home, protective services must explore placement with relatives to ensure children are placed in a "least restrictive environment" wherever possible. The spirit of this legislation is variously implemented from state to state. Nonetheless, the intent was to ensure that children retain a right to their family and cultural heritage. As a matter of public policy in protective service cases, a grandparent's home must be considered as a relative care placement for children, and grandparents and family members should be eligible for foster care reimbursement. This legislation and current debates as to whether grandparents should have custody of grandchildren increase the likelihood of preserving children's and grandparent's legal rights to family and cultural heritage. It also permits grandparents to intervene to protect grandchildren from placement outside the family when parents are unable or unwilling to care for them.

My sixth and final affirmative point on grandparents assuming full parental responsibility for grandchildren needs to be viewed within the context of broader government policies that affect the welfare of children and families and grandparents as extended family resources. Policies and social programs that address the needs of children, the welfare of vulnerable families, and the well-being of older adult family members, particularly older single women, are fraught with not-too-subtle class, race, and sexist agendas that highlight an exclusive and privileged definition of family for some, but not for all. For example, families are most often viewed as a homogeneous group with little, if any, emphasis on the value of extended family members or the diversity of families. A white middle-class nuclear family norm is generalized as the experiences of all families in society. The lifestyles, behaviors, and experiences of poor, working class, or families of color are minimized and viewed as deviant, disorganized, or pathological, when many of these families have maintained a strong collective identity and strong kinship ties. For example, the extended kin network in African American families that includes nonbiological or fictive family kin is often regarded as deviant rather than an important and enduring aspect of African American culture. Similarly, the strengths and resilience of poor or single-parent families are minimized because of a idealized two-parent nuclear family norm that renders *all* such families because different or deviant from the norm. Issues related to gender and autonomy are also important because the welfare of women is most often sacrificed to the welfare of the family, and the white middle-class values of privacy and autonomy that are implicit in family policy are also most often contingent on one's class, race, and, gender (see Hartman, 1993).

These six issues converge in a variety of ways to support my view that grandparents, if they are willing and able, should assume full responsibility of grandchildren. I assume this position in the absence of research suggesting otherwise. Whatever the future holds for grandparents who are raising grandchildren in the absence of parents, it is important to stress that love is not enough to guarantee children the right to develop to their fullest potential. Nor will love alone sustain those grandparents who are willing to assume surrogate parent functions with limited resources and few formal and informal supports to help them. The health and well-being of children is imperative to the prosperity of the future. Likewise, grandparents' needs and quality of life are equally imperative. The grandparent-parenting-grandchild situation must be viewed from a family resilience perspective because grandparents are family resources. The diversity that is typical of American families must also be recognized. If grandparents are to be used as resources to raise younger children in the absence of parents, it is imperative that they be provided with a variety of supplemental supports, as needed.

REFERENCES

Barth, R. P., Courtney, M., Berrick, J. D., & Albert, B. (1994). *From Child Abuse to Permanency Planning*. New York: Aldine de Gruyter.

Bengston, V. F. & Robertson, J. F. (1985). (Eds.), *Grandparenthood*. Beverly Hills, CA: SAGE.

Burton, L. M. (1992). Black grandparents rearing children of drug-addicted parents: Stressors, outcomes and social service needs. *The Gerontologist, 32*, 744–751.

Hareven, T. (1982). American families in transition: Historical perspectives on change. In F. Walsh (Ed.), *Normal family processes* (1st ed.). New York: Guilford Press.

Hartman, A. (1993). Challenges for family policy. In F. Walsh (Ed.), *Normal family processes* (2nd ed., pp. 3–72). New York: Guilford Press.

Minkler, M., Rose, K., & Price, M. (1992). The physical and emotional health of grandmothers raising grandchildren in the crack cocaine epidemic. *The Gerontologist, 32,* 752–760.

Robertson, J. F. (1995a). *Grandparents parenting grandchildren*. Unpublished manuscript, School of Social Work, University of Wisconsin, Madison, Wisconsin, 53706.

Robertson, J. F. (1995b). Grandparenting in an era of rapid change. In R. Blieszner and V. H. Bedford, *Handbook of Aging and the Family* (pp. 243–260). Westport, CT: Greenwood Press.

Walsh, F. (1993). Conceptualization of normal family processes. In F. Walsh (Ed.), *Normal family processes* (2nd ed., pp. 3–72). New York: Guilford Press.

Wilson, D. (1994). *Kinship care: A natural bridge*. Washington, DC: Child Welfare League of America.

Rejoinder to Professor Robertson   COLLEEN L. JOHNSON

It is virtually impossible to challenge the basic proposition here, that if grandparents are ready and willing, why should they not take full responsibility for their grandchildren? Such freedom of choice is so basic in our culture that it hardly needs stating. The underlying question is this: Can we really assume that grandparents are becoming surrogate parents out of free choice? At this point, we know enough to raise serious reservations about such a shift in family roles.

First, the statement that there is no evidence that such an arrangement is detrimental to grandparents or grandchildren is not completely accurate. Evidence does exist that grandchildren in custody of grandparents have more problems, granted a finding that must be tempered by the fact that one cannot identify whether such problems stem from grandparents child rearing or the family situation that forced the custodial arrangement in the first place.

There is better information about the impact on grandparents when they become surrogate parents. One source of information comes from my own work and that of others who, in the course of doing research on grandparents, incidentally encountered a few custodial grandparents. Since then, more information has become available from systematic research on the impact of surrogate parentage has on the grandparents' lives. Jendrek, in her study of white grandparents providing daily care to grandchildren, found that custodial grandparents were more negatively affected. Custody places more responsibility on grandparents that goes beyond child care. Such an arrangement also affects the grandparents' marriage, their relationships with their other children, and their friendship involvements. Needless to say, surrogate grandmothers also report fatigue and feelings of being emotionally drained.

More telling is Burton's research that takes into account the insidious changes taking place in our inner cities that have dramatically changed intergenerational relationships. No longer can we assume that these ties are strong and supportive, because the adult children are either unavailable or too distracted with their own lives to be instigators or supporters in the widely acclaimed black family helping networks that have long acted as buffers to stress. Instead, grandparents as surrogate parents live in fear for their grandchildren's lives because of drive-by shootings and crime-ridden streets. These grandparents must make extraordinary sacrifices because of the economic drain of having a drug-dependent child and because of the lack of supports they receive from other family members. Not surprisingly, 85 percent of the grandparents in her study reported depression and anxiety.

Thus, to return to my original point, to advocate a policy that grandparents should assume full parental responsibility for grandchildren places unnecessary burdens on women and minorities. In advocating such a policy, are we setting a precedent that may weaken the responsibility of the public sector for the care of dependent children? Do we really want to place additional stresses and burdens on already disadvantaged populations?

A QUALIFIED NO

COLLEEN L. JOHNSON

My opposition to the proposition "Should grandparents assume full parental responsibility?" stems mostly from the insistent and inflexible emphasis on *the shoulds* of grandparenting rather than the *maybes*. After a five-year study of grandparent roles in mostly middle-class divorcing families and two research projects with older urban blacks, I conclude that this issue should not be addressed in such mandatory terms. Because there are so many ambiguous issues about the grandparent role in our society, it is unwise to transfer responsibility to individuals forced often involuntarily to assume a parental role that is regulated by conflicting expectations.

We have found that difficulties arose for both white and black grandparents when their children could no longer care for their own children. When forced to assume full parental responsibility for their grandchildren, conflict and tension between generations in some cases arose that required outside assistance.

I speak as an anthropologist and family researcher, not as a policy advocate, and I naturally recognize the unfortunate situation many grandparents find themselves in today when they are forced to take over the care of their grandchildren. With the breakdown of a child's family and that child's failure to perform the parent role, some grandparents have no other options. But, one must ask, is it in the best interests of the grandchild and of the grandparents? Such added responsibilities are not in the best interests of most grandparents because of their own middle-aged agenda or, in some cases, because of their health problems. It also might not be in the best interests of grandchildren because of age and cohort gaps in values and interests. It also seems to me that such a possibility places a disproportionate burden on women and minorities and perhaps relieves the public sector of some responsibilities for dependent children.

It hardly needs stating that full responsibility for grandchildren rarely falls on grandparents as couples—the responsibility is likely to fall on the grandmother. Few grandfathers today have been influenced by androgynous norms, and when grandchildren are in need, we have found, grandmothers do the work, and grandfathers are usually distant and shadowy figures. It also needs to be emphasized that advocates of grandparents' parental responsibilities often illustrate their points by referring to inner-city black grandmothers who are caring for abandoned grandchildren. Black women may face particular problems when forced to parent grandchildren, because of the spacing of generations in black families. The grandmother may be in early middle age or even younger, a time in life when she has many other responsibilities. If the responsibility is assigned to older grandparents, most older black women are usually enjoying their leisure for the first time in their life and do not want to take on such burdens. Consequently, those who advocate turning responsibilities over to grandparents should also advocate social programs that would assist them in doing so. Given the political climate in the mid 1990s, such assistance is unlikely. In fact, efforts to turn responsibilities for dependent children back to the family would be a welcome excuse to cut current public assistance.

Any consideration of this proposition needs to take full cognizance of the underlying impediments inherent in the American family system and its scant resources to bring to times of family crisis. Consequently, some outside sources of assistance are usually necessary. Problems in raising children are likely to occur in families already burdened by divorce, poverty, substance abuse, and parental abandonment, all sources of stress that have ripple effects to grandchildren. The normative guidelines about what grandparents should do are unclear, making grandparents unprepared and hesitant about responding. That point when one's child can no longer perform the parent role is a time of crisis in intergenerational relationships. Because of these difficulties facing both black and white families we studied, most grandparents did not want to become surrogate parents, and many took major steps to avoid that possibility. Both white and black grandparents usually concluded that they were at a time in life when such sacrifices were inappropriate.

Three factors influence responses of grandparents in those critical times when an adult child can no longer function as a parent. First, it should be pointed out that the grandparent role in times of family crisis is influenced by their cultural background, gender, and lineal relationship to their grandchildren. The grandparent role is derived, meaning that their access to their grandchildren and any actions they take must be consistent with the wishes of the parents of their grandchildren. In times of marital breakdown or failures in parenting, the mothers are usually the ones who are attempting to care for the children, whereas fathers leave the family and often surrender parental responsibility entirely. In fact, a national survey found that half of the fathers had no contact with their children a year after the divorce. One would expect that in cohabiting and casual unions, the father would be even more distant. Consequently, the mothers of daughters are more likely to have direct access to their grandchildren, so one assumes that they are the ones who *should* take over responsibility. The mothers of divorced sons, however, are more concerned about the symbolic and emotional significance of the blood tie to their grandchildren than they are about taking over some parenting functions.

Black grandparents in our studies tended to have more flexible definitions of lineal relationships. For practical purposes, a child is defined as "someone I raised," and a person not related biologically but raised is often closer to older blacks than a biological child. Consequently, their definition of who is a grandchild is even more flexible because of the tendency to define family relationships in functional terms. The children and grandchildren who function as a source of social and emotional support to older blacks may not necessarily be biological descendants. Having to take responsibility for the children of a child who has not fulfilled filial duties may be particularly difficult for black grandparents.

Second, in contrast to some ethnic groups in this country, in which members endorse strong norms of responsibility in intergenerational relationships, the role of grandparent in the average American family is regulated by weak and ambiguous social norms. Several popular books on how to grandparent reflect the uncertainties grandparents have about their role. Some researchers label the role as a state of mind or a matter of style rather than a functioning role with clear-cut expectations. Consequently, grandmothers can decide whether to be the fun-loving grandparent, an "Auntie Mame," or "a cookie-baking grandmother, an aproned woman laboring over a hot stove." Not surprisingly, today's grandmothers favor an image of youth and vitality in their role, not one of domesticity and nurturance. In fact, without clear-cut guidelines, the role must be achieved and personally defined, and most grandparents define the preferred role dominated by expressive rather than instrumental content. Where grandparents in actuality are forced to play a more important role as a stabilizing force in a child's family, they are uncertain as to how to proceed.

Although it borders on a truism to echo assumptions about self-reliance and independence, it needs to be emphasized that one dominant American value adheres to the mandate that children should become independent in early adulthood, and particularly after their marriage. On marriage, children are expected to form not only a separate household but one that is private and autonomous. Grandparents usually respect that autonomy and privacy and, where forced to intrude, for example, to help a grandchild during the divorce process, such privacy is violated. In fact, one grandmother echoed the stance of many, "I never drop in unannounced at my daughter's, because I'm afraid of what I'll find." In other cases, their adult child is undergoing a developmental regression in which he or she once again becomes dependent on a parent, an unanticipated situation that has unsettling consequences for the parent–adult child relationship. Consequently, the ambiguous role of a grandparent is likely to become even more ambiguous. Moreover, with no clear guidelines as to what they should do for their grandchildren, their actions are further constrained by the parents of their grandchildren. Thus, most grandparents are wary about their role.

Our analysis of how grandparents define their role indicates that prescriptive norms are accompanied by proscriptive norms. The do's and don'ts of grandparents are contradictory: "Be there to help but don't interfere," "Be an advocate but don't buy love," "Be loving but don't be too protective," "Babysit but don't nag," "Be fun to be with; don't be dull." The "should nots" of grandparenting seemed to be more detailed than the "shoulds," suggesting that grandparents understand more about what they should not do than what they should do. When forced not only to grandparent but to act as a parent, they have only diffuse and unspecific norms to guide them.

My third and last point concerns the midlife of the grandparents, that age period when they are likely to have younger grandchildren. We have long recognized that "the empty nest" after the last child leaves home is usually a time of positive change for middle-aged people. Rather than feelings of loss and abandonment, most parents today look forward to that point when their children become autonomous, so they can embark on new interests, travel, return to school, and new leisure activities. "It is time for me to take care of myself" reflects a common attitude among grandparents. At the time of life when other responsibilities diminish, their grandparent role tends to be of secondary interest. Grandparents today like to establish clear-cut boundaries between parenting and grandparenting. The following comments were frequently heard: "I've paid my dues. I don't want to repeat the parent role," "My grandchildren should learn moral values from me—their parents do the rest," "The best thing about being a grandparent is being able to send them home when they misbehave."

Among the people I have studied, those grandparents who had initially taken over parental responsibilities for their grandchildren no longer did so after three years. Their initial response was a stop-gap measure intended to be only a temporary arrangement until children straightened out their lives. Thus, grandparents who were forced to become surrogate parents rarely viewed this role as a lasting commitment, but rather they looked forward to the time they could enjoy their new freedoms. If their responsibilities persisted, conflict with children invariably arose, conflict accentuated because they are in a socially and culturally dissonant arrangement incongruent with family norms. Black grandparents expressed similar values on independence and norms about grandparenting as did the whites, and they too expressed the same reservations as white grandparents.

From this evidence, we need to be cautious about advocating that grandparents *should* take over full responsibility for the most important function of a family, that of raising children. The weight of the burden will fall on women and minorities. If this policy is widely accepted, it may have important implications during this period of changing policies about public versus personal responsibilities for dependent children. If such responsibilities are turned back to the family, public support may decrease, and some children will have no safety net. Suggesting that older family members assume full parental responsibility might fuel the current efforts at the federal level to cut family benefits.

Rejoinder to Professor Johnson JOAN F. ROBERTSON

My first reaction to the position taken by Colleen Johnson is to disagree with her view that the question under consideration implies insistent and inflexible emphasis on the *shoulds* of grandparenting rather than the maybes. The question implies no more than is intended, a spirit of inquiry and dialogue into the strengths and limitations of grandparents assuming full-time custodial care of grandparents when parents are unable or unwilling to care for them.

Second, is it really the case that there are many ambiguous issues surrounding grandparents in American society or that grandparents who assume custodial care of dependent grandchildren are performing a voluntary family role guided by conflicting expectations? Until fairly recently, the expectations of grandparents or relatives was quite clear and not ambiguous—children were the responsibility of their parents. As my opponent suggests, for the most part, grandparents are comfortable with the nonobligatory roles and functions that they assume in family life with regard to grandchildren. Some are not. In the absence of longitudinal research that compares intervention samples of grandparents with normal population samples controlling for factors such as social class, age, ethnicity, and race, one can only speculate that weak and ambiguous social norms regulate the behaviors and styles of grandparenting.

The recent proliferation of books on "how to grandparent" reflects the value of grandparenthood in the United States and the marketplace and consumer demand for self-help books. In fact, we know very little about the health and mental health status of grandparents who assume full-time care of grandchildren. We also know little about the pros and cons of these situations for children except to suggest that if child protective service was involved in the removal of the child from the parental home, the grandparent provides a safety net for the children. Most of what we know about grandparent as caregivers stems from intervention samples that are biased toward low-income women of color, particularly blacks. It is important to guard against generalizing the experiences and behaviors of those who receive public support to all grandparents.

Grandparents raising grandchildren is not a new phenomenon in the United States. Families of color, particularly African Americans, Hispanics and Native Americans, have informally reared grandchildren in the absence of parents for many years, many without ever receiving public support. Then, as now, grandparents did not welcome parental surrogate roles, nor were they pleased with the failure of their adult children to provide for their offspring. These families exhibited strong family norms and placed a high value on children, strengths that one seldom reads about in the family or aging literature.

What is different from the past is a dramatic increase in the number of grandparents parenting grandchildren. These numbers reflect family and societal changes—increases in poverty, alcohol and drug abuse, teen births, dramatic changes in family structures and family processes, and changes in child welfare laws protecting a child's right to family life by placement with grandparents or in kin foster homes. The momentum of turning responsibilities for child welfare back to the family in these cases is motivated by economic and political forces, not a deep concern for the welfare of children or elders. Grandparents parenting dependent children in the absence of parents must be provided with supportive services to protect the grandchild and the grandparent. Unless policies are backed with fiscal resources to provide programs and supportive services, the grandparent caregiving situation will seriously risk the health and well-being of both children and grandparents, and will result in a disproportionate burden on women and minorities. The public sector will be relieved of responsibility for major social structural problems and, once again, children and the vulnerable will be held responsible to alleviate or buffer major social and structural problems.

Is Gerontology Biased toward a Negative View of the Aging Process and Old Age?

EDITORS' NOTE: It is not uncommon for those who work in the field of aging to cite repeated examples of ageism in their daily work. Ageism refers to instances of stereotyping of and discrimination against older people sheerly on the basis of their age. These negative attitudes toward older persons can be exhibited both covertly and overtly, and both younger and older age-groups are guilty of fostering such perspectives. Although the origins of ageist myths about older persons are unknown, much of the gerontological research conducted during the 1940s and 1950s was based on samples of elderly who were incapacitated or institutionalized. Findings from these studies highlighted decline, illness, and vulnerability in the old-age population. Various forms of media also must bear some blame for our skewed views of old age, given the scarcity of roles given to older actors and actresses and the propensity, until recently, of the few available elderly television characters to reflect such qualities as unhappiness, failure, and other undesirable behaviors. Our public institutions continue to be challenged to separate myth from reality and fact from fallacy when it comes to perceptions of the aging experience. Are professionals in the field of aging as guilty as those around them in fostering a negative view of the old-age experience? Does the message transmitted by our scholarship continue to reflect pessimism and negativism?

Robert C. Atchley, Ph.D., says *YES.* He is Director of the Scripps Gerontology Center and Distinguished Professor of Gerontology at Miami University in Ohio. Joining Miami in 1966, Atchley quickly established a nationally known research program on adjustment to retirement. He published the first widely used textbook in social gerontology, *Social Forces in Aging,* and has published more than a dozen other books. Dr. Atchley is a past President of the American Society on Aging and the founding Editor of *Contemporary Gerontology: A Journal of Reviews and Critical Discourse.*

    M. Powell Lawton, Ph.D., says *NO.* He was Director of Research at the Philadelphia Geriatric Center for thirty years and is now Senior Research Scientist. He is also Adjunct Professor of Human Development at Pennsylvania State University and Professor of Psychiatry at the Medical College of Pennsylvania. He has done research in the environmental psychology of later life, in assessment of the aged, the psychological well-being and quality of life of older people, caregiving stress, and evaluative studies of programs for the aged and for the mentally ill. Dr. Lawton is a past President of the Gerontological Society of America, has published numerous books in the field, and is Editor-in-Chief of the *Annual Review of Gerontology and Geriatrics.*

YES

ROBERT C. ATCHLEY

It is important to acknowledge that the issue here is not whether gerontology is absolutely negative. No responsible observer would contend that gerontology presents no affirmative or positive results concerning aging. The issue is whether gerontology pays undue attention to negative outcomes or problems of aging and is thereby biased. My position is that the field of aging pays much more attention to negative aspects of aging than to positive ones and that, by neglecting positive aspects of aging, gerontology presents a distorted view of aging to itself and to the public.

    A negative view of aging dominates academic gerontology, the media, and public opinion. Despite ample evidence that aging has both positive and negative outcomes, and that negative outcomes are in the minority, scholarship in all areas of gerontology emphasizes "problem" aspects of aging and generally places a low priority on looking at areas in which positive results are most likely. Thus, writings on physical aging mostly deal with aging's relationship to illness, disability, mortality, health care delivery, and health spending. In recent times, more attention has been paid to prevention, rehabilitation, and compensation, but research and program funding still emphasize medical and service delivery interventions and ameliorative social policies and downplay the positive solutions to challenges of aging that elders are able to achieve on their own.

    Discussions of physical aging pay little attention to the issue of whether physical well-being is possible with a body that is functioning at considerably less than peak performance. In this regard, the self-reports of older people generally present a much more positive picture than the clinical literature leads us to expect. Gerontology tends to portray disabled elders as "cases" to be "managed," with little indication that many disabled elders can and do make their own choices and manage their own lives.

Discussions of psychological aging emphasize cognitive declines with aging, particularly diminished sensory capacity and slowing psychomotor performance and information processing. From time to time, rays of hope appear, only to be extinguished by the harsh light of research reality. For example, in the 1970s, studies suggested that some of the cognitive changes associated with aging might be spurious correlations that disappeared when education was held constant or when practiced skills were studied. However, subsequent studies showed that these hopes were just that, and by now most cognitive researchers believe that age-related cognitive declines are real and cannot be prevented. At the end of lengthy books summarizing these research results, brief statements sometimes acknowledge that most aging people retain more than sufficient capacity to function effectively as adults. But this possibility, that life may demand far less than peak performance, is given scant coverage in comparison with the number of pages devoted to detailing the deficits caused by aging. This anomaly says something important about the concept of negative change. Functions can decline with age and individuals can still be able to function adequately. Thus, negative changes do not necessarily have negative consequences.

The adult development literature is more optimistic and in general presents a more positive view of aging. Many developmental theories contend that development continues throughout adulthood and that older adults retain their capacity to adapt effectively to change. But these perspectives are counterbalanced by the views of scholars who see aging mainly in terms of negative themes such as learned helplessness, loss of control, and chronic depression.

Scholarship on social aspects of aging focuses on social problems associated with aging. Poverty, substandard housing, lack of transportation, poor nutritional status, isolation, need for meaningful activities, problems securing adequate health and long-term care, lack of community services and facilities, and vulnerability to crime, economic exploitation, fraud, elder abuse, and medical quackery are just a few of the social problems said to be confronting older Americans. That most older people experience none of these problems is seldom discussed.

From the standpoint of social policies, aging and older people are seen as a burden. Very seldom are elders seriously portrayed as essential or important contributors to society, although most are. Instead, they are portrayed as a drag on our economy through their need for Social Security and Medicare as well as Supplemental Security Income (SSI) and Medicaid. Medicare is seen as breaking the back of Social Security, and Medicaid for older people is seen as the major state budget-buster. The older population is erroneously held responsible for a long list of social ills, including poverty among children, the national debt and federal budget deficit, and our lack of national savings.

Why is gerontology so negative with regard to aging and the old? Academic researchers and teachers, program administrators and professional service providers, and government bureaucrats and policy makers all contribute to the overly negative image of aging and old age.

1) Academic researchers often need grants to do their research. Funding agencies rarely give research grants to document that all is well. Both government and foundation research funders concentrate their scarce research dollars on developing information that can be used to solve problems and meet needs; therefore, they focus their funding priorities on problems associated with aging. It is assumed that, with better information, the problems can be fixed.

Researchers who want to study aspects of aging that are not a problem are not likely to get grants. As a result, the research that gets done is heavily biased toward problem aspects of aging, which by definition are usually negative.

2) Academic journals are usually open to both good and bad news about aging. But grant funding is also used to buy the time to write articles reporting the research as well. The bias toward negative reports in academic journals is thus mostly the result of who has time to write articles, and this ties back to what research topics are funded. For example, *The Gerontologist* is one of two major journals of the Gerontological Society of America, the premiere organization of researchers in the field of aging. In 1994, ninety-four of the ninety-nine substantive articles published in this journal concerned "problem" aspects of aging such as caregiver burden, Alzheimer's disease or other dementias, suicide, elder abuse, service delivery problems, long-term care issues, income problems, family problems, and so forth. Most of these articles acknowledged external financial support from government or private foundations.

3) Gerontology students are not planning on making a living watching healthy, competent elders successfully cope with what life brings. Most gerontology students plan to take up work aimed at meeting the needs of elders who need help. They plan to run agencies, provide professional services, or make policies that structure or finance services. These vocationally focused students are not very interested in the large majority of older people who live independently in the community without anyone's help. They want to know about the population they will be serving. They want an education biased toward negative outcomes and problems of aging.

4) Service providers who deal with frail and disabled elders make powerful witnesses. The struggles of disabled elders, and the conflicts raging within those who are responsible for helping them, create natural dramas that can be mesmerizing. Stories of elders conned out of their life's savings by scam artists can raise strong emotions. By contrast, tales of aging as gentle slope and later life as a satisfying enterprise filled with new life meaning play to a smaller audience. Action films generally do much better at the box office compared with slow-moving, thought-provoking stories. Our penchant for violence and tension in films reflects our morbid interest in the negative side of life, and gerontology's negative bias may be just an extension of this general cultural predisposition.

5) Even gerontologists in the humanities tend to focus on ethical dilemmas and conflicts, not on explaining amazing moral victories such as the fact that most adult children quietly and patiently make great sacrifices to care for their aging parents.

6) Social policy actors—legislators and their staff workers, government agency personnel, the gray lobby, the anti–gray lobby—see aging as a set of policy issues that are in competition with other issues. Not only are the needs of elders justified by citing negative effects of aging, but the growing size of the older population and the costs of their income security, health care, and long-term care needs create a double-negative valence on aging because the needs of aging people seem to be crowding out other desirable policy goals such as better care of our nation's children, lowering the national debt, or promoting economic growth.

The negative focus of gerontology probably stems from several sources. An 1) underlying ageism became prevalent around the turn of the twentieth century. It was based on erroneous views of aging as inevitable decline. Although many of the presumed "facts" that gave rise to ageism have been discredited or substantially qualified by research done since 1950, the culture today still contains strong beliefs that aging inevitably results in declining physical and mental capacity and loss of entitlement to full adult status. The entire institution of retirement was constructed to deal with the negative effects of age discrimination in employment that followed from these beliefs.

Also, a negative stereotype of illness, poverty, and isolation among elders was emphasized by early advocates for the older population in pushing for enactment of ameliorative legislation such as Social Security. Even gerontologists sometimes hold negative stereotypes about aspects of aging that are outside their fields of expertise. The negativity of gerontology also stems from the fact that 3) gerontologists are products of their society. Long before students begin to study gerontology, they experience many years of negative indoctrination about aging and old age. The images of aging we see just in television commercials constitute relentless negative conditioning. For example, physical aging is associated with denture adhesive, constipation, and leaky bladders. No one in their right mind would allow themselves to have wrinkled skin or gray hair. You certainly do not embrace aging; you fight it. Mental aging is illustrated by the goofy behavior that can be associated with senile dementia. By young adulthood, most Americans are conditioned to see aging as something to be dreaded, avoided, and denied, and to see older people as suffering from numerous social ills. It should not be surprising that these people go on to find negativity when they study aging. What is more surprising is that, in this environment, gerontology contains as many positive portrayals of aging as it does.

Rejoinder to Professor Atchley
M. Powell Lawton

My good friend Robert Atchley and I agree so much on the good news inherent in the aging process that it is curious to see us on different sides of the fence in interpreting the predominant tone of modern gerontology. We both enumerate the same litany of negatives that have plagued our discipline and we both note a host of positive features of aging. Yet, I see the glass as half full; he sees it as half empty.

I note that Atchley chose not to refer to his own very influential continuity theory (Atchley, 1987). Perhaps there was more than a trace of humility in this omission. Just as notable an explanation for the omission, however, is the fact that continuity is the essence of self-direction, a highly positive conception of the aging process, and continuity sells! Atchley's many depictions of the positive in human aging have been detailed in some of the all-time best sellers in the gerontological literature. His own productiveness and emphasis on what is right about growing old have influenced all gerontology and have been major contributors to what I see as "mature gerontology." So his position on the age-bias side ignores some of that most potent evidence.

When Atchley moves on to target academic researchers, students, service providers, ethicists, and policy makers. I have to concede him a few. It is a vulnerable spot in all of us. However, do look at what has happened in the branch of the National Institutes of Health (NIH) most concerned with our topic, the National Institute on Aging (NIA). Despite the NIH's general pull toward the study of poor health, it is the NIA to whom virtually all social scientists go for their support in conducting research on cognitive training, wisdom, attachment to place, intergenerational exchange, psychological well-being, self-efficacy, selectivity behavior, and many of the other assets seen by Atchley as neglected in gerontological research.

Why do Atchley and I take opposite positions on the bias questions, despite our looking at much of the same evidence? I suggest that the developmental trend of gerontology toward recognizing all that is good about old age is discernible and that it promises an even clearer plurality of good news about aging as the science continues to develop. The current trend and its promise for the future justify the position that gerontology has lost its negative bias.

NO

M. Powell Lawton

Gerontology has had its own developmental history. Like the developing person, the field itself can be said to have learned a few things over the approximately sixty years of its modern history. Scientific evidence is the focal issue in considering whether there has been age bias in the social structures that produce knowledge about aging. Therefore, at the very beginning we must dissociate two separate phenomena: negative facts about old age and negative bias in the pursuit and dissemination of knowledge. If knowledge shows something negative about aging, it is still a fact, not a bias. I plead that we not direct anger at the messenger who bears bad news.

Age bias, however, takes many forms. There are four main avenues potentially leading to age bias: (1) an incomplete or oversimplified approach to generating knowledge; (2) choosing only the negative aspects of aging for research attention; (3) overemphasis on reporting knowledge with negative implications for aging and old age; and (4) pursuit of a research agenda determined by political rather than scientific considerations. Gerontologists may have at one time contributed to these four types of age bias, but the field has overcome its early negative social stereotypes of old age. This section documents the developments that have led to the present enlightened state of gerontological research.

Oversimplified Questions

Basic statuses such as gender, marital status, and age constitute very appealing foci for research because they are admirably objective and accessible to ascertainment. What, then, could have been more reasonable than to initiate research that asked whether people of differing ages also differed on a whole variety of biological, psychological, social, cultural, and economic variables? Gerontology would never have had its start if there had not been a cohort of researchers who simply documented how people of differing ages differed (or did not differ) on such diverse measures as autonomic functions, skinfold thickness, abstract thinking, or living arrangement.

During this early period, the importance of health was unrecognized, and many studies showing age decrements when comparing old and young ignored health as an explanatory phenomenon. The landmark study at the National Institute of Mental Health (Birren, et al., 1963) provided the model for separating age and health. Even more importantly, it was not until the 1960s that the critical factors of age, cohort, and period in history were differentiated. Schaie (1974) and his colleagues set gerontology straight once and for all: The full story on age change can only be investigated by consideration of which age *differences* are related to the common experiences of an age cohort, the influences of historical and social changes over time shared by people of all ages, and true age changes. "The myth of intellectual decline" has been demythologized by well-controlled longitudinal research, whose findings indicate that intellectual changes were greatly overestimated. A whole series of studies and critical literature reviews have been based on such findings and have led to the reduction of age bias in employment, job retention, and job advancement. By my rough estimate, it took less than a generation of such research to begin to address the age-differences question in its deserved complexity. This revised question then became, are there phenomena that are caused by age that can be distinguished from those that are age related but not caused by age?

Choice of Negative Aspects of Aging for Research

A historical look at gerontological publications shows a progression that ran very much in parallel with the increase in sophistication in research design discussed earlier. Once having teased out artifacts from the apparent age-equals-decline conclusion, gerontological research has turned with a sense of mission to the task of directing study toward the processes that enhance the quality of age.

Ego-protective processes have been the focus of research dealing with positive states throughout the life span. We should not forget that two of the most ubiquitous constructs in gerontological research have been "morale" and "life satisfaction." Both the names and significant portions of the content of the dominant measures of these constructs clearly direct our attention to positive mental health.

Over the years since the introduction of these constructs, there have been steady streams of research devoted to the search for the positive. Robert Atchley's continuity theory portrays the active role that older people take in directing their everyday lives. Currently, a new look at psychological well-being idealizes autonomy, environmental mastery, personal growth, positive relations with others, purpose in life, and self-acceptance as definers (Ryff, 1989). Affect experiences on the positive side have been reinstated into our conceptions of psychological well-being (Lawton, 1989). Whereas gerontology focused for years on major loss events as characteristic of old age, the importance of positive events has been recognized (Zautra, Affleck, & Tennen, 1994). On an even more generalized level, the processes of "selective optimization with compensation" (Baltes, 1991) give central positions to the older person's ability to actively direct his or her life, to exercise good judgment in adapting to losses, and to maintain expertise in the life tasks considered important. A major study of productivity among older people continues to be reported (Herzog, Kahn, Morgan, Jackson, & Antonucci, 1989).

Selective Reporting of Negatively Toned Knowledge

The foregoing discussions should lead to the value-neutral conclusion that what gets published reflects the research being performed. Gerontology as a developing discipline published more bad-news reports in its earlier years, but a decreasing proportion as the science grew.

Political Uses of Research and Publication Agenda

This may be where the gerontological community is vulnerable to the criticism of bias. For example, when research funding is provided to determine how families could bear a greater portion of the burden of caring for an impaired elder in the community, it is difficult to ignore that potential source of research support. Just examine what actually happened in this case, however. The political push for more family care (and fewer public-fund expenditures) began in 1980. Since that time, the overwhelming amount of research on family care and community residence has actually documented far better than we had known previously the extent to which elders *contribute* support to the broader family and the mutual adaptations that caregivers and care receivers make. If we needed any further destruction of the myths of family abandonment and one-way assistance given to elders, these fifteen years of research have provided it.

Where Is the Bad News?

The accentuations of the positive, in growing number, stand out to this observer. Nonetheless, as scientists we cannot ignore chronic disease, activity limitations, slowing of some cognitive processes, interpersonal losses, social ageism, selective deprivations of the poor and some minority elders, the high cost of medical care, and so on. Is it negative age biasing to study and bring these problems to the attention of both gerontologists and the general public? Clearly, they have to be identified if they are to be ameliorated. They are age biasing only if they are offered as the sole characterizations of the quality of older life.

As a conclusion, let us review a few examples of how gerontology has counteracted that impression:

> *Old age is poor health.* Countless studies of the healthy aged and avenues toward optimizing their daily functioning have been performed.
>
> *Activity limitations.* Ethel Shanas (1962) began, and many have followed, to remind us that most elders are independent in their everyday lives.
>
> *Cognitive decline.* As noted earlier, cognitive decline of most types that affect everyday adjustment have been definitively identified with illness, not age.
>
> *Interpersonal loss.* Despite the reality and the tragedy of bereavement, enforced retirement, and other types of loss, the dominant research conclusions document the resiliency of most older people.
>
> *Social ageism.* Interestingly, the more specific the research investigating age biases on a personal level, the more verification there has been of an absence of age bias, or even a positive age bias (Crockett & Hummert, 1987). Although there is clearly more bias on a social structural level,

gerontologists have chipped away at such practices as employment bias, racial "double jeopardy," and so on.

In conclusion, no one can deny that there is a negative side of aging in some arenas. Research documenting loss is necessary to design counteractive strategies. Seen in historical perspective, gerontology has contributed heavily to the unfolding of the positive aspects of personal aging and the positive contributions made by elders to the larger society.

REFERENCES

Atchley, R. C. (1987). *Aging: Continuity and change.* Belmont, CA: Wadsworth Press.

Baltes, P. M. (1991). The many faces of human aging: Toward a psychological culture of old age. *Psychological Medicine, 21,* 837–854.

Birren, J. E., Butler, R. N., Greenhouse, S. W., Sokoloff, L. & Yarrow, M. (1963). *Human Aging.* PHS Publication No. 986. Washington, D.C.: National Institute of Mental Health.

Crockett, W. H., & Hummert, M. L. (1987). Perceptions of aging and the elderly. In K. W. Schaie (Ed.), *Annual Review of Gerontology and Geriatrics* (Vol. 7). New York: Springer Publishing Company.

Herzog, A. R., Kahn, R. L., Morgan, J. N., Jackson, J. S., & Antonucci, T. C. (1989). Age differences in productive activities. *Journal of Gerontology: Social Sciences, 44,* S129–S138.

Lawton, M. P. (1989). Environmental proactivity and affect in older people. In S. Spacapan and S. Oskamp (Eds.), *Social psychology of aging* (pp. 135–164). Newbury Park, CA: Sage.

Ryff, C. D. (1989). Happiness is everything, or is it? Explorations on the meaning of psychological well-being. *Journal of Personality and Social Psychology, 57,* 1069–1081.

Schaie, K. W. (1974). Translations in gerontology—From lab to life: Intellectual functioning. *American Psychologist, 29,* 802–807.

Shanas, E. (1962). *The health of older people.* Cambridge MA: Howard University Press.

Zautra, A. J., Affleck, G., & Tennen, H. (1994). Assessing life events among older adults. In M. P. Lawton and J. A. Teresi (Ed.), *Annual review of gerontology and geriatrics* (Vol. 14, pp. 324–352). New York: Springer Publishing Co.

Rejoinder to Professor Lawton
ROBERT C. ATCHLEY

Powell Lawton and I are both optimists who have been fully open to the positive side of aging, and who have both done significant work establishing that older people generally cope well with a variety of presumably negative changes, for example, physical and mental aging, disability, housing relocation, retirement, or widowhood. I agree that much of the empirical work that looks for positive outcomes finds them. I disagree that there is a growing balance of attention paid to both positive and negative possibilities. I also disagree concerning how far we have come in eliminating incomplete or oversimplified conceptualizations of aging, being open to both positive and negative aspects of aging, and being balanced in reporting both positive and negative research results. Lawton does not address the negative bias that occurs as a result of gerontology's predisposition to look at aging as a set of problems that need to be solved.

Lawton loads the dice by singling out the exceptional investigators who have taken a balanced view. These researchers are exemplars of how to do a proper job of being willing to look for positive as well as negative outcomes and looking at aging as an opportunity as well as a problem. But the bulk of work in gerontology portrays a different picture. For example, excluding papers dealing with research methods, in 1994, the *Journal of Gerontology: Psychological Sciences* published thirty-six substantive research papers, of which 58 percent (twenty-one) took a neutral, "just give me the facts" approach. The remaining 42 percent (fifteen) took a "problem" approach to aging. But in the *Journal of Gerontology: Social Sciences,* only 21 percent of the twenty-nine research reports were balanced or not problem oriented, and in the *Journal of Gerontology: Clinical Medicine,* only 5 percent of the thirty-seven reports published were oriented toward balanced or nonproblem aspects. Most areas of gerontology still contain many oversimplified and overly negative statements of research results or approach aging mainly as a social problem.

If we look at the contents of the professional journals over time, we can see a growing conceptual and methodological sophistication, better sampling, better research designs, better statistical methods, and other improvements. But the list of topics in the 1994 volumes of *The Gerontologist* and the *Journal of Gerontology* were dominated by a problem orientation to aging every bit as much as the 1974 volumes.

Lawton contends that the negative balance in portrayals of aging results from the realities of aging. But how then do we account for the absence of topics such as establishing life meaning, preserving self-esteem, the contributions elders make to their communities, the role elders play as spiritual mentors, and a host of other important but neglected topics? The realities of aging do not fund research or write research reports; researchers do. And researchers' choices of topics do not occur in a vacuum. If a researcher wants to succeed, he or she must be aware of the topics that funding agencies have set as their research priorities. And the research priorities of funding agencies are tied to political or ideological definitions of aging as a set of problems in need of solution.

Retirement research is a good example. Gerontological research from the 1960s and 1970s strongly contradicted the "common knowledge" that retirement increased the probability of physical and mental illness or death. This robust finding was repeated in several well-done studies. But the finding that retirement had no substantial negative effects on physical and mental health led to a sharp reduction in funding for research on retirement. If retirement is not a problem, why spend scarce research funds to study it? Studies of retirement are relatively sparse today, compared with the 1970s. Thus, we have relatively few studies of how the changing economic realities of the 1980s or 1990s have affected the experience of retirement. These trends are not just a by-product of the "realities" of retirement; they reflect a politics of gerontology.

As research funding has become scarcer and scarcer, it has become more and more difficult to justify research that does not presume to address a serious physical, mental, or social problem associated with aging. In this context, where is the space for studies that look at self-reliance, at enlightenment, or at creativity or wisdom among older people?

Aging is a double-edged sword that can be both positive or negative. To have a realistic gerontology, we must be able to devote equal attention to both potentials. But the problem-centered, overly biomedical research agenda of current gerontology prevents us from giving equal attention to the positive potentials of aging.

Should Gerontology Be Considered a Separate Profession?

Editors' Note: A number of decisions face students preparing for careers in service to older adults. Among them is determining the most advantageous route to take in terms of educational preparation and the securing of credentials that will be valued by prospective employers. Should the individual be trained in a traditional profession such as social work, public health, or business administration with a subspecialization in gerontological practice, or should that individual pursue his or her education in an educational program whose primary focus is gerontology? This decision, certainly not an easy one, should be determined in no small part by whether one considers gerontology to be an emergent domain of professional practice in its own right. Such a question has been debated for a number of years among gerontological educators. It remains a matter worthy of consideration.

Pamela Francisco Wendt, Ph.D., and David A. Peterson, Ph.D., say *YES.* Dr. Wendt is a Research Assistant Professor at the Andrus Gerontology Center at the University of Southern California in Los Angeles. Originally educated and credentialed as a registered dietitian, she has become a multidisciplinary-educated gerontologist. Her teaching, research, and publications focus on the areas of professional gerontology, gerontological education, and nutrition and aging. Dr. Peterson is Director of the Leonard Davis School of Gerontology and Associate Dean of the Andrus Gerontology Center. As Professor of Gerontology and Education, he has had four research grants from the Administration on Aging, which have focused on the extent, consistency, and operation of educational programming in gerontology. Dr. Peterson regularly teaches a graduate course on professional issues in gerontology and has authored a book in the area titled *Career Paths in the Field of Aging.*

Jordon I. Kosberg, Ph.D., says *NO.* He is Professor and Coordinator of the Ph.D. Program in the School of Social Work at Florida International University (North Miami) and Faculty Associate in the University's Southeast Center on Aging. He is a member of the editorial board of the *Journal of Gerontological Social Work* and a Fellow of the Gerontological Society of America, and he has been elected to the board of directors for the National Committee for Gerontology in Social Work Education. He has published extensively, including six books on elder abuse and maltreatment, working with and for the aged, family care of the elderly, international aging, and elderly men.

YES

Pamela Francisco Wendt
David A. Peterson

In this article, we support the statement that gerontology should be considered a separate profession. Our emphasis is on the phrase "should be considered," rather than attempting to convince the reader that gerontology "is currently" a separate profession. Our report is divided into two sections. In the first, we discuss the nature of professions and present evidence that gerontology is acquiring the necessary attributes of a profession. In the second, we identify the need for and value of gerontology becoming a profession.

Gerontology Is Becoming a Profession

Professions typically have a developmental pattern that results in a common set of attributes. Although there are numerous descriptions of a profession, the Carr-Saunders and Wilson (1964) model (Figure 18.1) incorporates this developmental pattern particularly well and allows us to show how an employment area, moving from left to right, becomes more professionalized as it acquires specific characteristics. Rather than designating an employment area as being or not being a profession, this model allows us to track progress toward and refer to the degree of professionalization.

As the left side of the figure indicates, professions are full-time occupations, often supported by government and private funding sources. In gerontology, this occurred in 1965 with the passage of Medicare, Medicaid, and the Older Americans Act, which provided funding for individuals who planned, conducted, coordinated, evaluated, and advocated for services and programs for older people. Federal and state support was supplemented by private and corporate foundations, and a modest legislative appropriation grew to nearly a billion dollars annually,

Full-time occupation	Body of literature	Accreditation of academic programs	
	Formal university training program	Fee for service	
Full-time occupation	Academic journals disseminating knowledge	Specific body of literature	Formal association with strict entrance requirements
Appeals, foundations, etc.	Formal association with flexible requirements	Promulgates specific legislation	State licensure required

◄───►

Nonprofessionalized or Deprofessionalization	Would-be Professionals	Semi-professionals	New Professionals	Established Professionals	Professionalization

FIGURE 18.1 ILLUSTRATION OF A CONTINUUM MODEL OF PROFESSIONALIZATION. Carr-Saunders and Wilson, 1964. *The Professions.*

employing tens of thousands of professionals serving older adults and their families in public and private organizations as well as in private practice, where a *fee for service* is collected.

Carr-Sanders and Wilson suggest that professions can be distinguished from occupations by the amount of specialized knowledge and skills that must be mastered before becoming an effective practitioner. Occupations typically involve on-the-job learning, whereas professions require formal college or university pre-service education. The acquisition of this professional knowledge and skill is usually verified by professional and governmental bodies (certification or licensure). The value of professionals with specific gerontological knowledge and skill was recognized in the most recent version of the Older American's Act. In section 307(a)(11)(B), it states, "special consideration shall be given to individuals with formal training in the field of aging (including an educational specialty or emphasis in aging and a training degree or certificate in aging) or equivalent professional experience in the field of aging."

The body of specialized knowledge rapidly increased as information from research and professional practice became available. The first comprehensive compilation of aging knowledge was undertaken in the late 1950s with the publication of the *Handbook of Social Gerontology* (Tibbitts, 1960), *Handbook of Aging and the Individual* (Birren, 1959), and *Aging in Western Societies* (Burgess, 1960). Three decades later, the handbooks are no longer a comprehensive compilation but are limited to the biology, psychology, and social sciences of aging. In addition to these disciplinary surveys, more than 10 thousand books and a hundred journals address such applied areas of practice as direct services, program planning and evaluation, administration, and policy development in health, mental health, and social services, as well as in industrial, financial, and entrepreneurial gerontology.

Since the late 1950s, classification of the knowledge base has been along disciplinary lines. This changed in 1992 when the Association for Gerontology in Higher Education (AGHE) put forth six transdisciplinary themes that reflected a significant maturing of the educational field and the profession: diversity and contexts, theories and frameworks, stability and directions of change, ethical issues, scholarship and research, and application (Wendt, Peterson, & Douglass, 1993). They are evidence of the development of an integrated knowledge base compared with the previous segmented one.

College and university instruction in professional gerontology got its initial support when the U.S. Administration on Aging (AoA) used its financial support to encourage institutions of higher education to develop instructional programs leading to separate degrees in gerontology, aging, and human development. A 1991 national survey of institutions of higher education indicated that there were 185 degree/major programs in gerontology, with 730 others offering specializations, minors, or certificates in aging for students majoring in other fields (Peterson, Wendt, and Douglass, 1994). A large proportion of these have a professional orientation, systematically teaching the facts, concepts, and principles embodied in the knowledge base, as well as including a supervised practicum/internship experience in which knowledge is applied to the needs of older persons.

AGHE has been actively involved in improving the quality of college and university education in gerontology. It has developed curriculum and program development standards and guidelines, published instructional materials, and conducted faculty development workshops. Currently being studied are alternative mechanisms for recognizing educational programs that meet national criteria for quality and relevance (e.g., accreditation, voluntary seal of approval).

Membership associations in aging were organized as early as 1945, with the American Society on Aging (10 thousand members) and the National Council on the Aging being the largest organizations. Membership in these organizations is virtually unrestricted, being open to all persons working or interested in the field of aging. In 1994, the Association of Professional Gerontologists (APG) began organizing. Its professional membership is restricted to individuals with college or university education in gerontology, who work in the field of aging, and who identify themselves as professional gerontologists. When fully operational, professional gerontologists, as members of APG, will adhere to a Code of Ethical Practice and be subject to peer review of their professional practice. APG is also developing plans to initiate a credentialing process that will recognize those professionals who have acquired the specialized knowledge and skills necessary to practice effectively as entry-level registered professional gerontologists. State licensure has not yet been attempted by any group of professional gerontologists. It is expected to be a future step that will not be undertaken until a national organization such as APG is fully functional in credentialing gerontology professionals.

Based on the existence of a specific body of knowledge taught in college and university educational programs, academic journals, formal associations, fee for services, and legislative activity, it can be seen that gerontology is becoming professionalized. Using the Carr-Saunders and Wilson model, gerontology falls on the continuum between new and established professions and is moving toward becoming a full profession.

Gerontology Should Be a Profession

A profession develops when there is a need for specialized services, even when its functions are not completely unique; frequently there is considerable overlap among related professionals. The profession exists, however, because it has a characteristic role that is needed and valued. Gerontology, for example, has a characteristic role, although numerous other professionals also contribute to its practice by applying their own skills to benefit older adults. However, their professional education lacks in-depth knowledge of the complex and interrelated nature of older persons. Gerontologists know more about aging and its impact on individuals; therefore, they provide services and develop programs in more effective ways. They are aware of the successes and failures of previous programs; they are familiar with the special service delivery system for the elderly; they know government policies that affect older persons and their families; and they are aware of the diversity requiring service delivery professionals who are familiar with the uniqueness of older people.

Conclusion

Gerontology continues to acquire the characteristics of established professions, and because our society needs and increasingly appreciates the distinctive services that professional gerontologists offer, it should be considered a separate profession. Moreover, professional gerontologists contribute to the effectiveness of agencies and institutions, and they should be recognized as professionals.

REFERENCES

Birren, J. E. (Ed.). (1959). Handbook of aging and the individual. Chicago, IL: University of Chicago Press.

Burgess, E. W. (Ed.). (1960). *Aging in western societies.* Chicago, IL: University of Chicago Press.

Carr-Saunders, A. M., & Wilson, P. A. (1964). *The professions.* London: Frank Cass & Co.

McLeran, H., Pope, H., Logan, H., & Jakobsen, J. (No date). *Career pathways for graduates of midwestern gerontology programs.* Iowa City: University of Iowa.

Peterson, D. A., Wendt, P. F., & Douglass, E. B. (1994). *Development of gerontology, geriatrics, and aging studies programs in institutions of higher education.* Washington, DC: Association for Gerontology in Higher Education.

Wendt, P. F., Peterson, D. A., & Douglass, E. B. (1993). *Core principles and outcomes of gerontology, geriatrics and aging studies instruction.* Washington, DC: Association for Gerontology in Higher Education.

Tibbits, C. (Ed.). (1960). *Handbook of social gerontology.* Chicago, IL: University of Chicago Press.

Rejoinder to Professor Peterson and Professor Wendt

Jordan I. Kosberg

The argument given by Wendt and Peterson in support of gerontology as a profession is based—in part—on the historical development of gerontological education (driven by government funding), the existence of (unspecified) special knowledge and skills, and surveys of those working in the aging field and graduates of gerontology programs. I remain unconvinced that gerontology should be a profession, based on either meeting the criteria of a profession or because of any imperatives for such a profession.

Although I am better convinced that there is specialized knowledge, rather than skills, for those working in the aging field, it is still unclear whether only "professional" gerontologists (that is, those from gerontology programs) would possess such attributes. Furthermore, I am not certain that the existence of membership organizations, academic journals, and fee for services are necessary criteria of a profession. And I am also not certain whether AOA or AGHE had envisioned gerontology to be a profession (or currently see that as a high priority). Although it is suggested that there is a move toward national standards (with a code of ethics, peer review, and credentialing process) by the Association of Professional Gerontologists (APG), it is not known whether these efforts are related to the employment interests of APG members or whether a significant proportion of those working in the aging field will be APG members.

Let there be no doubt, those who work with elderly persons need to be skilled (and knowledgeable and well motivated). But what are these special skills, and are they taught only in gerontology programs, and do only graduates of such programs possess such skills? Although 80 percent of those working in the aging field or graduates of gerontology programs believe aging knowledge is necessary, why only 80 percent? I will not quibble with the authors' assumption that those with education in aging and old aged can provide or plan more effective types of intervention (although empirical verification would be welcome), but does this education come only from gerontology programs, or can it come from gerontological content integrated into more traditional academic and professional programs?

Finally, an age-specific professional focus may stigmatize and discriminate against that population it intends to help. Should the goal of gerontological education be the preparation of a relatively few "professionals" or the enlightenment of the majority (many of whom will find themselves—rather unexpectedly— working in the aging field)?

Although Wendt and Peterson envision gerontology to be between a new profession and an established profession, I see it as a semi-profession. Gerontology lacks uniformity, controls, exclusivity, and many other characteristics of a profession. And an unambiguous and undisputable imperative to support the notion that gerontology should be a profession is lacking as well.

NO

Jordan I. Kosberg

It is inappropriate to view gerontology as a profession, necessitating specialized programs and gerontological degrees, inasmuch as gerontology does not meet the criteria for a profession, has not generated the number of graduates to fill the increasing number of personnel needed in the aging field, and cannot produce widespread awareness of (and sensitivity to) aging and old age in contemporary society. Increased and broader attention to gerontology within higher education is best accomplished through the integration of such content within traditional academic disciplines and professional schools rather than in specific gerontology programs.

Definitions of a Profession

Over the years there have been many descriptions and definitions of a profession. Greenwood (1957) indicated that there are five components of professionalization: a systematic body of theory, professional authority, sanction of the community, a regulative code of ethics, and a professional culture. Wilensky and Lebeaux (1965) stated that a profession claims exclusive possession of competence in a particular area that results from a systematic body of skill and knowledge acquired over a lengthy period of "prescribed training." Additionally, a profession represents a monopoly of skills that are related to training standards and practice competence, and to moral integrity ensured by a professional code of ethics.

Although professions exist along a continuum of professionalization, it does not appear that gerontology meets the basic criteria by which to be considered a profession. Simply put, there is no systematic body of knowledge, no monopoly of skills, no exit examinations for graduates and entrance examinations for those entering the aging field, and no codes of ethical imperatives. Moreover, not only is there reason to question whether gerontology should be considered a profession, but there is also reason to wonder whether it represents a discipline with its own theory, body of knowledge, research methodology, and practice skills. Atchley (1985) has written that gerontology, as an academic discipline, "shares concepts, theoretical perspectives, classifications, factual knowledge, and research methods with other social sciences...." Is "sharing" sufficient for designation as a discipline?

Lack of Standardization

Generally, there are no standards to be met by educational programs in gerontology (a criterion for a profession). Without accreditation standards for gerontological programs, and minimum requirements for graduates, there has been some concern about the great variation in such education. Standards would require a minimum level of preparation and commonality of education for those who become (and are considered to be) gerontologists—whether in academia, practice, or in other settings. Although many persons who consider themselves gerontologists have received substantial preparation in higher education, many others working in the aging field have not had such preparation.

The need for accreditation standards for gerontology programs has been debated over the years. In 1985, Seltzer advocated for accreditation of gerontology programs and raised questions about the criteria to be used for accreditation, the accrediting organization, and the accreditation of practitioners (Seltzer, 1985). Although curricula have been suggested for gerontology programs, the Association for Gerontology in Higher Education (AGHE) has not set accrediting requirements for programs or credentials for graduates and seems reluctant to do so. As such, there is great variation in gerontology programs and the graduates from such programs.

Challenges to and from Gerontology Programs

Several potential problems result from the existence of gerontology programs. First of all, such programs can suffer from a lack of understanding by some faculty from other disciplines and some university administrators, who view the program as no different than other "fringe disciplines," such as Women's Studies and Afro-American Studies. Faced with misunderstanding, whenever a university budget faces strains, undergraduate and graduate gerontology programs have often faced the prospects of being discontinued or being "downsized" (which threatens the educational goals and integrity of the program). Additionally, Rich, Connelly, and Douglass (1990) have indicated that the diversity of names under which gerontology programs are being offered (i.e., aging studies, elderly services programs, human life programs) has confused students (and others) and hinders the understanding and acceptance of the subject area.

2/ A second problem is that often gerontology programs represent a sociopsychological focus as opposed to a biomedical focus, and an applied educational focus (i.e., middle-management, recreation workers, housing administrators) as opposed to a theoretical or research-oriented focus. This has accorded the gerontology programs (and degrees) a lower status on campuses where biomedical developments (especially in geriatric medicine) are proceeding rather rapidly (Estes & Binney, 1989).

3/ Third, programs in gerontology can be seen to offer only limited generic skill preparation for those preparing for mid-management or mental health counseling positions in programs and services for the elderly. Thus, not only do graduates compete with those from more traditional academic and professional disciplines who have specific skill training (in such disciplines as social work, management, public administration, nursing, psychological counseling, etc.), but their career options tend to be limited to the field of gerontology, and they do not have the same career options as those with specific preparation from more traditional disciplines and professions.

4) Fourth, when there are programs in aging, educators and administrators in other academic units may believe that there is no need for gerontology courses in their programs. Indeed, at one university, in the college within which exists a department of gerontology (a college that includes departments of social work, sociology, psychology, and anthropology, among others) there are no other specific courses in aging and old age. Inasmuch as there may be few students from outside disciplines taking courses from programs in gerontology, the existence of such programs may have the unintended consequence of reducing the probability of nongerontology students being introduced to material on aging and old age.

5/ A fifth area of concern pertains to the possibility that the perception of gerontology as a profession (or a discipline) may deter student interest. This is to suggest that gerontology can be viewed as the antithesis of professional education and training (Kosberg & Harris, 1984). Most professional programs educate students for the rehabilitation, restoration, convalescence, and other improvements in the condition of clients and patients. Pessimism may exist regarding the ability of elderly populations to respond to professional assistance in a relatively quick, dramatic, and easy manner, and of the results to endure for a number of years. Admittedly, such a perception is both unfair and incorrect, but it can keep individuals away from gerontology programs.

Sixth, and somewhat related, there are those who believe that any gerontologically based educational program (or service, policy, or organization, for that matter) is guilty of ageism (Binstock, 1983; Neugarten, 1979), for it stigmatizes and artificially removes the elderly from a more normative life-span perspective. Preferred would be aging content integrated into more generic, less age-specific courses and programs of studies. Such educational content and practice would be based on function, rather than chronological age (although electives or special courses could be available for those who are motivated to seek coursework on aging and old age).

An Integrated Approach to Gerontology

Gerontological knowledge should be integrated within the content of non–age-specific courses and gerontology courses integrated into traditional academic disciplines and professional programs, so as to retain a normative life-span perspective. In addition to the infusion of gerontology into generic courses, specializations in aging are advocated for academic and professional education. Such concentrations would ensure adequate education and training for those wishing to pursue careers in aging and old age (whether as researchers, teachers, or practitioners), as well as a core of courses that focus on generic principles, skills, and methodologies of the specific discipline or profession. Graduates represent their field, first (as social workers, psychologists, physical therapists, nurses, sociologists); specialists in gerontology, second. Thus, regardless of the job prospects in the field of aging, or the recognition of gerontology as a discipline or profession, the graduates have a conventional degree in their discipline or profession and have the (research, clinical, theoretical) skills that can be applied to all populations, including the aged. Both the specialization model and the integrated model, which would inculcate all courses with gerontological content, are preferable to gerontology degree programs for educating both future professionals and future citizens who will be familiar with, and sensitive to, contemporary gerontological issues.

Conclusion

It has been argued that gerontology cannot be considered a profession because it fails to have a systematic body of knowledge, specific skills, and prescribed training, accredited and standardized educational programs, criteria by which to judge the competence of new professionals, and a code of ethics. Moreover, there is reason to question whether gerontology warrants designation as a separate academic discipline. Gerontology programs offer generic skill preparation and limited career options to graduates. Such programs are not necessarily well understood, may not reach students from other educational programs, and have been criticized as being contrary to a more normative life-span perspective. Finally, the slow growth in doctoral degree programs in gerontology (or aging studies) might underscore questions about gerontology being a profession and raises additional questions as to whether the degree is too specialized and limited to have relevance for careers in and outside of academia.

REFERENCES

Atchley, R. (1985). *Social forces in later life* (4th ed., p. 15). Belmont, CA: Wadsworth.

Binstock, R. H. (1983). The aged as scapegoat. *The Gerontologist, 23*(2), 136–143.

Estes, C. L., & Binney, E. A. (1989). The biomedicalization of aging: Danger and dilemmas. *The Gerontologist, 29*(5), 587–596.

Greenwood, E. (1957). Attributes of a profession. *Social Work, 2,* 45–55.

Kosberg, J. I., & Harris, A. P. (1984). Attitudes toward elderly clients. *Health and Social Work, 3*(3), 67–90.

Neugarten, B. L. (1979). Policy for the 1980s: Age or need entitlement? In J. P. Hubbard (Ed.), *Aging: Agenda for the eighties* (pp. 48–52). Washington, DC: The Government Research Corporation.

Rich, T. A., Connelly, J. R., & Douglass, E. B. (1990). *Standards and guidelines for gerontology programs* (2nd ed.). Washington, DC: Association for Gerontology in Higher Education.

Seltzer, M. M. (1985). Issues of accreditation of academic gerontology programs and credentialing workers in the field of aging. *Gerontology and Geriatrics Education, 5*(3), 7–18.

Wilensky, H. L., & Lebeaux, C. N. (1965). *Industrial society and social welfare.* New York: The Free Press.

Rejoinder to Professor Kosberg

DAVID A. PETERSON
PAMELA FRANCISCO WENDT

Despite current realities in the educational and employment arenas, the fact remains that gerontology is developing into a profession. It is important to take a long view of where gerontology began, how it has progressed, and where it is going, to avoid being overwhelmed in details. The topic of debate is whether gerontology should be a profession, not whether it currently is one, and we continue that line of thought in this rebuttal.

We have already discussed the development of gerontology instruction as it moves toward becoming a full profession; we believe that sufficiently addresses a number of Dr. Kosberg's points. Now we describe gerontology's capacity to continue and complete that progress.

First, gerontology has the capacity to develop and maintain a system of professional education. AGHE is encouraging gerontology faculty to consciously determine the focus of their instruction and to identify outcomes that are consistent with that orientation. Gerontology programs with a professional orientation (as differentiated from those with liberal arts and scientific orientations) will be the ones that prepare professional gerontological practitioners with the in-depth knowledge and skills necessary to provide comprehensive and effective services to older adults. The AGHE Core Principles and Outcomes document provides the foundation for this developmental process and standardization. With this type of organized plan, the admittedly difficult details (e.g., organizational structure, interdepartmental liaisons, scheduling negotiations, funding, etc.) will be systematically addressed, just as they have been by previously developing professions.

Second, there is a demonstrated capacity for graduates of professionally oriented gerontology programs to deliver needed services. Professionally oriented gerontology programs are no more "non-normative" than are educational programs in neonatology, pediatrics, early childhood education, adolescence, or obstetrics. On the contrary, all of these acknowledge unique characteristics of a subset of the life span and successfully educate practitioners to provide valuable services to them. Virtually all published personnel forecasts project the need for greater numbers of well-trained gerontological practitioners to serve unprecedented numbers of older adults and their families. Furthermore, several studies of the graduates of professionally oriented gerontology degree programs report that they have appropriate jobs in the field of aging, and that they value the aging education they received.

Third, there is the capacity to monitor and control professional practice in gerontology. With the establishment of the Association of Professional Gerontologists, its professional code of ethics, and plans for credentialing professional practitioners, a major step has been taken toward ensuring public safety and quality of professional gerontological services. Progress has been made, and more will be made in the future as professional gerontologists contribute to the professionalization of the field.

Will Future Elderly Persons Experience More Years of Disability?

EDITORS' NOTE: There is widespread concern about the specter of chronic illness and disability in later life. Individuals look with fear and trepidation at the likelihood of spending the final years of their lives dependent on family members and other care providers, while policy makers question society's ability to afford the care that they will require. But, others have claimed that the final years of our lives, rather than being years of disability and dependence, can be years of health and activity. This position is most clearly expounded in the "compression of morbidity" hypothesis, which postulates that we have the ability to live virtually our entire lives in good health and to reduce to a bare minimum any final period of illness or disability. This position, first proposed by Dr. James Fries in 1980, is predicated on three assumptions: (1) that there is some maximum expectable life span that is not likely to increase appreciably; (2) that death rates will remain low until we reach that particular age and then rapidly accelerate; and (3) that we can essentially eliminate premature disease. But, can we really expect to have good health almost until the time of death, or is this still a vision available only to a select group of advantaged individuals? For the rest of us, are Alzheimer's disease and other afflictions of old age inevitable? Should we expect to spend increasing years of our lives with disabling conditions such as these?

Edward L. Schneider, M.D., says *YES*. He is Executive Director of the University of Southern California's Ethel Percy Andrus Gerontology Center, where he is Dean of the Leonard Davis School of Gerontology, William and Sylvia

Kugel Professor of Gerontology, and Professor of Medicine at the University of Southern California School of Medicine. Dr. Schneider also serves as the first Scientific Director of the Buck Center for Research on Aging in Novato, California. Previously, Dr. Schneider spent fourteen years at the National Institute on Aging, first as the head of a laboratory studying genetic aspects of aging, later as Associate Director for Biomedical Research, and finally, as Deputy Director.

James F. Fries, M.D., says *NO*. He is Professor of Medicine at Stanford University School of Medicine. His research interests include long-term outcomes of chronic illness, strategies for reducing morbidity in rheumatoid arthritis and osteoarthritis, and public policy issues related to altering the need and demand for medical services. He presented the compression of morbidity paradigm in 1980.

YES

EDWARD L. SCHNEIDER

"It is the best of times and the worst of times." Charles Dickens's opening to the *Tale of Two Cities* may be as appropriate today as in the nineteenth century. We have witnessed a remarkable increase in life expectancy in the twentieth century unrivaled in human history. Life expectancy has increased for residents of developing as well as developed countries. In Japan, life expectancy for women exceeds eighty years, and in Okinawa, it exceeds eighty-two years. But it is not yet clear whether the additional years of life expectancy that we have experienced will be years of health or years of disability, dependency, and disease.

Dr. James Fries, in a compelling article written more than fifteen years ago, postulated that we were experiencing a compression of mortality and morbidity. He speculated that more and more deaths were occurring over a narrower period of the life span (compression of mortality) and that disease and disability would also be compressed into a shorter period (compression of morbidity). He proposed that we were rapidly approaching a human maximum life expectancy of eighty-five years and further proposed that the survival curve would continue to "rectangularize" as we experienced a compression of mortality. Lecturers, excited by Dr. Fries's hypothesis, in their enthusiasm would often omit the "hypothesized" part and expound on the "current trend in rectangularization of the survival curve." Kenneth Manton (1982) and Eileen Crimmins (1981), reviewing data on mortality shortly after the Fries article was published, clearly demonstrated that mortality was not being compressed. There were also a number of articles at that time that examined the compression of morbidity and demonstrated either a compression, a decompression, or no change of morbidity.

In this article, I would like to offer the following argument: that the critical issue is not whether there is a compression of morbidity, but that there is a larger issue for this nation. Namely, if there is a compression of morbidity, will it offset the vast numbers of older Americans who are reaching the decades in which the diseases of aging take their terrible toll? For example, if morbidity is compressing at a rate of 1 percent a year for those ages eighty-five and older, could it offset a 100 percent increase (5 percent per year) in the number of individuals aged eighty-five years and older, which occurred during the last two decades?

Several trends bear on these issues. First, over the last few decades we have witnessed a steep decrease in mortality from two of the three leading causes of death, heart attacks and stroke. As a result, many individuals who might have died in their sixties and seventies of these conditions are now living long enough to develop some of the chronic and disabling diseases of aging. If we find successful treatments for most cancers, and I believe that we are on the verge of this important accomplishment, this trend will further accelerate, and the leading causes of death in the twenty-first century may well be chronic and disabling conditions, such as Alzheimer's disease. Another critical trend is the exponential risk of developing certain diseases with aging, such as Alzheimer's and Parkinson's diseases. Thus, as we live longer, our cumulative risk of getting these disorders increases.

To measure any change in the compression of morbidity, you would need to examine populations of individuals of specific ages at different times. For instance, you might measure the level of disability and disease in individuals aged sixty-five to seventy-five in ten-year intervals from 1965 to 1995. You would hope that measures of health and disease have not changed, that new diseases have not been introduced, and that the demographics of the populations are equivalent (difficult assumptions at best). There have been health interviews (subjective estimates) performed periodically that can be analyzed. These show either no change or a slight improvement in reported health over the last few decades.

One of Fries's hypotheses in his landmark paper on the compression of mortality and morbidity was that health care costs for an aging population would decline as a result of the compression of mortality and morbidity. In the fifteen years since this article was published, every measure of health care resources used by an aging population has shown exponential increases. For example, substantial increases in Medicare costs are expected over the next decade. In the past, the escalating costs for Medicare and Medicaid were blamed on the extraordinary inflation of health care costs. However, we are finally realizing that what is driving the increasing costs for Medicare is no longer merely the inflating costs of medical care, but also the rapidly increasing numbers of frail aging Americans.

Because of my views, my colleagues and I have been termed "pessimists." I prefer the term "realist" in the tradition of Paul Revere, who announced that the British were indeed coming! I share the view of "optimists" that we can make some headway in compressing morbidity by modifying our diets and by following the best prescription for successful aging, exercise. For example, we might be able to reduce the number of hip fractures by 50 percent or more if we could build up bone mass through diet and exercise in young men and women and maintain bone mass throughout the life span by exercise and nutrition. However, I do not foresee that, even with universal adherence to strict dietary and exercise programs, the costs of medical care for an aging population will decline. There are too many other conditions that disable an aging population and do not appear to be altered by even the best health habits. The best example is Alzheimer's disease. I have seen many individuals aglow with the shine of healthy living, fit and trim, who have never smoked or drank, but with severe mental impairment caused by Alzheimer disease. Exercise and diet will not yet protect you from Parkinson's disease, amyotrophic lateral sclerosis (Lou Gehrig's disease) or osteoarthritis. Exercise may have some benefits for the last condition, but it will not be curative.

I am, however, "optimistic" about finding ways to prevent or successfully treat the diseases of aging. If this nation would invest a reasonable amount of resources into research on these conditions, even just a fraction of the Medicare budget, we might have a way to make a real dent in the morbidity facing this nation. We spend a third of a trillion dollars a year on health care for Americans aged sixty-five and older, but we spent only $807 million in 1995 for aging research. That is approximately one-quarter of a cent on research for every dollar spent on medical care for an aging population. If we taxed Medicare 1 or 2 percent and spent this money to find a way to prevent or cure Alzheimer's and Parkinson's disease, amyotrophic lateral sclerosis, osteoarthritis, and all of the diseases of aging that cause so much disability, not only could we potentially compress morbidity, but we also could save this nation trillions of dollars. Few corporations survive if they do not invest 3 or 4 percent of their sales into research, yet we spend approximately one-quarter of 1 percent of our health care dollar on aging research!

Therefore, although I might finally concede that we will probably see a very small compression of morbidity over the next decade, I think we are missing the opportunity to make a big dent in the morbidity facing the 70 million baby boomers if only we would invest now in aging research to find ways to prevent the diseases that cause the greatest disability in the last decades of life. Instead, the budget for the National Institute on Aging is barely keeping up with inflation. Furthermore, we are cutting back on payments to doctors and hospitals, which, I believe, will result in a deterioration of medical and nursing care and in even greater disability for an aging population.

References

Crimmins, E. M. (1981). The changing pattern of American mortality decline, 1947–1977, and its implications for the future. *Population and Development Review, 7*(2), 229–254.

Manton, K. C. (1982). Changing concepts of morbidity and mortality in the elderly population. *Milbank Memorial Fund Quarterly/Health and Society, 60,* 183.

Rejoinder to Professor Schneider
James F. Fries

Dr. Schneider rapidly leaves the subject at hand to argue that the future will have more old and very old people (true), that cures for cancer are just around the corner (questionable), and that more money for research into aging is needed (it is). When he does speak to the issues of compression of morbidity, his data are dated. For example, he cites an article by Ken Manton from 1982, whereas I cited Manton in a far stronger article in 1993, in which he observed very substantial compression of morbidity in a study involving data from 1982 through 1989. (Even more recently [1994], Manton has focused on the "compression of *mortality*," and finds the evidence equivocal; the compression of morbidity is not dependent on the compression of mortality.)

The first major article critical of the compression of morbidity hypothesis was by Schneider and Brody (1983). Dr. Brody now writes (Brody & Butler 1995):

> We have not directed enough serious attention to the concept of postponement and the enormous benefits to be accrued. Most of the fatal diseases and all of the nonfatal diseases we discussed increase exponentially with age. Postponing, therefore, has a magnified effect since delaying a process by one doubling will reduce by half the future incidence. We are living too long not to direct more of our efforts toward diseases which make aging a burdensome process.

Drs. Brody and Butler have titled their current book *Strategies to Delay Dysfunction in Later Life.* This is morbidity compression.

Dr. Schneider himself has been associated with programs with titles such as "Successful Aging," in which individuals are encouraged to exercise, eat good diets, and maintain satisfactory body weight. Were he to believe truly in his arguments, one would have to term such programs "unsuccessful aging" and deplore them, because they would just be increasing the incidence of Alzheimer's disease. When he cuts to the chase, Dr. Schneider is concerned about research funding for gerontology and has seemed to carry the opinion that the compression of morbidity hypothesis is in some way a threat to such funding. In contrast, I also favor increased funding in gerontological research in all areas, with a new emphasis on primary prevention and delay in chronic disease onset (Fries, 1993).

Twenty years ago we declared "war" on cancer. Age-adjusted cancer mortality, however, instead has shown a slight increase over the subsequent twenty-year period. Belatedly, the National Cancer Institute now stresses that 70 percent of cancer mortality and morbidity results from known risk factors and is preventable. Had we instead made war on the "causes of cancer," we might today have the ability to claim at least a partial victory. Other chronic diseases have equally well-defined risk factors, whether these are fatal or nonfatal diseases. If we can "make war" on the *causes* of chronic illness, we may then as a society began to see the pronounced compression of morbidity that is theoretically accomplishable.

REFERENCES

Brody, J. A., & Butler, R. N. (1995). *Strategies to delay dysfunction in later life.* New York, NY: Springer Publishing Company.

Fries, J. F. (1993). Compression of morbidity 1993: Life span, disability, and health care costs. *Facts and Research in Gerontology, 7,* 183–190.

Manton, K. G., Corder, L. S., & Stallard, E. (1993). Estimates of change in chronic disability and institutional incidence and prevalence rates in the U.S. elderly population from the 1982, 1984, and 1989 National Long-Term Care Survey. *Journal of Gerontology, 48*(4), S153–S166.

Manton, K. G., & Singer, B. (1994). What's the fuss about compression of morbidity? *Chance, 7,* 21–30.

Schneider, E. L., & Brody, J. A. (1983). Aging, natural death, and the compression of morbidity: Another view. *New England Journal of Medicine, 309,* 854–856.

NO

JAMES F. FRIES

We already know how to postpone disability substantially. The theoretical issues are largely resolved. But, national resolve, changes in public policy, and a realignment of priorities from "cure" to "prevention" are essential if we are to achieve a mentally and physically vital senior population.

The basic issue is whether individuals in the future will have a larger increase in "health span" than in "life expectancy." The "compression of morbidity" paradigm holds that if the average age at first disability (or other sign of morbidity) increases more rapidly than the average age at death, then morbidity will be compressed into a shorter and shorter period at the end of life. The ideal is seen as a population in which the norm is vigorous and vital physical, mental, and social health until a terminal collapse near the end of life (Fries, 1980).

Mortality

How much longer can we live anyway? Evidence shows no increase in life expectancy from advanced ages for more than a decade, yet these data are often ignored, for various reasons: perhaps because of hope that a gloomy prognosis will draw greater funds into a particular field; perhaps because, for some, immortality is a tempting ideal; perhaps because the medical model implicitly refuses to accept the notion of death absent disease or trauma; or perhaps because our view of longevity is based on "life expectancy from birth," an artificial concept, estimates of which march fairly steadily upward as long as we can continue to eliminate premature deaths. Somehow people have gotten the idea that human genetics are changing and that people are living longer and longer. The truth is that the genetics of a species do not change rapidly, and that life expectancy from advanced ages is historically rather constant. Here follow three observations not generally appreciated.

First, life expectancy from age eighty-five has been essentially constant since at least 1700, a period of nearly 300 years. Leonid Gavrilov and co-workers at Moscow State University have recently examined life span data for men (18,435 cases) and women (5,062 cases) born in 1700 through 1899, extracted from Russian genealogical publications, bibliographic dictionaries, and encyclopedias (Gavrilov, 1994). In 1700, life expectancy at age eighty-five was 4.1 years for men and 4.2 years for women, and this did not change significantly over the following two centuries. These values are close to modern data based on cross-sectional life tables: 4.3 years for men, and 4.9 years for women in the former USSR in 1985. These results substantiate that increases in life expectancy from birth are not associated with a significant increase in human longevity and are caused mainly by elimination of premature deaths at younger ages.

Second, since 1980 life expectancy for the total population has risen from 73.9 to 75.4 years (Kranczer, 1994). Thus, there is a slow but definite increase in average life expectancy from birth amounting to approximately a year and a half over thirteen years. However, life expectancy from ages sixty-five, seventy-five, and eighty-five has hardly changed at all. In 1980, life expectancy at age eighty-five, combining both sexes, was 6.0 years in the United States. In 1993 it was also 6.0 years! No change. At age seventy-five, the overall increase was 0.4 years, with men increasing 0.6 years and women increasing only 0.3 years. From age sixty-five, the total increase was 0.7 years, for men 1.0 years, and for women only 0.5 years. Thus, over the past thirteen years there has been minimal change in life expectancy over ages sixty-five and seventy-five, and *none at all* over age eighty-five.

Third, international comparisons also are of interest, because in countries with the greatest longevity the approach to longevity limits might be expected to occur earlier. The most recent international data (1988) from the 24 Organization for Economic Co-operation and Development (OECD) countries (Schieber, Poullier, & Greenwald, 1991) shows that the greatest life expectancy from age eighty is seen in Canada and Iceland, both at 8.9 years. These are followed by the United States at 8.7 years and by France at 8.6 years. Japan is at 8.4. Thus, the much-reported poor performance of the United States in international comparisons does not hold at the oldest ages; the United States merely has more premature deaths than do many other countries. Its genetic stock looks pretty good. There is, in longevity from extreme ages, no international target for us to aim at and no hint from international data that a major increase in these numbers is on the horizon.

Morbidity

What are the possibilities for postponing morbidity? Evidence shows clearly that morbidity at advanced ages may be reduced. Manton and colleagues have perhaps performed the most elaborate studies, using the 1982, 1984, 1989 National Long-Term Care surveys (Manton, Corder, & Stallard, 1993). These authors, reversing their previous conclusions, find a dramatic decrease in age-specific chronic disability rates over the seven years from 1982 to 1989.

By far the most provocative data come from studies of what might be. Here, the idea is to study a group that on theoretical grounds might be expected to have less morbid lives. The postulate is that the favored group will have substantially decreased morbidity as compared with the nonfavored group, and that this advantage will be preserved despite taking into account the greater longevity of the favored group. The three independent variables used to define "favored" status in these studies are socioeconomic status, education level, and the diligent practice of aerobic exercise.

House and colleagues (House, Kessler, & Herzog, 1990) for example, found huge differences in functional status scores at all ages between lower, lower middle, upper middle, and upper socioeconomic classes, but the more favored classes begin to crash rapidly at ages over seventy-five and disability rates begin to converge with data from the lower socioeconomic classes. Thus, the more favored populations lead more "rectangular" lives, with disability postponed until a terminal collapse. Similarly, a study by Paul Leigh and myself (Leigh & Fries, 1994), using data from the epidemiological followup to the National Health and Nutrition Survey, found that lifetime cumulative disability over age fifty was 21 percent to 60 percent less for persons with sixteen or more years of schooling as compared with those who had eleven or fewer years of schooling. If higher education level is an appropriate surrogate for the effect of good health practices, then extending such practices, we concluded, will result in less, rather than more, lifetime disability.

Our group has also studied long-distance running and the development of disability with age, in an ongoing longitudinal study, over the past nine years (Fries et al., 1994). We studied 451 members of a runner's club and 330 community controls who initially averaged fifty-nine years of age, with appropriate controls for self-selection bias. After eight years of longitudinal study, the differences in initial disability level (0.026 compared with 0.079) steadily increased to 0.071 for runners compared with 0.242 for controls ($P < .001$). Differences persisted after adjusting for age, sex, body mass, baseline disability, smoking history, history of arthritis, other comorbid conditions, and other variables. Rates of disability progression, adjusted for these variables, in the exercising group were only one-third the rate of those in the control group. These large differences in disability persisted through age eighty, and then the runners began to develop disability at an accelerated rate, converging toward the level of the control population. Older persons who engage in vigorous aerobic activities thus have slower development of disability than do members of the general population. This association is probably related to increased aerobic activity, strength, fitness, and increased organ reserve. Similar results have been reported by Stewart and colleagues (Stewart, King, & Haskell, 1993). These findings strongly support the notion of greatly decreased lifetime disability in "favored" groups. If it is already occurring in some, we should be able to extend these benefits more widely.

The Issue of Fatal and Nonfatal Disease

Most of the discussion and controversy about morbidity compression (whether it is happening, and whether it can be made to happen) has focused on the fatal diseases. Here, pessimists have assumed a scenario such as the following: a fatal heart attack is prevented, the patient lives another twenty years, the last ten of which are spent with slowly progressive Alzheimer's disease. The more accurate scenario is this: first heart attacks are not usually fatal, but begin a series of events that include subsequent heart attacks, strokes, congestive heart failure, and other cardiovascular problems that result in death after chronic illness in a number of years. Because heart disease is the most prevalent cause of death, the more likely scenario for the individual is that a postponed first heart attack also postpones the rest of the sequence, but this individual will more likely than not still eventually die of a cardiac event. No one has yet performed the meticulous decision analytic modeling that would be needed to estimate the number of people for whom a postponed event presages more chronic problems and the larger number of people for whom a postponed event also postpones these problems for a later death with less cumulative disability.

There is, however, incontrovertible evidence about the effects on mortality rates of postponing heart attacks. Multiple large randomized controlled trials designed to prevent or postpone heart attacks have been successful at their goals. However, these studies have not changed total mortality. Thus, preventing a heart attack *must* reduce lifetime morbidity because the patient does not have the morbidity of the heart attack, and preventing that attack does not on average measurably extend life. This paradoxical ability to reduce specific disease mortality rates but not total mortality rates raises complex questions, and may result from fallacies in the independence assumption of statistical "competing risk" models.

There are also nonfatal diseases, and these also may be prevented. A partial list would include osteoporosis, hemorrhoids, hernias, gallbladder disease, back pain, varicose veins, thrombophlebitis, hip fractures, spinal fractures, and the musculoskeletal disability associated with aging. These are very major contributors to morbidity. Postponement and prevention here represent pure gains in terms of compression of morbidity, because they reduce the amount of lifetime morbidity and do not affect life duration. A fatal disease prevented involves trade-offs, because the alternative future is uncertain. Postponement of nonfatal diseases is a win–win.

Thus, morbidity can be compressed. Probably most of us are attempting to live our lives so that our own morbidity is in fact compressed. Based on the data, it is appropriate to be optimistic. But there is a dark side. When we look at the population as a whole, we find little major movement toward improved lifestyle and preventive practices. Only 22 percent of the U.S. population exercise regularly, some 28 percent still smoke, and an astounding number of people are very substantially over a desirable weight. We now have established interventions that can improve health and reduce morbidity, documented by randomized controlled trials (Fries et al., 1993). But we are not adequately disseminating such programs.

The Cost Corollary

Finally, we have a national health care cost crisis. The most desirable way to surmount this crisis is to reduce the national illness burden; to decrease the need for medical services (Fries et al., 1993). We now have operational, documented health education programs that are able to do this, and in the process they can save 20 percent or more of our current health care dollars. Another win–win; better health, perhaps a somewhat longer life, and a more solvent economy.

REFERENCES

Fries, J. F. (1980). Aging, natural death, and the compression of morbidity. *New England Journal of Medicine, 303,* 130–135.

Fries, J. F., Koop, C. E., Beadle, C. E., Cooper, P. P., England, M. J., Greaves, R. F., Sokolov, J. J., Wright, D., & The Health Project Consortium. (1993). Reducing health care costs by reducing the need and demand for medical services. *New England Journal of Medicine, 329,* 321–325.

Fries, J. F., Singh, G., Morfeld, D., Hubert, H. B., Lane, N. E., & Brown, B. W. (1994). Running and the development of disability with age. *Annals of Internal Medicine, 121,* 502–509.

Gavrilov, L. (1994). [*Personal communication.*]

House, J. S., Kessler, R. C., Herzog, R., et al. (1990). Age, socioeconomic status, and health. *Milbank Quarterly, 68,* 383–411.

Kranczer, S. (1994, July/September). Changes in U.S. life expectancy. *Statistical Bulletin,* pp. 11–17.

Leigh, J. P., & Fries, J. F. (1994). Education, gender, and the compression of morbidity. *International Journal of Aging and Human Development, 39*(3), 233–246.

Manton, K. G., Corder, L. S., & Stallard, E. (1993). Estimates of change in chronic disability and institutional incidence and prevalence rates in the U.S. elderly population from the 1982, 1984, and 1989 National Long-Term Care Survey. *Journal of Gerontology, 48*(4), S153–S166.

Schieber, G. J., Poullier, J. P., & Greenwald, L. M. (1991). Health care systems in twenty-four countries. *Health Affairs, 1,* 22–38.

Stewart, A. L., King, A. C., & Haskell, W. L. (1993). Endurance exercise and health-related quality of life in 50–65 year-old adults. *Gerontologist, 33*(6), 782–789.

Rejoinder to Professor Fries
Edward L. Schneider

Because there is a limited amount of space for this rebuttal, I will focus on two of Dr. Fries's arguments. The first is a continuation of his original argument that we are experiencing a compression of mortality, a rectangularization of the survival curve. He uses data on mortality in Russia over two centuries at age eighty-five to make the case that mortality has not changed substantially during this time. Yet, Russia may not be the best example to choose when looking at mortality. Although both developing and developed countries have observed continuing increases in life expectancies at all ages, life expectancy has actually been decreasing for at least the last two decades in Russia (United Nations, 1995). Therefore, examinations of life expectancy using this population are misleading!

Dr. Fries's second argument relates to the compression of morbidity. The premise for the compression of morbidity contends that individuals, on average, are experiencing a delay in the onset of disability. Dr. Fries uses the example of heart disease. He suggests that there has been a decrease in the rate of heart attacks without a change in overall mortality. Once again, Fries is off target! The real health issue facing older Americans is not any one specific disease, it is the consequences of many diseases on disability. Although heart disease is extremely frequent in an aging population and is the chief cause of death, it is not the largest cause of disability at older ages. It is not even close to arthritis and dementia as a cause of disability in older populations, especially when you look at the oldest age-groups. Therefore, it is misleading to make conclusions about trends in morbidity using heart disease as an example.

Finally, I am in agreement that education has been shown by several studies to have a positive correlation with life expectancy. However, I must, once again, disagree that more education will decrease morbidity. We have just concluded a study of education and its effect on disability and disease in Dr. Fries's backyard, Northern California (Reed et al., 1995). In this highly educated and affluent population, we found that mortality rates were lower in this population than in the general U.S. population. However, comparisons of life-threatening diseases, chronic conditions, measures of physical performance, and limitations of the activities of daily living did not show any clear pattern of reduced disability in this highly educated population when compared with other less-educated populations.

In conclusion, although I once again agree with Dr. Fries's emphasis on health behaviors as a way to reduce disability in aging populations, I am very concerned that this effort alone will not solve the great future health needs of an aging population. The real solution is prevention accompanied by sufficient research support to find effective ways to prevent or cure the devastating diseases of aging such as Alzheimer's and Parkinson's diseases and osteoarthritis.

REFERENCES

Reed, D., Satariano, W. A., Gildengorin, G., McMahon, K., Fleshman, R., & Schneider, E. (1995). Health and functioning among the elderly of Marin County, California: A glimpse of the future. *Journal of Gerontology, 50A:* M61–M69.

United Nations, Population Division, Department of Economic and Social Information and Policy Analysis. (1995). *World Population Prospects, 1994 Revision.* New York: United Nations.

Will Tomorrow's Elderly Be Better Off?

EDITORS' NOTE: Today's elderly Americans represent one of the most economically advantaged old-age cohorts in history. Living their adult years in the post–World War II period of economic prosperity and expanding public policies, they enjoy Social Security benefits that typically far exceed their individual contributions, nearly universal health care coverage through Medicare, and nearly universal long-term care coverage through Medicaid once their own resources are exhausted. Yet, the possible bankruptcy of the Social Security Trust Fund, efforts to contain Medicare expenditures through managed care and similar mechanisms, dramatic reductions in support for Medicaid and other public programs, and reductions in the percentage of individuals covered by private pension plans all suggest that future cohorts of elderly persons may not fare as well. This may particularly be the case for the baby-boom generation, those Americans born approximately 1945 to 1964, whose large numbers simply may overwhelm society's ability to provide needed support. Yet, baby boomers always have managed to prosper in spite of such skepticism, and it is possible that they may continue to do so as they enter old age. Will the advantaged conditions that baby boomers generally have enjoyed throughout their lives continue into their later years, or will old age be a rude awakening? Can the next generation of elderly really expect to experience better conditions than their parents?

Neal E. Cutler, Ph.D., says *YES*, tomorrow's elderly will be better off. He is Director of the Boettner Center of Financial Gerontology at the University of

Pennsylvania and holder of the Boettner/Gregg Chair of Financial Gerontology at Widener University. Dr. Cutler is co-author of *Aging, Money, and Life Satisfaction: Aspects of Financial Gerontology* and *Can You Afford to Retire?* and he is a Consulting Editor of the *Encyclopedia of Financial Gerontology.*

Paul C. Light, Ph.D., says *NO.* He is Director of the Public Policy Program at the Pew Charitable Trusts and a former Associate Dean and Professor at the University of Minnesota's Hubert Humphrey Institute of Public Affairs. He is the author of eight books on American government and public policy, including the award-winning *Still Artful Work: Continuing Politics of Social Security Reform.*

YES

Neal E. Cutler

Although the "elderly" population in the United States includes substantial demographic, financial, and social heterogeneity, and the issues relevant to our question are therefore complex, I argue that tomorrow's elderly will be better off financially than older persons of today and yesterday. Although I certainly agree that many men and women, including identifiable groups of individuals, will not be well off (or "better off" in some comparative sense), three sets of indicators suggest that, in general, tomorrow's elderly will be better off: (1) income diversity, (2) pension coverage, and (3) financial planning.

Income Diversity

Over the past several years the profile of retirement income among older households has become increasingly diverse. Many retirees do not have to rely only on Social Security or primarily on their savings. Recently published analyses demonstrate that over the period 1974 to 1992, although almost all older households received Social Security income, the percentage of retirement income received from employer pensions and from income-producing assets increased substantially (Employee Benefit Research Institute, 1994).

To be sure, not all elderly participated equally in this expanded diversity of retirement income. Economists typically divide the population into fifths ("quintiles") based on household income, and then compare the wealthiest, least wealthy, and middle-income groups. As might be expected, households in the poorest quintile rely almost exclusively on Social Security for their retirement income. Perhaps somewhat surprising, however, is that even among the middle-income households (third quintile), retirement income from assets and from pensions is widespread, and has increased substantially from 1974 to 1992. The point is not that these sources constitute great wealth for working-class and middle-class elderly. What it does signify is that the trend among older households is toward greater diversification of their retirement income, which at least produces some insulation from the current uncertainties of Social Security politics.

Pensions

Employer pensions became widespread in the United States after World War II. This means that among today's elderly, the opportunity to accumulate lifetime pension funds during their working years was less than it will be for future elderly. Nonetheless, each decade produces a larger percentage of current retirees who receive pension income. What about tomorrow's elderly? Will they be better off in this regard? Yes. 1988 Census Bureau data show that although 44 percent of workers aged sixty-five or older were covered by a pension, 66 percent of workers aged forty-five to sixty-four were covered. This suggests that more of today's middle-agers (i.e., tomorrow's elderly), compared with today's older men and women, have a work experience that for a variety of reasons is offering them a future pension income.

A major factor is "vesting." When a worker is vested in a pension, it means that after meeting certain job requirements, including working for a minimum number of years, the worker now has a legal right to that pension even if he or she quits, is fired, changes jobs, or whatever (Cutler, 1996). Years ago, before federal law encouraged more "worker-friendly" vesting rules, if a pension plan required twenty-five years of continuous service for the worker to qualify for pension/retirement income, and if that worker quit or was fired after twenty-three years, the entire pension could be lost. In 1974, Congress passed the Employee Retirement Income Security Act (ERISA), which, among other policies to protect pensions, directed companies to use significantly reduced vesting requirements. Workers can now become vested in the pensions they earn by working as few as five or ten years. 1988 Census data show that although 50 percent of people aged sixty-five years or older had vested ownership of their pension, 69 percent of workers age forty-five to sixty-four were vested, suggesting an additional reason that tomorrow's elderly are more likely to receive pension income than today's elderly.

Financial Planning

Finally, tomorrow's elderly have a number of advantages compared with yesterday's elderly in the realm of financial planning. First and foremost (despite the tone of today's political trends) is the existence of Social Security and Medicare. Even as Social Security benefits become part of taxable income, and even with increased premiums and co-payments within Medicare, these two highly successful programs provide a core of financial security that yesterday's elderly did not have.

Consider the connection between (a) the year of a person's birth and (b) the year when each of these programs began, and the influence of this connection on financial planning. A person (or the cohort) born in 1900, for example, was already entering middle age when the first Social Security benefits were paid out in the early 1940s, so Social Security could not have played a major role in that generation's retirement planning. A man (or the cohort) born in 1930 knew that Social Security would be part of his future, but was already an adult when Medicare was enacted in 1965. By contrast, a baby boomer born in 1950 entered the labor force with both Social Security and Medicare as part of his or her everyday financial environment. With this core of financial resources, plans could be made for retirement finance—if not with absolute certainty, then at least with the likelihood of public program resources.

Even as the politicized debate over the size, cost, and certainty of Social Security and Medicare heats up in the late 1990s, this front-page debate itself helps to educate tomorrow's elderly about their own individual and family retirement financial planning needs. To be sure, a public debate over lowered financial expectations is not as satisfying as a debate over how to allocate expanding wealth, but alongside the pension and other resources discussed here (and appropriately recognizing inevitable exceptions), tomorrow's elderly are in a better position to look ahead and knowledgeably plan for their future.

DIPPIES

A special dimension of financial planning concerns what our research refers to as the *DIPPIES,* an acronym (*Double Income, Plural Pensions*) describing couples in which both partners work, and each is independently earning a future pension. That is, these couples have *D*ouble *I*ncome during their working years, and can look forward to *P*lural *P*ension income in retirement. This does not mean that families characterized as DIPPIES are necessarily rich; for many families it takes two incomes just to make ends meet. Rather, the point is that DIPPIES have a greater set of financial planning opportunities and responsibilities to make the most of their future plural retirement income resources. A couple could have two employer pensions, two Social Securities, as well as work-related savings bonds or life insurance, home equity, and other financial resources. For a variety of social and cultural reasons, two-earner couples are more prevalent among baby boomers than in previous generations. And so, when combined with the general income and pension vesting trends just mentioned, tomorrow's elderly have a substantial chance of being better off.

Better Off Than Whom?

A 1993 study by the Congressional Budget Office (CBO), titled *Baby Boomers in Retirement: An Early Perspective,* compared the accumulated net wealth (that is, assets minus liabilities) in 1989 of the first-half boomers at age thirty-five to forty-four years (born 1945–1954) with the birth cohort of 1918–1927, who were examined using data from 1962, when that group was also aged thirty-five to forty-four years. Thus, in a kind of gerontological–demographic version of *Back to the Future,* boomers were compared with their parents at the same age (an age when both groups were about to enter middle age). And because of the importance of family-connected factors, the study separately compared married and unmarried individuals.

What the CBO study found (using appropriately inflation-adjusted financial data so that the 1962 and 1989 profiles can be validly compared) was that boomers are doing substantially better than "their parents." Married boomers at age thirty-five to forty-four (in 1989) had an average accumulated wealth of $61,000, whereas "their parents" (at age thirty-five to forty-four in 1962) had an average accumulated wealth of half that amount, at $29,300 (both groups compared using 1989 dollars). Unmarried boomers did better than "their parents" too, although not twice as well ($17,900 versus $10,300).

Finally, using a different basis for comparison, a Census Bureau study published in early 1995 compared first-half boomers (that is, boomers born 1947 to 1956) at ages thirty-seven to forty-six in 1993 with themselves at ages twenty-seven to thirty-six in 1983. The specific comparison focused on the percentage who were covered by employer pensions. Both men and women boomers (analyzed separately) had increased their pension coverage by 10 percent from their younger to their pre–middle-age stage of life. In 1993, among tomorrow's elderly, 67 percent of the men and 59 percent of the women were covered by pensions.

In sum, in answer to the basic question, will tomorrow's elderly be better off? I would argue that there is clear evidence for an affirmative answer. It should be kept in mind, however, that this argument focuses on aging baby boomers as "tomorrow's elderly," and different definitions of what constitutes "elderly" and which "tomorrow" we should look at might produce different answers and arguments.

Given the realities of gerontological demographics, however, the 1946-to-1964 baby boom will constitute "tomorrow's elderly" for many years to come. For example, under current Social Security eligibility rules, the first boomer becomes eligible for early retirement at age sixty-two in 2008 and the last boomer achieves this eligibility on December 31, 2026. Add twenty-three years so as to focus on age ninety, and the boomer generation will be entering the portals of the "old old" from 2036 to 2054. In other words, the "tomorrow" of our debate stretches from 2008 through 2054 and beyond. Given this definition of tomorrow's elderly, the evidence suggests that—alongside the need for increased financial literacy and public policy vigilance—tomorrow's elderly will be financially better off.

REFERENCES

Cutler, N. E. (1996). Pensions. In J. E. Birren (Ed.), *Encyclopedia of gerontology.* San Diego: Academic Press.

Employee Benefit Research Institute. (1994). *Baby boomers in retirement: What are their prospects?* Washington, DC: Employee Benefit Research Institute (EBRI), Special Report SR-23.

Rejoinder to Professor Cutler
PAUL C. LIGHT

Neil Cutler's insightful and hopeful portrait of the future of retirement confirms that predictions about the future of retirement depend largely, if not entirely, on about whom one asks. Professor Cutler reaches his more hopeful forecast by comparing tomorrow's elderly against both elderly of the present and the past, while I reach mine by comparing tomorrow's elderly against each other.

Under Cutler's hopeful gaze, even the current fears of future Social Security collapse improve the forecast, for "this front-page debate itself helps to educate tomorrow's elderly about their own individual and family retirement financial planning needs." Facing certain financial doom if they count on Social Security alone, today's middle-aged baby boomers will build savings, invest wisely, and enter the coming century well girded for retirement sans government support.

Would that the scenario were certain. As Cutler himself agrees, the baby boomers are only doing well on *average*. There are deep pockets of poverty within the generation, and stunning problems in the accumulation of wealth. Although Cutler is quite right to note the financial performance of married boomers at age thirty-five to forty-four in comparison with their parents a quarter century earlier, he does not factor in the much higher probabilities of divorce, nor the greater chance that large numbers of these middle-aged baby boomers will be severed from future work by corporate and government downsizing. The literature is replete with evidence on the problems of recently divorced women, for example, whose financial fortunes are anything but average.

It is not yet clear whether these income gaps will widen throughout the coming years, and whether government has any role to play in assuring a more even performance. For now, the laissez-faire futurists seem to be in command, arguing that the future is fine as long as we let it happen. This philosophy clearly holds in Washington, where sweeping disinvestment now is underway in critical research programs and data-monitoring efforts. As a result, we may enter the

2000s not even knowing the dimensions of the problem, let alone the nature of the solution.

NO

PAUL C. LIGHT

It does not take long before talk about the future of the elderly becomes talk about the future of the baby-boom generation. And it does not take long before talk about the future of the baby boomers becomes talk about the future of Social Security. If the baby boomers knew the true dimensions of the future crisis, or so the macabre joke might go, half of the generation would die of fright, thereby solving the crisis immediately.

The question is just how bad the future looks. The answer depends not so much on whom one asks, but *about* whom one asks. The distinction is critical. If one asks about middle- and upper-income baby boomers, the answer is that the future looks pretty good. Savings rates are likely high enough, pensions good enough, and investments promising enough to offer some confidence about healthy, comfortable retirements. If one asks about middle-aged baby boomers who have healthy, wealthy parents, the answer is also good. As those parents pass on, they will leave much of their wealth to their children, thereby curing the most careless investment strategy. But if one asks about poor African American baby boomers, middle-class single parents, or never-married single women who spend their careers in gender-segregated work, the answer is much less sanguine. These baby boomers may have a much less hopeful future indeed.

Wealth is not everything, of course. Those who project the future of retirement are quite sensible to write about multigenerational families, new technologies, evolving social services, and a host of other dreams that seem just within reach. Just imagine what retirement might look like, they tell us, for the most educated generation in American history, one familiar with the Internet, schooled on change, ready to accept the new.

There are three problems with the image. The first is that not everyone is likely to share in this future. The 75 million baby-boom generation is not some monolith that rises and falls in unison. Although there are shared experiences—for example, a one-time wage penalty from being part of such a large collection of people, or the shared impact of Vietnam—the baby boom is actually sharply divided along gender, educational, income, racial, and social lines. Baby boomers who served in Vietnam are very different politically, for example, than baby boomers who protested the war back home.

The most important divisions for the future may be economic. There is no doubt, for example, that the 1980s were very profitable for America's wealthy. Tax rates on the richest Americans went down, as did tax rates on corporate earnings and investment. According to the Internal Revenue Service, the number of millionaires grew 1,400 percent over the decade. In 1980, only 4,400 Americans reported $1 million in adjusted gross income (the figure listed at the bottom of the tax return); by 1990, the number was up to 63,642 (Farhi, 1992).

Alas, the rising tide did not raise all boats. Even as the number of rich increased, so did the number of poor. The rich did get richer, and the poor did get poorer. According to the Center on Budget and Policy Priorities, the average income for the top fifth of Americans grew nearly $14,000 over the 1980s, rising from $83,000 to $97,000, whereas the average for the bottom fifth dropped $600, from $10,900 to $10,300 (Rich, 1992). Not only were the rich getting richer, the gap between the top and bottom appeared to be growing. Along the way, poverty among working Americans increased. By 1990, experts at the Population Reference Bureau argued that "the traditional assumption that holding a job will keep an individual out of poverty no longer seems to apply." Two of five adults in poverty now work at least part of the year. Three of five families in poverty had at least one person working somewhere; one of five had two people working (Population Reference Bureau, 1990).

It is not yet clear whether the baby boom will carry the mark of the 1980s and early 1990s all the way through retirement. Nor is it clear that these past few years of unexpectedly poor performance cancel out the above-average returns during the 1950s and early 1960s. What is clear is that the baby boom will likely enter its retirement years with serious income inequalities. Although some baby boomers will be quite comfortable, a much larger number appears to be well on the way to economic distress.

The second problem with images of a more hopeful future is that Social Security will enter a new funding crisis early in the next century. As the ratio of workers to beneficiaries shifts downward, the tax rates required to maintain even a modest rate of return will rise. According to the 1992 *Report of the Trustees of the Federal Old-Age and Survivors Insurance and Disability Insurance Trust Funds,* Social Security's assets will continue to rise until fifteen years or so after the turn of the century. After that, in the traditionally dry language of all trustees' reports, "tax rates scheduled in present law are expected to be insufficient to cover program expenditures and it will be necessary to use interest earnings and to redeem assets held by the combined OASI and DI trust funds to make up the shortfall." Translated, by roughly 2016, Social Security will be eating into its interest earnings and drawing down its substantial reserves. Depending on the estimates used, the Social Security trust funds will be exhausted sometime during the 2030s, a prognosis that prompted former Social Security Commissioner Dorcas Hardy to title her recent book on the subject *Social Insecurity: The Crisis in America's Social Security System and How to Plan Now for Your Own Financial Survival* (Hardy & Hardy, 1991).

The situation would look even worse if death rates, birth rates, and immigration rates were all to fall below current best-guess estimates. According to an analysis of the worst–worst case by population experts Jacob Siegel and Cynthia Taeuber:

> ...There could be serious dislocations in the economy as it tries to adjust to changing needs for jobs, goods, and services. Societal ageing calls for increasingly larger financial contributions to the federal treasury on behalf of older non-workers. Tax rates could become oppressively high and serve as a disincentive to work. The productive capacity of the economy could be diminished as the proportion of persons of working age shrinks and vast expenditures have to be made for the 'maintenance' of elderly persons (Siegel & Taeuber, 1986, pp. 113–114).

Get this kind of forecast out to the baby boom and no wonder half the generation would be distraught.

There are ways to address the coming crisis, of course, including steep tax increases, deep benefit cuts, and a significant increase in retirement age. Because many of these options envisage moving money from one generation to another, doomsayers often warn of coming intergenerational warfare between the young and old. The much more likely scenario, however, involves an *intra*generational war between rich and poor baby boomers, with the rich elderly fending off the steep taxes needed to cover the poor. It is the rich, for example, who will be able to buy themselves out of longer working years, protect themselves against lower relative Social Security benefits, and insulate their earnings against the kinds of cost-of-living freezes that may become commonplace after 2015 or so. And it is less affluent baby boomers who likely will bear the burden of the increasing poverty rates that may accompany the baby boom's movement into retirement. The resulting conflict will make retirement anything but comfortable, whether to individual elderly or to the politicians they elect.

The question, as Ebenezer Scrooge once put it, is whether this is the future that must be, or just a future that might be. It is a question that leads to the third problem with images of a more hopeful future: it requires hard work that is even now being postponed by the current budget and policy battles.

There are really two futures facing the baby boom. One is the more frightening future foretold above—deep economic divisions, and sharp political conflict. The other is the more hopeful outlook offered by Neil Cutler. In this future, there is more than enough economic growth to support baby boomers through their retirement years, more than enough savings to support needed health care and catastrophic coverage, and more than enough societal compassion to assure that all the baby boomers live their later years in comfort.

The problem with this more hopeful future is that it takes work now. The list of needs is great: investments in preventive care, renewal of the economic infrastructure, improvements in the education of future workers, strengthening of the civic culture, even healing of social divisions. Weaving the social fabric for a more vibrant future does not happen by accident, nor is it wished into being at the last minute. It is the product of tough choices and careful investments today, choices and investments that are not yet being made.

REFERENCES

Farhi, P. (1992, July). They're in the money. *Washington Post National Weekly Edition,* pp. 20–26.

Hardy, D., & Hardy, C. C. (1991). *Social insecurity: The crisis in America's social security system and how to plan now for your own financial survival.*

Population Reference Bureau. (1990). *America in the 21st century: Social and economic support systems.*

Rich, S. (1992, September). The rich got richer, again. *Washington Post National Weekly Edition,* pp. 14–20.

Siegel, J., & Taeuber, C. (1986). Demographic perspectives on the long-lived society. In A. Pfifer & L. Bronte (Eds.), *Our Aging Society.* New York: W. W. Norton.

Rejoinder to Dr. Light

NEAL E. CUTLER

Dr. Light defines the terms of the question too narrowly when he says that to talk about the future is to talk about how aging Boomers will fare under Social Security. Although Social Security is, of course, part of the financial future, it is simply wrong to presume that it is the only issue relevant here. To ignore the other facets of the question serves only to perpetuate two fallacies: first, to limit the discussion to Social Security alone means that the answer to the question "will tomorrow's elderly be better off?" must be, virtually by definition, *wrong* because it is misfocused to only a piece of the question; second, such an incomplete statement of the question summarily dismisses the proposition that we need to address the broader range of human concerns that reflect the social and financial heterogeneity of our rapidly aging society. It is not only the concerns of poor elderly that are the legitimate focus of our attention.

Although Dr. Light recognizes that the baby boom (as do the generations both before and after it) includes middle-income and upper-middle-income families, after his opening paragraphs, his world becomes narrowly divided simply into rich and poor. This is truly a shame because there are issues to explore, problems to define, and solutions to consider for the whole of an aging society. To have only disdain for the rich and sympathy for the poor is to abdicate our full range of social and intellectual responsibilities. The available information documents the proposition, as mentioned in the text of my essay, that working-class and middle-class families have an increasingly diverse profile of retirement income, including a growing share of future retirees who will have pensions. Compared with their own parents, many boomers will be better off financially, yet the effective protection of those retirement income resources remains an important public policy as well as private and personal challenge.

I close this comment with the story of a family that is indicative of American upward mobility, but is also indicative of the continuing challenges that face even successful older men and women. The husband went to work after the sixth grade, and his wife graduated from high school during the Depression and had a lifetime career as a secretary. They raised their children in a rented apartment, but eventually managed to save enough for a down payment and purchase a small home. When he died, there was little life insurance, but she managed what there was fairly well, continued to work, retired a decade later with Social Security, a defined-benefit company pension, and a few bonds and mutual fund shares purchased mainly through payroll deductions and the careful massaging of that little bit of life insurance proceeds. She lives alone in her own condo apartment, worries appropriately about her finances, especially about interest rates, inflation, Medicare taxes, and the cost and availability of health services. Because she is neither poor nor rich, she would appear not to warrant Dr. Light's attention. Yet there are millions similar to her (identified as people in the "middle quintiles" in my essay), both today's elderly and tomorrow's, who deserve the attention, support, and perhaps even the financial and social policy protection of a benevolent society.

I continue to believe, as I have written here, that on balance tomorrow's elderly will be better off as measured in various ways. I agree with Dr. Light that this does not mean that we should abandon those of tomorrow's elderly who will not be better off. At the same time, however, those working-class and middle-class elderly who are better off financially still have challenges in the areas of finance, health, long-term care, and quality of life—and we must not ignore and abandon them either.